More Praise for
UNEASY STREET

"Sherman's analysis is informative, insightful, and nuanced."
— GLENN ALTSCHULER, *Psychology Today*

"Sherman's book does take absorbing measure of what has become a corrosive reality in New York: the tendency among well-off people to regard their circumstances as entirely ordinary—'Manhattan poor' as others have put it."
— GINIA BELLAFANTE, *New York Times*

"Although it is easy to judge the rich for [their] 'anxieties', Rachel Sherman suggests that this often distracts us from examining the wider 'systems of distribution that produce inequality'."
— MATTHEW REISZ, *Times Higher Education*

"*Uneasy Street* is an insightful guide through the struggle faced by elites in reconciling extreme wealth with the desire for moral legitimacy. Sherman writes with great nuance and subtlety."
— JONATHAN YONG TIENXHI, *LSE Review of Books*

"*Uneasy Street* is an important book. It is an all too rare empirical study of how the rich see themselves."
— DANIEL BEN-AMI, *Spiked Review*

"Sherman transcends the cartoon caricatures of the wealthy to provide a profound and nuanced picture of the lived experience of affluent New Yorkers. *Uneasy Street* is an original and insightful look at the complex ambivalence that many wealthy people feel in a time of extreme inequality and the narratives they sometimes tell themselves to rationalize, justify, or ignore their wealth and advantage."
— CHUCK COLLINS, author of *Born on Third Base*

"At a time of growing class inequality, how do the wealthy grapple with their privileged economic position? In *Uneasy Street*, Sherman offers a remarkable look inside the world of affluence and shows how the liberal elite struggles to attain moral worthiness. This book skillfully advances our understanding of social class and makes an important contribution to the sociology of money."
— VIVIANA A. ZELIZER, author of *Economic Lives*

D1712080

"*Uneasy Street* looks at how rich people talk about the choices they make about money, and how that talk constructs a moral universe in which they can claim legitimacy for their advantages. This book is full of astute observations and sensitive interpretations, and its argument is new and profoundly important."

—ALLISON J. PUGH, University of Virginia

"This exceptionally interesting book examines how one group of wealthy people understands and experiences its extraordinary privilege. Sherman's analysis of elites is long overdue, especially as the popular discourse on inequality has exploded. Beautifully written, *Uneasy Street* is an exceptional piece of work."

—JULIET SCHOR, author of *True Wealth*

UNEASY STREET

RACHEL SHERMAN

UNEASY STREET

THE **ANXIETIES** OF **AFFLUENCE**

PRINCETON UNIVERSITY PRESS
PRINCETON AND OXFORD

Published by Princeton University Press
41 William Street, Princeton, New Jersey 08540

In the United Kingdom: Princeton University Press
6 Oxford Street, Woodstock, Oxfordshire OX20 1TR

press.princeton.edu

Cover image courtesy of Shutterstock
Cover design by Karl Spurzem

First paperback edition, with Discussion Questions, 2019

Paperback ISBN 9780691191904

The Library of Congress has cataloged the cloth edition as follows:
Names: Sherman, Rachel, 1970– author.
Title: Uneasy street : the anxieties of affluence / Rachel Sherman.
Description: Princeton : Princeton University Press,
[2017] | Includes bibliographical references and index.
Identifiers: LCCN 2017010629 | ISBN 9780691165509 (hardback : alk. paper)
Subjects: LCSH: Wealth—United States. | Rich people—United States. | Social
stratification—United States. | Social class—United States.
Classification: LCC HC110.W4 S54 2017 | DDC 305.5/2340973—dc23
LC record available at https://lccn.loc.gov/2017010629

British Library Cataloging-in-Publication Data is available

This book has been composed in Adobe Text Pro

Printed on acid-free paper. ∞

Printed in the United States of America

For Laura

The fortunate man is seldom satisfied with the fact of being fortunate. Beyond this, he needs to know that he has a right to his good fortune. He wants to be convinced that he "deserves" it, and above all, that he deserves it in comparison with others. . . . Good fortune thus wants to be "legitimate fortune."

—MAX WEBER, "THE SOCIAL PSYCHOLOGY OF THE WORLD RELIGIONS"

CONTENTS

5

LABOR, SPENDING, AND ENTITLEMENT IN COUPLES

6

PARENTING PRIVILEGE

Constraint, Exposure, and Entitlement

CONCLUSION

METHODOLOGICAL APPENDIX

Money Talks

NOTES

REFERENCES

INDEX

DISCUSSION QUESTIONS

ACKNOWLEDGMENTS

First and foremost, I am enormously grateful to all the people I interviewed for this book. They shared with me not only their time but also their thoughts, experiences, and emotions, which are not always easy to talk about. Their generosity made this project possible. I also want to thank the friends, colleagues, and acquaintances who helped me find the interviewees. For reasons of confidentiality I prefer not to name them here, but they were essential to this research.

Generous institutional and individual support made this project possible. The New School offered research funds and research assistance. Eric Klinenberg and the staff of NYU's Institute for Public Knowledge offered me the physical and mental space to begin writing this book in 2013–14, and a faculty fellowship at the New School's Graduate Institute for Design, Ethnography and Social Thought (GIDEST) allowed me to continue writing the following year. Lisa Keister generously responded to an out-of-the-blue request for data. Anna Matthiesen and Jussara Raxlen carefully and insightfully coded many interviews. Guillermina Altomonte and Tania Aparicio reviewed much of the secondary research, and Guillermina combed through late drafts and proofs to identify both intellectual and grammatical inconsistencies.

As I discuss in the appendix, working on this project has been intellectually and emotionally challenging. I could not have completed it without the support of a wide range of friends and colleagues. My greatest debt on this front is to Laura Liu and Miriam Ticktin, who have been both devoted friends and central intellectual interlocutors throughout the entire project. They offered astute and often transformative comments on many, many versions of papers and chapters and provided equally indispensable moral support on more occasions than I can count. I am also deeply grateful to Karen Strassler, with whom I have been discussing the core issues of this project for more than half our lives. Her interventions throughout, especially her uniquely perceptive reading of a full draft of the book, have been essential. Juliet Schor, Teresa Sharpe, and one anonymous Princeton reviewer offered incisive and useful comments on the entire manuscript, for which I am thankful.

Many people have read parts of this work at various stages, and the book has been enormously improved by their contributions. Jeff Alexander, Angèle Christin, Cindi Katz, Annette Lareau, and Robin Wagner-Pacifici offered insightful feedback at crucial moments. I am also indebted for comments and ideas to Leslie Bell, David Brody, Sébastien Chauvin, Bruno Cousin, Priscilla Ferguson, Melissa Fisher, Teresa Gowan, Rachel Heiman, Shamus Khan, Leslie McCall, Ashley Mears, Tey Meadow, Julia Ott, Devah Pager, Hugh Raffles, Lisa Servon, Lissa Soep, Millie Thayer, Florencia Torche, and Caitlin Zaloom. Carolina Bank Muñoz, Penny Lewis, and Stephanie Luce helped me hone my analysis in the early stages of writing. I am grateful to participants in the Craft of Ethnography workshop at Columbia, to members of the New School's GIDEST seminar, and to students and colleagues at my department's Brown Bag series, who read and commented on this work, as well as to the many audiences who have listened to me present on this project during the long course of its development. For their continued interest, encouragement, and help in a range of ways, I thank Michael Burawoy, Oliver Burkeman, Jeff Golick, David Herbstman, Dara Levendosky, Ruth Milkman, Debra Minkoff, Deirdre Mullane, Tim Murphy, Andy Perrin, Allison Pugh, Raka Ray, Juliet Schor, Steve Shohl, Sandy Silverman, Kim Voss, Paul VanDeCarr, and Viviana Zelizer. I also thank the Mentos, who always made me laugh, and my longtime crew of Neskowinners, who helped come up with the title.

I am fortunate to have worked with the whole team at Princeton University Press. Eric Schwartz was delightfully enthusiastic in the initial stages of the process. As I wrote the chapters, Meagan Levinson was an attentive and engaged editor, cheerfully reading multiple drafts with her eye on the prize of general accessibility. Marilyn Martin's careful and perceptive copy editing much improved the book, and Blythe Woolston's indexing made it searchable. Samantha

Nader, Mark Bellis, and Al Bertrand kept everything going smoothly behind the scenes. Finally, I want to recognize everyone who worked on the fantastic jacket design and the publicity, as well as all those whose labor was invisible to me but contributed in essential ways to making this book.

I feel very lucky to have a family that finds the work I do worthwhile and interesting. My mother, Dorothy Louise, engaged enthusiastically with this project from the first interview to the last punctuation mark. Tom Sherman and Nancy Middlebrook, my father and stepmother, were always eager to talk about the work and offer ideas and comments. Doug Sherman and Jeanne Henry encouraged me many years ago to think about some of the issues I explore here, and I have been fortunate to continue talking with them during the course of this project. Margaret Hunt provided unconditional love and plenty of Peruvian chicken. Last but never least, Laura Amelio contributed in more ways than I can possibly name here. I dedicate this book to her.

UNEASY STREET

INTRODUCTION

Scott and Olivia, both 39, live with their three children in a large pre-war apartment in Manhattan. They spend weekends and vacations at their second home in the Connecticut countryside. Their children attend a prestigious private school. They employ a part-time personal assistant as well as a nanny-housekeeper and occasionally a personal chef. On airplanes they usually travel in business class, though when the children were small the family often flew on private planes. Fueling this lifestyle is Scott's inherited wealth, generated by a business his grandfather founded. After earning Ivy League BA and MBA degrees, Scott worked in finance for several years before deciding that the benefits of this employment did not compensate for the time he had to spend on it. He now focuses on a small technology business he started that supports nonprofits, as well as playing an active role on the board of his children's school. Olivia is also Ivy League educated, although she comes from a working-class family. She has an MA in social work but works for pay only occasionally, spending most of her time taking care of the children and maintaining the household.

Scott told me he had been self-conscious about his wealth since he was a child. He recalled feeling sensitive to comments classmates and others would make about the size of his family's house. He said, "I just felt like, 'Yeah, this is kind of different. And, it's something to hide.'" In college he became a leftist and obscured his background as much as possible, but classmates ultimately found out that he was a "secret rich guy" and taunted him about the family's company, which was associated with abuses of workers' rights. When I talked with Olivia, she described feeling uncomfortable having married into wealth. Although she felt that it was easy to spend money helping other people or creating a home for her children, she had trouble spending only on herself, particularly because it was money she hadn't earned. Quite liberal politically, she and Scott were both

1

especially aware of those who had less. They also worried about their children and how to instill in them the desire to work.

Scott and Olivia's internal conflicts about their wealth cropped up especially in their feelings about their living space. When I interviewed Scott in 2009, he was overseeing renovation of an Upper West Side apartment worth $4.5 million, which they had bought primarily because they believed that each of their children should have his or her own room. But they felt conflicted about living there. When I asked why, Scott said, "Do we want to live in such a fancy place? Do we want to deal with the person coming in and being like, 'Wow!' You know, like, that wears on you. . . . We're just not the type of people who wear it on our sleeve. We don't want that 'Wow.'"

When I talked with Olivia a few years later, the family was living in their new home. But the transition had not been easy for her. In fact, she had initially been so uncomfortable with the apartment that they had considered not moving into it. The previous owner had done a significant renovation, which she found unbearably ostentatious. The apartment was "dripping marble" and had other aesthetic features Olivia hated. She said, "I mean, we're doing our best, with our clutter and junk, to, like, take the majesty and grandeur out of it. But, when I come [home], I feel like, 'This isn't me.' You know. This doesn't reflect who I feel like I am in the world, and who I want to be in the world."

In the renovation Olivia had planned to change the aesthetic elements that bothered her. But expensive unexpected structural problems ate up the money they had allocated, and Scott had balked at shelling out another million or so. Olivia told me, "We could have spent it. He just didn't—psychologically, he didn't want to. And I didn't either. But I also really didn't want to live with it the way it was." The conflict that ensued was, as Olivia described it, "traumatizing," destabilizing their marriage, and it resulted in their not doing anything to their new home for over two years. Olivia said that the renovation conflict "was a fight about a lot of things. But at root, I think it was about money. And what is okay to spend or not spend."

Their struggle was also partly about the *visibility* of their wealth, as their discomfort with the aesthetics of the apartment shows. As Scott noted, standing out had been a sore spot for him since his childhood. Olivia elaborated on this issue in talking about the opulence of her home vis-à-vis those of their peers and friends, whom she described as "normal." She said, "I always feel a certain level of awkwardness about having people over. Especially people—I mean, we don't hang out in society circles. In society circles, I don't think our apartment would be that exciting. We hang out with more normal people. And so, even having kids' friends over, there's always this, like, inner hurdle that I have to get over." She was still so uneasy with the fact that they lived in a penthouse that she had asked the post office to change their mailing address so it would include the floor number instead of *PH*, a term she found "elite and snobby."[1] Not surprisingly, neither invited me to their home; I talked with Scott in his office and with Olivia in mine.

But their discomfort was not just about how their consumption choices would look to others. It was also about how to set a limit on spending when there was, essentially, no objective ceiling, and what that limit meant about what kind of people they were. Scott said it had taken them nearly two years to buy an air conditioner when they first moved to New York. He said that kind of decision "typifies us." He continued, "We have to feel like we're doing it the hard way. I mean, the way we shop, the way we do our sort of like [family] stuff. And, you know, the way life works is, we do normal-Joe everyday stuff. We ride the trains. You know, for some reason it's important to us to feel that way." Olivia described creating these discomforts as "the mental trick I have to play, in a way, to be okay with having so much. And coming from so little."

Yet Scott and Olivia seemed to be growing more comfortable with their lifestyle over time. Olivia told me their annual spending had reached $800,000, up from $600,000 a few years before. She had a new attitude about the apartment, saying, "If we're going to live there, like, let's really live there. Let's really kind of embrace it, and not try to pretend like we don't live there, in a funny sort of way, by not getting the door fixed. You know, we had a broken closet door for the whole time we lived in our old apartment. So there's some, like, little mental game, again, about keeping it just a little bit uncomfortable. You know, we're here, but we're not really here, kind of thing. So that's finally starting to wear off. I'm kind of getting really tired of doing that." She was even planning to embark on another renovation.

Scott and Olivia are two of the fifty affluent and wealthy New York parents I interviewed for this book, who ranged from Wall Street financiers and corporate lawyers to professors and artists with inherited wealth. In talking with these people, I initially wanted to know how privileged New Yorkers made choices about consumption and lifestyle—that is, how people who had economic freedom decided what was worth spending money on. How did they make decisions about buying and renovating a home, placing children in school, hiring domestic workers, and using their leisure time? What counted as "real" needs versus "luxuries"? These questions mattered because they were related to a broader issue: how people who were *benefitting* from rising economic inequality experienced their own social advantages. Did they think of themselves as having more than others? If so, did this self-conception affect the life choices they made? What might these decisions and discourses have to do with their personal histories; their networks of friends, family, and colleagues; or their political views?

What stood out from the beginning of these conversations was how much my interviewees, like Scott and Olivia, had struggled over these decisions. I first noticed conflicts about how much money it was acceptable to spend, and on what. Was it okay to spend a thousand dollars on a dress? Two thousand on a purse? Half a million on a home renovation? Sometimes these were questions about how much they could afford, given their resources. But more often they were about *what kind of people they would be* if they made these choices. When a stay-at-home mother paid for a lot of babysitting, for example, was she "a snob"? If she sent back a light fixture she thought was too big for the kitchen, was she a "princess"? Did a couple with tens of millions in assets have to live with a sofa they hated because it felt "wasteful" to change it? These questions were loaded with moral judgment and language; my interviewees criticized excess and self-indulgence while praising prudence and reasonable consumption.

I therefore shifted the focus of the interviews to explore these issues more fully and started hearing about other kinds of dilemmas related to money and identity. How could these affluent parents give their children high-quality (usually private) education and other advantages without spoiling them? How should they resolve disagreements about spending priorities with their partners? How could those who did not earn money be recognized for contributing to their households? How should they talk with others, including me, about these decisions? Interior designers, financial planners, and other service providers I interviewed confirmed that their clients often had trouble talking about money and were conflicted about spending it.

Ultimately, I realized that these were conflicts about how to be *both wealthy and morally worthy*, especially at a historical moment of extreme and increasingly salient economic inequality. This book is about how these affluent New York parents grapple with this question.

CLASS INEQUALITIES AND IMAGINARIES IN THE UNITED STATES

In the United States, social class is a "touchy subject,"[2] which is "vast, amorphous, politically charged, [and] largely unacknowledged."[3] Free of the aristocratic and monarchical histories and social distinctions of Europe, the United States imagines itself as egalitarian.[4] The "American Dream" narrative tells us that anyone can "make it" with hard work and intelligence.[5] This commitment to equality of opportunity has long gone hand in hand with a taboo on explicit conversations about class and money, both among individuals and in public discourse. For centuries Americans have avoided terms such as *master* and *servant*, which explicitly recognize economic and status differences, in favor of euphemisms such as *help*.[6] Politicians rarely use the language of social class—though it has cropped up more in recent years, as I discuss later.

We do talk often about one class, of course: the "middle class." But, as Benjamin DeMott has shown, the "imperial middle"—the idea of the middle as all-inclusive—has actually fostered the idea of classlessness, because it portrays nearly all Americans as in the same boat.[7] In the period following World War II, this image was increasingly (though not entirely) accurate as the middle class grew both in real numbers and in symbolic power. Economic expansion, state policy established during and after the New Deal, and labor union strength allowed incomes and home ownership to rise enormously, especially for white people, and permitted many more people to attend college. Radical movements were decimated by anticommunist ideology and legislation during the Cold War, and poverty largely became invisible, allowing for the ascendance of the "middle class" as the central category of political discourse. Pundits believed that the future would simply entail managing affluence.

Yet this state of affairs was not to last. Beginning in the 1960s and gaining steam in the 1970s, international competition, outsourcing and deindustrialization, employer attacks on unions, and political realignments spelled the end of the broad prosperity of the postwar period. Single incomes no longer sufficed to support families. Since the Reagan era of the 1980s, these trends, plus neoliberalism, globalization, financialization, technological innovation, and the continued decline of both manufacturing jobs and union strength, have given rise to an economy based primarily on knowledge and services. Employers are less committed to workers than they were in the past, and vice versa. Concomitant with these economic changes, the welfare state has lost power and the social safety net has weakened. Tax policy has increasingly favored the wealthy. Most recently, the "gig" economy, based on short-term or freelance work, has emerged. Although some analysts laud such arrangements for their flexibility, these shifts have generated greater economic and occupational insecurity for many people.[8]

One of the most significant consequences of these transformations has been a dramatic increase in economic inequality in the United States since the 1970s, giving rise to what some have called "The New Gilded Age."[9] The benefits of economic growth have gone to the richest Americans—the top .01 percent, or the top 1 percent of the 1 percent—as CEO compensation and financial returns have skyrocketed.[10] Americans without college degrees have seen their incomes stagnate since the 1970s. The level of upward mobility is lower than most people believe, and inequality is higher.[11] Although the precise effects of rising inequality are debated, they may include increasing consumer debt, educational disparities, unequal health outcomes, and family problems, and in general high levels of inequality are thought to be socially detrimental.[12]

As the level of inequality has grown, the middle class has shrunk. The decline holds whether we define the middle class—a notoriously fuzzy concept—according to position in the income distribution, type of job, or lifestyle. The share of adults living in middle-income households in metropolitan areas is decreasing as more people are living in higher-income or lower-income households.[13] The number of middle-wage jobs, such as those of bus drivers and retail clerks, has stagnated relative to others as job growth has occurred mostly at the top and the bottom of the wage scale.[14] And even people in traditionally middle-class occupations (including teaching, social work, office work, and government employment) can no longer afford the traditional trappings of a middle-class lifestyle, such as owning a house and a car and paying for kids to go to college.[15]

Thus the middle class has become a kind of ghost category, existing more in the popular imagination than in reality. The symbolic power of the middle class persists, however, even as the referent disintegrates; this image remains ideologically critical in American cultural and political life.[16] Politicians still eternally refer to the "middle class" as the backbone of America, consisting of deserving, hardworking, family-oriented Americans. The morally worthy middle class is also symbolically attached to the "Protestant ethic," the idea that hard work and prudent consumption form the moral bedrock of

American society.[17] The use of the term *working families* to connote this same moral worth (and the implied counterpart of *nonworking families*) is an even clearer allusion to the importance of "hard work" in achieving the American Dream.

Although we rarely talk openly about class as a social category, popular culture and politics are both rife with images of wealthy and poor people. In contrast to the worthy middle, both the rich and the poor are often represented as *lacking* the basic values of hard work and prudence. Poor people have often been portrayed as lazy spendthrifts, typically in racially coded images such as that of the "welfare queen" of the 1980s, and therefore as "undeserving."[18] Wealthy people have likewise been cast as both lazy and profligate, at least since 1899, when critical economist Thorstein Veblen wrote *The Theory of the Leisure Class*, the book that introduced the concept of "conspicuous consumption." In Veblen's theory, highly visible consumption primarily functions as a mechanism of status competition among men. Veblen also paints the wealthy as uninterested in work—indeed, one of the functions of conspicuous consumption (and the complementary concept of "conspicuous leisure") is to demonstrate publicly the wealthy man's distance from productive labor.[19]

The theme of wealthy people as conspicuous consumers remains a mainstay of American culture, especially in moments of greater inequality. Such consumption marks the wealthy as both exotic objects of fascination and aspiration and as morally suspect in their materialism. Perhaps the most canonical American novel, F. Scott Fitzgerald's *The Great Gatsby*, portrays the American Dream gone awry in the character of arriviste Gatsby and the hedonistic, morally empty moment of the Roaring Twenties. In the 1980s, as the level of inequality rose again, Robin Leach took television viewers into the "lifestyles of the rich and famous." Now "reality" TV has made a cottage industry of representing wealthy lifestyles, spotlighting everyone from the Kardashians to the "real" housewives to the buyers and sellers of million-dollar real estate. Tabloid magazines trumpet the details of celebrities' astronomically expensive destination weddings and vacations, complete with full-page photo spreads.

The mainstream media also portray wealthy people in this way. In 2016, for example, both the *New York Times* and the *New Yorker* ran feature articles on the community of wealthy Chinese young people in Vancouver who, to judge from this reporting, are prone to drive Lamborghinis and buy gold-plated Apple watches for their dogs.[20]

The wealthy are often represented not only as status-seeking and lazy but also as morally deficient in terms of personality and behavior. They are snobby, greedy, rude, braggy, and self-absorbed. Social psychological research based on experiments and widely reported in the press indicates that rich people are more unethical, more narcissistic, less generous, more isolated, and generally less "pro-social" than other people.[21] The word *entitled* is the catch-all critical term for this kind of selfhood. It is nearly always used as a dirty word, describing people with an *illegitimate* belief that they should get whatever they want because of who they are and/or that they can treat other people badly because they have money.[22]

Finally, representations of both lifestyle choices and personalities cast the rich and famous as completely other, echoing F. Scott Fitzgerald's famous dictum that "the rich are different from you and me." By the same token, rich people are often represented as exotic, as if they live in another country or on another planet from "regular" people. Even relatively serious nonfiction books such as *Richistan* and *Plutocrats* reinforce this idea, even in their titles.[23]

Positive images of wealthy people do exist—especially of male entrepreneurs such as Bill Gates, Warren Buffett, and Steve Jobs. Yet these positive representations make the same point as negative ones: they reiterate the moral importance of hard work and the moral transgressiveness of elitism and excessive consumption (which has become, a century after Veblen, increasingly associated with wealthy women). Represented as hard workers who used their smarts to get ahead, good rich people are also often seen as minimalist consumers. Buffett, despite his billions, has famously lived since the 1950s in the same modest house in Omaha. Silicon Valley billionaires are known for their understated self-presentation (think of Jobs's black mock turtleneck or Mark Zuckerberg's gray sweatshirt).[24] Gates, Buffet,

Zuckerberg, and others are also lauded for their significant philanthropic enterprises across the country and the globe. Possessing a down-to-earth affect is another plus; in 2004 George W. Bush, despite his own extraordinary wealth and exclusive upbringing, managed to paint his opponent for the presidency, John Kerry, as an elite snob, while representing himself as the guy voters could imagine themselves having a beer with.

So being wealthy is not always good. Even words such as *well-off, wealthy, rich, affluent, privileged,* and *upper-class* have negative connotations and are rarely used by wealthy people to describe themselves. More frequently, we hear euphemisms such as "comfortable," "fortunate," and the hefty but neutral-sounding phrase "high net worth individual" (abbreviated HNWI).[25] In 2014 former first lady and secretary of state Hillary Clinton caused a minor scandal when she claimed that she and her husband were "dead broke" when they left the White House. She also contrasted herself with the "truly well-off," who, she said, don't pay "ordinary income taxes" and have not become wealthy "through dint of hard work." These verbal missteps reveal a deep discomfort with the idea of being wealthy in America. Clinton's comments, contrary to what we might assume, actually indicate that she would *rather* be perceived as "dead broke" than "truly well-off." And to be truly well-off, in her formulation, is to be a nonworking tax evader. Thus "real" rich people are morally compromised. Because Clinton pays taxes and works hard—despite her income of well over $100 million over the previous several years—she is not "really" rich. Whether one is wealthy in this connotative way is defined by how much moral integrity one has—not how much money.

In the past ten years, rich people have faced another symbolic challenge as economic inequality has emerged as a dominant issue on the national stage.[26] The 2008 housing market collapse and the subsequent "Great Recession" brought economic struggles front and center. In 2011 the Occupy movement's critique of "the 1 percent" dominated even the mainstream media. In 2014 French economist Thomas Piketty's 700-page book on inequality became a bestseller in the United States. Strikes by fast-food workers and prominent debates about raising the minimum wage to fifteen dollars per hour also put the spotlight on low-wage workers in this period. The 2016 presidential campaigns of Bernie Sanders and Donald Trump, despite their differences, kept outrage about economic disparities in the public eye. The language of class, especially the "working class," appeared in political discourse often in the period both before and after Trump's election. Public opinion critical of inequality has increased since 2000 as perceptions of the possibility of upward mobility have grown gloomier.[27]

INVESTIGATING AFFLUENCE

Given these contradictory ideas about wealthy people, how do the beneficiaries of growing inequality feel about and manage their privilege? Although images of the wealthy proliferate in the media, we know very little about what it is like to *be* wealthy in the current historical moment. Contemporary scholarly accounts of elite experience are in short supply, due largely to the difficulty of gaining access to wealthy people. The few studies of elite consumption that do exist focus on its explicitly or implicitly competitive dimensions, whether they embody Veblenian conspicuous consumption or other forms of social distinction.[28] Other research on elite lifestyles looks at how privileged people maintain and reproduce their privilege through social closure in elite clubs and elsewhere.[29] Researchers are skeptical of allusions to hard work, interpreting them mainly as shallow justifications.[30] Although scholars in recent years have stressed the importance of morality in the study of social class, they have theorized moral values primarily as another basis for exclusion.[31]

Research on class that foregrounds the lived experience of participants themselves, what Diane Reay has called "the psychic landscape of social class," has focused mainly on poor or working-class people or on the middle class.[32] Comparative studies of aspects of daily life such as parenting tend not to look at classes higher than the broad "middle" or occasionally the "professional middle."[33] Perhaps the only study analogous to mine is Susan Ostrander's 1984 book *Women of the Upper Class*. Ostrander interviewed thirty-six women in an unnamed city who met one or more of the classic criteria of upper-class membership: being listed in the *Social Register*,[34] belonging to exclusive clubs, or having attended elite prep schools. She talked with them about their lives as wives, mothers, and volunteers and argued that despite their gender subordination, these women played a key role in the reproduction of an upper-class lifestyle and community.[35]

However, the composition of U.S. elites has changed significantly since Ostrander conducted her research nearly four decades ago. In that period, as in most of the twentieth century, the upper class was exclusive and homogenous, dominated by old-money families such as the Rockefellers and Astors, the WASP elite chronicled (and so named) by sociologist E. Digby Baltzell.[36] Elite college and professional education were typically closed to all but white men; wealthy women rarely worked for pay. Social status was largely inherited, and the old elite looked down on newcomers. In the past few decades, in contrast, elites in the United States have become more diverse in terms of race, ethnicity, religion, and class of origin.[37] The *Social Register* has fallen into obscurity. The postwar opening of higher education, especially in elite institutions, to people besides elite WASP men was a major catalyst for this shift.[38] Globalization has also both helped create a more diverse upper class and generated a need for upper-class people to be able to navigate diverse cultures.[39] Importantly, not only the composition but the outlook of elites in the United States has changed, from a view that accepted inherited status as legitimate to one that stresses meritocratic achievement through hard work and cultural openness to a diverse world.[40]

Given the rise of this belief in meritocracy as well as increased and increasingly visible economic inequality in the context of contradictory discourses about wealth, I wanted to know how elite people would talk about questions of privilege and lifestyle. I wasn't seeking their opinions or attitudes about social class or inequality, like those we might find on a survey, but rather investigating what it *felt like* to be wealthy in this historical moment. As noted earlier, I thought looking at consumer decisions would be one avenue into this experience.

New York is an ideal place to explore these issues. It is a "global city" in which finance and related industries are concentrated. Indeed, astronomical compensation in these industries, the low-wage service jobs they generate,[41] and city development strategies favoring the rich have made New York the most unequal large city in the United States,[42] creating a situation Mayor Bill De Blasio has labeled an "inequality crisis."[43] In 2014 the gap between the poorest and the wealthiest in Manhattan was the largest in the country, as the average earnings of the top 5 percent were more than eighty-eight times those of the bottom 20 percent.[44] New York's levels of residential segregation by income as well as race are also among the highest in the nation.[45] As more wealthy professionals have stayed in the city rather than move to the suburbs, real estate prices have shot up. Many neighborhoods, especially in Manhattan and Brooklyn, have gentrified rapidly, pushing nonwealthy people farther into the outer boroughs. Issues of wealth and inequality are also extremely visible in the city. It is where the Occupy movement first appeared in the United States in 2011. Activists took over Zuccotti Park, in the heart of the financial district, thrusting these issues into the public spotlight. Finally, Manhattan is the backdrop for many of the most dominant images of the morally suspect wealthy, from the "Primates of Park Avenue"[46] to the "wolves of Wall Street."[47]

But who counts as "elite"?[48] As I discuss further in the appendix, defining *elites* is complicated. It is tempting to think of wealthy people as only the ones we see talked about in the media. But these representations tend to feature the super-wealthy, those in the top .1 percent or above. We might, instead, choose the top 1 percent, a definition often used in scholarly analysis and popularized by Occupy. The political focus on this category, through the slogan "We are the 99%," brought attention to inequality in a powerful way. But it also homogenized the 99 percent rather than acknowledging differences between, say, the top 2 percent and the bottom

50 percent.[49] Noting some of these issues, Lauren Rivera has advocated defining *elites* as the top 20 percent because of this group's educational advantages.[50]

I chose to start my study by seeking participants with annual household incomes of $250,000, which is in the top 5 percent in New York City.[51] I also decided to look for people in their thirties and forties who had children, as I believed that such people would be especially likely to be making important lifestyle decisions such as buying homes and choosing schools. I wanted to talk with both inheritors and earners of wealth. And I wanted to make sure to include people of color as well as gays and lesbians to investigate their underrepresented perspectives on these questions. In general, I was seeking a range of perspectives rather than a representative sample, as I discuss in the appendix. I found participants primarily through my own social networks, using snowball sampling; I located a few through nonprofit organizations oriented toward progressives with wealth.[52] After interviewing ten or fifteen participants recruited on the basis of different lifestyle decisions, I narrowed the focus to those engaged in home renovation, which combined aesthetic, familial, and financial elements and seemed like a clear place to start.

I ultimately interviewed fifty parents in forty-two households (including both members of eight couples).[53] Most families had two or three children, usually under 10 years old. Annual incomes across the group ranged from $250,000 to over $10 million; the range of assets was $80,000 to over $50 million. Most households (thirty-six, or 86 percent) had incomes of over $500,000 per year, assets of over $3 million, or both. About half earned over $1 million annually and/or had assets of over $8 million. The median household income of the sample was about $625,000, which is twelve times the New York City median of about $52,000.[54] The estimated median net worth was $3.25 million compared to $77,000 in the United States as a whole in 2010 and $126,000 in 2007.[55] About half had earned their primary assets; 25 percent had inherited the majority of their wealth (from $3 million to over $50 million); the remaining 25 percent both earned income of at least $400,000 per year and had inherited significant assets. Most were what Shamus Khan calls "new elite" in that they believe in diversity, openness, and meritocracy rather than status based on birth.[56] Even most of the inheritors of wealth were not from old-money families, having gained their wealth in the previous generation or two.

Those I interviewed lived in Manhattan, Brooklyn, or the nearby suburbs (all those in the suburbs had lived in the city before having children). About three-fourths were women. About 80 percent were white; the rest were South Asian, Asian American, African American, or mixed-race. About one-fifth identified as gay or lesbian. Fifteen interviewees had grown up at least partly in New York City or in the surrounding suburbs; the remainder hailed from all over the country except for a few who had been born outside the United States. All were college-educated, nearly exclusively in elite institutions. Two-thirds had earned advanced degrees, most often MBAs but also JDs, MAs in various fields, and PhDs.[57] They worked or had worked in finance, corporate law, real estate, advertising, academia, nonprofits, the arts, and fashion. Eighteen had left their full-time jobs to take care of children.[58]

These well-educated New Yorkers tended to share three characteristics. First, they had high levels of cultural capital. They were worldly and culturally curious. They enjoyed the arts and liked to travel; most said they valued experience more than material goods. Second, like most New Yorkers, they were politically liberal relative to their class.[59] (My sampling strategy also likely generated especially liberal and progressive respondents.) Most identified as Democrats, although a few located themselves to the left of the Democratic Party. Yet several voted Republican or independent or were married to Republicans, and many were economically conservative even if they voted Democratic. Finally, most were not especially religious. Slightly over half the people I talked with had been raised Catholic or Protestant; about one-third had been raised Jewish; the remainder practiced some other religion or combined Jewish and Christian traditions. Only about ten families, however, were seriously observant or regularly attended religious services.

In the course of this research I visited all kinds of homes: sub-urban houses, spacious urban apartments (often renovated to combine two or three original units), Manhattan townhouses, Brooklyn brownstones, and second homes in the Hamptons and Connecticut. Some were traditionally decorated, with antique furniture and spaces for formal entertaining; others were modern, marked by sleek lines and stark angles; still others were comfortable country homes surrounded by outdoor space. A few featured furniture designed by famous makers or valuable contemporary art. I conducted interviews in open kitchens, often outfitted with white Carrara marble or handmade tiles; at handcrafted dining tables; or on back decks in city gardens. I poked into bathrooms with soaking tubs or steam showers, living rooms decorated in palettes of gold or white, bedrooms with expansive views of the city or the river, and brightly decorated children's playrooms.

It was striking to me how customized these homes were and how deeply these homebuyers and renovators had thought about their lifestyles and their families as they considered what they needed and wanted in their living spaces. They talked about having to decide whether to have a separate dining room, whether their kids needed their own rooms or bathrooms, whether a stay-at-home mother needed an office. Where they lived was connected to a whole host of larger questions, including where they worked, where their children would go to school, and where they spent time on the weekends. They wanted to customize their homes aesthetically, too, seeking to express their individual styles through their choice of sofas, dining tables, wallpaper, faucets, paint colors, flooring, cabinets, appliances, countertops, and so on.

But despite these differences, most of the people I talked with described relatively similar lifestyles and consumption patterns. Nearly all had purchased at least one home, usually their primary residence; several had bought their homes outright or carried very small mortgages.[60] About a third of these families owned or were actively shopping for second homes (or third homes, in a few cases). These parents had slightly older children, suggesting that the purchase of additional homes occurs at least a little later in the parents' lives. Several of those with younger children rented summer or weekend houses or used those of family members, and they seemed likely to buy additional homes in the future. As we might expect, given the focus on renovation in my recruitment, about 90 percent had done significant renovation on an apartment or house or had built a primary or second residence from the ground up. Most children attended private schools, especially after sixth grade. Although their lifestyle choices varied according to whether they had incomes of $500,000 or $5 million, only the five or so families in the sample with the most limited resources (relative to the rest) had lifestyles significantly different from this one. I focus less on these families in this book.[61]

Maintaining these lifestyles requires a considerable amount of work. Among the heterosexual couples I studied, women usually had primary responsibility for the households, even when both partners worked for pay. As I will show in chapter 2, this "labor of lifestyle" involved extensive "consumption work,"[62] including planning and buying most of what was needed for the household, from food to furniture; carrying out renovations; maintaining second homes; overseeing children's care and education; and supervising and communicating with paid workers. Every household except one employed a housecleaner; all but one hired nannies or babysitters on a regular basis or had done so when their children were young. Some had also employed baby nurses, professional chefs, and personal assistants in their homes.

All my respondents had hired other expert service providers, including, for example, financial advisors, architects, interior designers, real estate brokers, personal chefs, and personal assistants. I conducted thirty interviews with people in these and related occupations (such as personal concierges and art advisors). I was interested in talking with such "cultural intermediaries"[63] because they facilitate their clients' consumption choices; in fact, their labor makes these lifestyles possible. They also have extensive and intimate knowledge of their clients' experiences of spending, accumulating, and giving away money, and their accounts therefore complement those of the wealthy consumers.[64]

TALKING (OR NOT) ABOUT MONEY

Perhaps not surprisingly, given the American cultural taboo against discussing money and class, most of my respondents were uncomfortable talking about their incomes and assets.[65] My first indicator of this reticence was an unusual difficulty finding people willing to participate in the project. As I describe in more detail in the appendix, this challenge seemed connected to the centrality of the topic of spending to the project.

In the interviews, most people described themselves as reluctant to talk about money in any detail with anyone except their partners and sometimes other close family members. They described money as deeply private—"more private than sex," in the words of one psychotherapist I interviewed. When I questioned one very wealthy woman about her assets, she said "No one's ever asked me that, honestly. . . . No one asks that question. So it's up there with, like, 'Do you masturbate?' That's just not something that people say." When we talked outside, they kept their voices down so their neighbors wouldn't hear; inside, some closed the door when the nanny was in the next room. Although most were ultimately fairly open with me, a few refused to answer certain kinds of questions, especially about specific amounts.[66] Several women mentioned that they would not tell their husbands that they had spoken to me at all, saying, "He would kill me" or "He's more private."[67] Linda, an academic whose husband had inherited wealth, believed there was too much stigma in "our culture" about discussing money. But she also refused to tell me her family's net worth, saying "I don't think I can really answer that, I'm sorry. I just feel like that's too much and it's too private for [her husband]. . . . I think he would hit the roof."

I also got the strong sense from many people that they were underreporting their income and/or assets, whereas I never suspected that they were exaggerating how much they had. Ursula, a stay-at-home mother whose husband was a technology executive, was uncomfortable telling me her husband's income. She asked, "Do we really have to get into that?" I offered, "You can give me a range." She said, "A million plus." Later in the interview, she corrected herself to say that her second home had cost $250,000 more than she had originally told me. Suspecting that she had underreported the income as well, I asked, half-joking, "So when you said 'one-plus' on the income, was it one plus . . . ten?" She laughed, and I asked, "One plus more than one?" She nodded. I said, "So, two plus?," and she nodded again—signaling affirmation while literally maintaining silence. Public records of home sales confirmed that others had quoted lower amounts to me than they had actually paid, while no one had inflated the purchase prices of their homes.

A few participants became extremely anxious about having shared financial information. One woman told me, speaking of her assets and home value, "I don't think that anybody knows our pocketbook. Like, there's nobody who knows how much we spend. I mean, you're the only person I ever said those numbers to out loud. . . . I don't say numbers to anybody, not my parents, nobody knows anything about anything. We try to be as discreet about it as possible." After the interview she emailed me and asked me to call her; when I did, she voiced concern about confidentiality, asking me not to talk about where she lived or how much she and her husband had paid for their home because they could conceivably be identified using public data on home purchases in a particular neighborhood. (These concerns about confidentiality were so extreme that I have taken significant pains to avoid making it possible for anyone to identify my respondents, particularly the people who introduced them to me, as I describe in the appendix.)

Despite this discomfort, many of the people I interviewed also acknowledged that they *thought* about money and lifestyle issues constantly and discussed them often with their spouses. Beatrice, who worked in a nonprofit but had inherited wealth, said she and her husband talked about these subjects "every minute of every day that we're not at work." Some described sharing their money conflicts with their therapists. Others admitted speculating about what their friends and neighbors earned and sometimes judging friends and family members for certain kinds of spending. By the same token, some said they enjoyed the interview because it allowed them to speak about these issues. It was "cathartic," said Alice, a stay-at-home mother, "to talk about things that you are always thinking about." Beatrice reflected at the end of the interview: "I've now told you everything that I even feel like is vaguely private about our lives." She told me she'd have been more comfortable talking about her sex life. "But," she added, "it's a bit of a relief. It does feel a little bit like an unburdening. It's, like, making all this stuff that you normally keep to yourself or between you and your intimate partner kind of tightly controlled, kind of letting it out and seeing it does not cause shock or horror." As it turned out, these silences about money were closely connected to ambivalence about being wealthy.

THE ANXIETIES OF AFFLUENCE

The wealthy women Susan Ostrander studied around 1980, who had been born mainly from 1900 to 1940, appeared comfortable with their class privilege. For the most part raised in a homogenous wealthy community, they saw themselves as pillars of that community, publicly carrying out charitable works and preparing their children to follow in their upper-class footsteps by organizing their prep school educations and debutante parties. Ostrander sees this community participation as an attempt to justify their privilege, but she does not describe any significant conflict about their class advantages (although some felt constrained by their gender roles). In fact, these women saw themselves as "being better than other people," expressing "a sense of moral, as well as social, superiority."[68] They seem never to have mentioned any desire for diversity in their communities. Indeed, some were doubtful about or openly hostile to admitting nonwhite, non-Protestant people to their clubs.[69]

The New Yorkers I spoke with, in contrast, were much less complacent about their social advantages. As I have noted, I was surprised at how many conflicts they expressed about spending. Over time, I came to see that these were often moral conflicts about *having* privilege in general. Some, like Scott and Olivia, talked about these struggles quite openly with me, while others were more indirect. As I discuss in detail in chapter 1, some of those I interviewed tended not even to think of themselves as socially advantaged because they were focused on others around them who had the same resources or more than they did. I call these people "upward-oriented," while "downward-oriented" people, including Scott and Olivia, were more likely to see themselves as privileged. Downward-oriented people tended to have more economically diverse social networks and thus to compare their own lifestyles to a broader range of other possibilities. Either way, the vast majority implicitly or explicitly indicated that they had some kind of moral concern about having wealth.

One way they addressed these conflicted feelings was to try to *minimize* the importance of privilege, or the privilege itself, by obscuring it. Whether they were oriented upward or downward, nearly all my interviewees also observed the cultural norm of not talking about money with people besides their partners. Like Scott and Olivia, who were ambivalent about having visitors, they also sometimes wanted to avoid *showing* their wealth to those with less. They asserted that money didn't influence how they thought about other people. And they believed that referring explicitly to their advantages might make those with less feel bad. But they also acknowledged that talking about their privilege made *them* feel vulnerable to negative judgments from others.[70]

Monica, who worked in real estate and had a household income of about $400,000, used this strategy of silence. She refused to tell me what her monthly expenses were, saying, "That's not for you to know." When I asked her to explain why she felt that way, she responded (slipping into the more distant second-person "you"), "I don't think people need to know what you're willing to spend, what you're willing to do. I mean, some people think it's crazy that we send our kids to private school. I don't need to have to argue that." She continued, "I do think people assume, or make assumptions, and create personalities of who you may or may not be, and what your choices are. And I think it is based on—a lot of it is financial." She also said her spending "is not a value. It's not a value about who I am, or what I am." Monica, like many others, also said she treated all people with respect, regardless of their economic status.

For the people I talked with, these general norms of civility—not talking about money, not "showing off," treating others as one wants to be treated—were also mechanisms for silencing and obscuring their own privilege, to others and sometimes to themselves. Following the culturally prominent idea of classlessness, they opted for a kind of "blindness" to class difference analogous to the widespread (though problematic) ideal of race-blindness.[71] These themes of silence and visibility run through their accounts, as the rest of the book will show.

At the same time, however, my interviewees did recognize that they were privileged. So, although they were silent with others, they struggled with themselves over the question of how *to be worthy* of this privilege in a moral sense. In order to feel that they deserved their advantages, they tried to interpret themselves as "good people." My reading of these efforts constitutes the core of this book.

My respondents' narratives delineated three characteristics of "good people." First, as I show in chapter 2, good people work hard. Across the board, these affluent parents described themselves as hard workers, drawing on general associations in American Dream ideology between work and worth.[72] They valued self-sufficiency and productivity and rejected self-indulgence and dependence. Those who had earned their wealth wore their paid employment proudly, although they often felt anxious about the risk of losing their jobs. Those who had inherited wealth or did not currently work for pay resisted stereotypes of laziness or dilettantism and offered alternate narratives of themselves as productive workers.

Second, good people are prudent consumers. The consumption aspect of the Protestant ethic has become less prominent in contemporary discourses of meritocracy, which focus on work,[73] but it surfaced strongly in these accounts. It may be counterintuitive to associate wealthy New Yorkers with Puritans, whom we imagine as self-denying ascetics, when they have large homes full of material goods, travel widely, raise their children in comfort, and for the most part are not very religious. Yet, as I show in chapter 3, they described their desires and needs as basic and their spending as disciplined and family-oriented. They asserted that they "could live without" their advantages if they had to, denying that they were dependent on their comfortable lifestyles. They distanced themselves from the negative images of consumption often associated with the wealthy, such as ostentation, materialism, and excess—all markers of moral unworthiness. These interpretations allowed them to believe that they deserved what they had and at the same time to cast themselves as "normal" people rather than "rich" ones.

In these ways, good people are *ordinary* people, belonging symbolically to the broad middle. The third requirement for being a good person—the obligation to "give back"—more explicitly recognizes privilege. But, as I discuss in chapter 4, this imperative meant different things to different people, which entailed publicly acknowledging privilege to varying degrees. Often to "give back" meant to "be aware" of and "appreciate" their advantages rather than to take them for granted—an essentially private state of feeling. Many gave away money, and time as well, in charitable enterprises of various kinds. But these practices were marked by ambivalence over what it meant to identify and be visible as a wealthy person. Those who faced upward, who moved in relatively class-homogenous communities, were more likely to take for granted that they would play this kind of role. Those who were more "downward-oriented" were often more ambivalent.

As we will see throughout, for my respondents to be a "good person" was *not* to be "entitled."[74] Betsy, for example, was a management consultant turned stay-at-home mother with a household income of about $1 million. She said of her lifestyle, "I don't think we feel entitled to it." When I asked what she meant by "entitlement," she said, "Feeling that you deserve it because you were born into it or had the right education, and [that] it *should* be this way." Monica, who worked with people much wealthier than she, said she would not want to "have the money they have, and be the ass that they are. . . . They're just not nice people. And part of it is that they feel that they're owed things because they either have money or they're famous."

Notably, being morally worthy and avoiding entitlement involve both *behaving* and *feeling* in particular ways. *Practices* of working hard, consuming prudently, and giving back are matched by *affects* of independence, modest desire, and appreciation rather than a feeling of being "owed things," in Monica's words. Yet it is not easy to adhere to all of these imperatives of merit or to interpret oneself as adhering to them, and the people I interviewed often struggled to do so. In chapter 5 I show how these struggles play out in couples. Partners look to each other for recognition of themselves as worthy workers and consumers, but they do not always find this recognition. They clash over what kinds of needs are legitimate, as Scott and Olivia did over their renovation. And they experience gendered conflicts over whether unpaid labor "counts" symbolically as a contribution to the family's lifestyle.[75]

Finally, the parents I talked with want to pass these behaviors, feelings, and values on to their children. As I show in chapter 6, anxieties about children's entitlement were especially prominent throughout my interviews. Parents want to raise nonmaterialistic, hard-working, nice people rather than, in Scott's words, "lazy jerks." Of course this desire is widespread among parents regardless of class. But for these affluent people the concern about entitlement harbors a deep contradiction. They want their children to see themselves as "normal" (and therefore just like everyone else) but also to appreciate their advantages (which make them different from others). In the end, they instill and reproduce ideas about how to occupy privilege legitimately without giving it up—how to be a "good person" with wealth.

This book challenges two common ideas about the wealthy: one, that they are always engaged in a competitive struggle for status or distinction, and two, that they are complacent about their privilege. I also highlight their desire to be moral actors. My goal is not, however, simply to understand the experiences and perspectives of affluent people or to "humanize" them in the face of sensationalistic media representations. Instead, these ideas about what it means to be a good person with wealth matter, I argue, because they draw on and thus illuminate broadly held notions of what it means to be *legitimately* privileged. Illegitimate privilege means excess, ostentation, and entitlement. In contrast, legitimate privilege means being ordinary, down-to-earth, hard-working, and prudent.

These ideas are not unique to my respondents. Much the opposite, in fact; these ways of thinking about legitimacy and moral worth resonate, I contend, precisely because they constitute "common sense."[76] The fact that some people have much more than others comes to be taken for granted as long as those who benefit *inhabit* their privilege appropriately. It's about what individual people do, how they feel, and who they are, not what they have. Even negative judgments of individual behavior are legitimations of wealth in general. That is, judging "bad" wealthy people means "good" wealthy people can also exist. In the end, ironically, inhabiting privilege in an "unentitled," morally worthy way actually legitimates entitlement.

As a result, it becomes hard to articulate a distributional critique rather than a behavioral one: that some people should not have so much while others have so little, regardless of how nice or hardworking or charitable they are. Furthermore, the focus on individual behavior and affect also draws attention away from social processes that foster the unequal distribution of resources, including the decline of public education and social welfare programs, employers' assault on trade unions, and tax policy that favors the rich.[77]

VARIETIES OF EXPERIENCE

Although all the people I interviewed wanted to be morally worthy, they described their emotions, conflicts, and choices in different ways. These variations seemed linked especially to class background and upward mobility, the source of wealth (inherited or earned), occupation, and political stance. High earners, for example, were especially likely to talk about valuing self-sufficiency and to feel economically at risk, regardless of gender. Inheritors talked more about experiencing discomfort or guilt about their wealth—unless they were also earners. The microcultures of work and consumption in which respondents were embedded also mattered. Earners who lived in uptown Manhattan and in the suburbs, for example, tended to have less diverse social circles than those who lived downtown or in Brooklyn. I attend to these differences in various ways throughout the book, beginning with chapter 1, and return to them in the conclusion. But it is impossible in this small and unrepresentative sample to see exactly how these many factors, which often work together, may "cause" certain kinds of orientations.[78] More important than parsing the causes of differences, I believe, is to trace the common discourses about legitimate privilege that emerged in these conversations.

I did not see major, patterned differences among my interviewees on the basis of race and ethnicity. I believe this is not because such differences do not exist but because my sample of people of color was too small and too crosscut with other factors to reveal such tendencies. A more systematic comparison by race with a larger number of interviewees of color might reveal patterned differences.[79] I do discuss questions of race and ethnicity where they seem especially salient. Because of concerns about confidentiality, described in the appendix, I have chosen not to identify named respondents by race; where I discuss race and ethnicity I use separate pseudonyms or I do not name the interviewees. Readers should not assume that quoted respondents are white.

A NOTE ON JUDGMENT

As I have suggested, accounts of wealthy people's consumption are often treated with voyeurism, skepticism, and moral judgment. It is easy to be fascinated by the details of my interviewees' lifestyles, especially by the seemingly astronomical amounts they possess and spend. And it is easy to feel suspicious of their accounts. Are they "really" working hard? Is their spending "actually" reasonable? Do they "truly" avoid display? Many of my respondents live in houses and apartments worth millions, own second homes, shop in expensive stores, travel widely, fly first class, and/or pay for a wide variety of household and other services. Their children, for the most part, lack nothing material. They go to the best schools and receive historically unprecedented amounts of adult attention from parents, tutors, therapists, coaches, and others.

I have seen such skepticism and judgment among people who have read parts of this work or heard me talk about it, and I have experienced them myself. Indeed, I sometimes find it tricky just to describe my subjects' lifestyles and some of their comments without sounding disparaging, because we almost automatically attach value judgments to these choices. These reactions, I believe, come from the exact assumption I am trying to challenge: that rich people are unpleasant, greedy, competitive consumers. And to ask such questions about my interviewees, from my perspective, is to miss the point. The issue is that they *want* to be hard workers and prudent consumers. Whether they actually *are* is, for one, impossible to adjudicate, because definitions of hard work, excess, display, and so on are always relative. More important, attempting to determine the "truth" about wealthy people's actions and feelings ensnares us in precisely the normative distinctions I am questioning. These classifications ultimately legitimate privilege by representing some rich people as "good" while others are "bad" rather than critiquing systems of distribution that produce inequality. My goal is to avoid this kind of orientation in favor of illuminating larger cultural processes of legitimation that are, in the main, taken for granted in the United States.

So I ask readers of this book to be aware of their evaluations of wealthy individuals as deserving or not and to consider how these assessments may in fact obscure critiques of resource distribution. If we did not see wealthy people as exotic or evaluate them as morally worthy or unworthy, how might we see them? And how might we then think about what it means to be deserving of privilege?

1

ORIENTATIONS TO OTHERS

ASPIRING TO THE MIDDLE OR RECOGNIZING PRIVILEGE

I interviewed Ursula in her spacious apartment on the Upper West Side, in a living room with a view of the Hudson River. Ursula is in her mid-forties, with two children and a husband who earns "two million plus" per year in his job as a high-level executive at a technology company. She has an MBA and a long work history in business. But several years ago she left paid employment, with some ambivalence, when she could not find a meaningful part-time job. She now primarily takes care of her home and children, as well as volunteering at their private school. She and her husband employ a nanny/housekeeper/cook who works about forty hours each week. Their apartment, which they have renovated significantly, is worth approximately $4 million. They spend weekends at their house in the Hamptons, valued at over $1.5 million.

Despite these advantages, which place her well into the top 1 percent, Ursula tends to situate herself primarily in relation to those who have more than she does. During the interview, Ursula characterized her upbringing as "middle-class." When I followed up by asking if she would describe herself now the same way, she said, "Yeah. You know, New York City, I feel like, no matter what you have, somebody has about a hundred times that." She does not feel that she lacks for anything; when I ask what she would do if her household income suddenly doubled, she can only think of "marginal" items such as improvements to the house in the Hamptons. And she does not express envy of people wealthier than she. Yet she is primarily oriented to people with as much as or more than she has, and she rarely talks about herself as privileged or explicitly expresses conflicts about it. Asked if she ever felt guilty about having more than other people, she responded, "No. Maybe there are more people that I know that have more, so, no."

Contrast Ursula to Keith and Karen, a couple also in their forties, also with two kids, who, like Ursula's, are around ten years old. Both Keith and Karen work, though Keith's job as an academic brings in most of their $300,000 household income. Both have advanced degrees. They own a house worth over $1.2 million in a desirable neighborhood in Brooklyn. They were able to buy the house when they sold their first apartment, which they had bought with funds lent by Keith's parents. They have assets of about $500,000 in retirement and college savings, but they dipped into their "emergency savings" and took out a loan to pay for a recent renovation. They do not own a second home, and their children go to public school. They often worry about money.

Because Karen and Keith have significantly less income and fewer assets than Ursula and her husband, live in a more modest home, and send their kids to public school, we might expect that they would see themselves as less advantaged than she does. In fact, however, they were much more likely to talk about feeling privileged, both relative to others in their social worlds and in general. Keith called the loan from his parents for their down payment "the ultimate white-person advantage." Karen said, of the renovation, "We're both horrified by how much money we make and that we even have to have these decisions. I mean, it's ridiculous." She worried that people they knew would see their renovation as "profligate." Keith said, "My feeling is it's a bottomless pit, renovation and home improvement. And I think that six Chinese people are camping out in some one-bedroom hovel in Beijing right now. So, like, the notion that you 'need' something is all BS." He characterized his kids as "living like kings two hundred years ago." Made without prompting from me, these comparisons invoked people with less rather than those with more.

As we have seen, the people I interviewed are objectively advantaged in terms of income and wealth. But like Ursula and Keith and Karen, they varied in terms of whether they *talked about themselves as privileged* and what kinds of feelings they expressed about it.[1] Because privilege is always relative, their orientations had a lot to do with which kinds of other people they compared themselves to. People like Ursula, whom I call "upward-oriented," downplayed their advantages by comparing themselves to others in a similar position or to those who had more. In fact, they were likely to locate themselves, implicitly and sometimes explicitly, "in the middle." They tended to recognize privilege only indirectly, using euphemisms such as "lucky" or "fortunate." They talked less about money unless I asked them directly about it, and they expressed fewer conflicted feelings about privilege per se. Instead, they talked more about feeling anxious and at risk. I describe taking this stance as "aspiring to the middle." "Downward-oriented" people like Keith and Karen, on the other hand, were more likely to describe themselves as privileged and to talk about people with less. They also talked more frankly about money and described struggling with feelings of discomfort about their advantages.

These orientations were not set in stone. Many people used both upward- and downward-oriented discourses over the course of our conversations, as I will show. And even when they seemed consistently upward- or downward-oriented, these stances might have had more to do with the conversational situation we were in than with some "permanent" orientation. Yet I did find patterns. Overall, those who openly recognized their privilege lived in more diverse worlds, both literally and imaginatively, than those who did not. They were more likely to have colleagues, friends, and/or family members from more varied backgrounds and with fewer resources. And they were usually more liberal or progressive politically, which made them more likely to have a structural understanding and critique of inequality.[2] Upward-oriented people, in contrast, moved in more homogenous social and family circles, had experienced less class mobility, and espoused more conservative politics (relatively speaking).

The one exception to this pattern was among women in the highest-earning families in my sample, those with household incomes of over $5 million per year and assets of over $20 million. These stay-at-home mothers described themselves as privileged even when they did not have especially liberal politics or diverse social networks. They were "upwardly mobile" in the sense that they had been raised upper-middle-class but were now much more wealthy than that. More important, I think, was that it was essentially impossible for them to face upward, simply because there were so few people above them. For the most part, however, income and assets were not correlated to whether people would face upward or downward.

We might imagine that upward-oriented people simply don't notice that they are privileged. Social-psychological research on relative advantage, though much less developed than that on relative deprivation, has suggested that people in advantaged groups may not recognize their advantages because they see their situation as "normal" or "neutral," while the minority position stands out. The classic example of this tendency comes from studies of race and whiteness: white people's experience tends to be seen as neutral, while that of people of color is seen as "exceptional."[3] But my interviewees are not in the numerical majority, as whites have historically been in the United States; nor is wealth analogous to whiteness, because it is not taken for granted in the way that whiteness is. "Middle-class" status and cultural capital, as opposed to "working-class" status, are often taken for granted, but wealth is not. Furthermore, as I have noted, the people I spoke with live in or just outside the most unequal city in the United States at a moment when economic disparities are especially prominent. And of course downward-oriented people do recognize and talk openly about their privilege relative to a wide range of others, indicating that it can be visible.

So, I argue, it is not that the advantages of upward-oriented people are actually mysterious to them. Instead, like Hillary Clinton defining herself as "dead broke," they are working hard to avoid defining themselves as privileged. Rather than trying to include themselves in exclusive categories of those who have more, they try, interpretively, to have *less*. In fact, by framing themselves as "in the middle" they try to attach themselves to the morally worthy category of the "middle class." At least to some extent, I suggest, these self-interpretations deflect conflicts they feel about having more than others.[4] Instead of making them feel worse, as theories of relative deprivation might suggest,[5] seeing themselves as having less actually makes them feel better. Downward-oriented people are more willing to acknowledge their conflicted feelings openly. As we will see in later chapters, however, people in both categories care about *inhabiting* their privilege in a morally worthy way.

LOOKING UPWARD FROM THE "MIDDLE"

Like Ursula, the people who tended to situate themselves "in the middle" typically shared several characteristics. First, they or their spouses earned all or a significant portion of their income rather than inheriting it. Some also had family wealth, but their incomes from earnings were significant and seemed likely to cover most of their expenses. They worked (or had worked, in the case of stay-at-home mothers) mainly in finance, business, real estate, or corporate law—fields in which incomes are typically quite high. Second, their friends were relatively similar to them. A few said they desired more diverse social circles, but they tended to be talking about occupational rather than socioeconomic diversity—for instance, businesspeople wished they had more friends who worked in the arts. Finally, they were also likely to identify as Republicans or more conservative Democrats. Most called themselves socially liberal and economically conservative. And all who talked about tax increases on wealthy people were opposed to them.

Like Ursula, upward-oriented people described New York City as an environment in which they were not especially privileged. Maya was an attorney turned stay-at-home mother, married to a corporate lawyer, with an income of over $2 million. She told me, for example, "I don't think of us as really wealthy or not really wealthy. I think part of it is if you take where we are and you put us in Spokane, we're actually really wealthy. But if you put us in New York, we're just—in our circle, we're fine. I mean, there are all the bankers that are heads and heels, you know, way above us." Maya uses the reference to those with more to frame herself as not having that much and casts herself as essentially the same as the people she socializes with ("our circle")—who were primarily her husband's business associates and their families.

These people sometimes characterized themselves *explicitly* as "in the middle" when referring to those above them. Helen was a stay-at-home mother who had worked in banking and was married to a lawyer, with a household income of over $2 million and assets I estimate at well over $8 million, including two homes. She told me, "I feel like we're somewhat in the middle, in the sense that there are so many people with so much money. They have private planes. They have drivers. They have all these things. . . . You know, money makes everything easier. It makes it easier for you to do much more, actually. And, you know, we don't have that luxury in that way." Helen's focus here is on the privilege she lacks rather than the advantages she has; although she is not complaining, she is situating herself relative to a particular set of others.

Willa worked in advertising and, with her husband, garnered a $2 million annual household income. They and their children lived in a brownstone worth about $5 million, and she came from a wealthy family. When I asked if she felt either privileged or underprivileged relative to others in her life, she responded: "No. There are always going to be people who make more money than we do. And there are people who don't make as much money as we do. And, you know, we found what works for us, and we're happy with it. I mean, we were joking the other day, when we played the Powerball. And it's like, nothing would change. You know? I mean, we're happy with this house. You know. We have everything that we need. Our life is not going to change if we win the Powerball." Willa also told me, of her kids' position in their private school, "You know, they're right in the middle. There are people [at the school] who have much more money than they do, and there are people who have less money than they do." Willa seems less dissatisfied than Helen. But both women exaggerate the ratio of the people above them to those below. Helen looks up and sees "so many" people with more; Willa creates an equivalence between those above and those below. (Notably, Willa also frames social disparities as permanent, something that will "always be.")

I asked Allison, a nonprofit lawyer turned stay-at-home mother in her forties, how her current lifestyle compared to the one she grew up with. She told me, "You know, I'm definitely much more affluent. But I still feel middle-class." She described her father's managerial job and her parents' household income, when she was growing up, as about $120,000 (itself well above the median at the time). She said, "We didn't take any vacations. We never went anywhere." This sounded very different from her current household income of about $3 million and two family vacations a year (plus millions in assets and real estate). I asked, echoing what she had said, "And so you feel like now it's more affluent, but it's still middle-class?" She responded: "We're definitely middle-class. In New York City, and in that school community, we're def—we're—yeah. I feel like—yeah. Upper-middle-class." I read Allison's hesitant shift from "middle-" to "upper-middle-class" as a result of her desire to define herself as middle-class, combined with recognizing that she can't quite do that, given the obvious differences between her childhood lifestyle and her current one. To support her interpretation, she invokes both her kids' private school and the New York context.

Other upward-oriented people similarly characterized themselves as in the middle, often implicitly, by framing their environments in particular ways. Zoe is a stay-at-home mother with an MBA and a household income of at least $1 million, plus family wealth, whose home is worth over $3 million. She told me "New York is a bubble. Everyone that can afford to live here is pretty well off. So you don't see the downside. Even the [parents of] kids that are going to the schools that we're sending our kids to. They're able to pay forty grand a year to send their kid to school, which is crazy. So you don't see the underprivileged. . . . It's sad, but it's kind of like the out-of-sight, out-of-mind thing, where you don't think about it in your—everyone's so busy that you don't think about it." Zoe's comment makes clear that the people she is most aware of are those who are most similar to her, as she conflates "everyone" in New York with the "pretty well off." Her idea that "you don't see the under-privileged" is also notable given that nearly everyone with whom she is likely to come into casual contact is less well off than she, raising questions about whom Zoe chooses both to "see" and to define as "underprivileged." Zoe does not locate herself as "in the middle" because she says she is "pretty well off." Yet she classifies those who are *not* pretty well off as "the underprivileged," which does situate her, in a sense, in the middle.

I found Zoe's view especially intriguing because, as we talked in her apartment, her housekeeper was working in the next room, offering living proof that not everyone in New York was "pretty well off." So I asked Zoe if she thought about these issues in relation to the housekeeper and the nanny she employed. She responded, "We treat them very well," by which she meant paying them generously, al-lowing them days off, and giving them used clothing that Zoe would otherwise donate elsewhere. She said, "For sure, with them, I take it into account that they're seeing our lifestyle. And I think it's not fair to try to demand—I want them to be happy." Zoe knows she is priv-ileged in relation to her domestic employees, and that matters to her to a certain extent, particularly because these individual women "see [her] lifestyle" (rather than because they belong to a larger group of less privileged people). She sees them because they see her. But she is not hyperaware of or conflicted about the inequality between herself and her employees in the way that others I introduce later are. Instead Zoe uses a "maternalistic" approach, which positions her as a "benefactor" and does not challenge inequalities between domestic workers and their employers.[6]

As noted in the introduction, Monica is a real estate agent mar-ried to an advertising executive, with a household income of about

$400,000. She told me of herself, her family, and her community of friends, "In New York, we're middle-income." She alluded almost immediately not to their actual income but to their consumption, saying, "None of us are ostentatious. None of us have big, fancy cars." Here "middle-income" signals a spending style, not a dollar amount. Later she described her family's lifestyle as follows: "I live modestly, I mean, I don't have jewels. . . . There's no flash. We're just normal. I mean, in *my* world, it's not flashy. To somebody that lives in a trailer park, I don't know. But we live a fairly simple life." She described the family's evening routine of having dinner, helping kids with homework, watching TV, and going to sleep. As we will see in chapter 3, it was common for my interviewees to allude, as Monica did, to a family life that is "just normal," comprising household habits that any family might have.

Notably, Monica does compare herself to those below her, by mentioning "somebody that lives in a trailer park." With this allusion, she casts herself as privileged, but only vis-à-vis people much poorer than she. Her rhetoric acknowledges disparity, but because a trailer park is a common signifier of poverty, it presents the disparity as between the middle (Monica) and the poor rather than as between the wealthy and the middle. And trailer parks are rare, if not unknown, in New York City. This trope of poverty thus becomes even further removed from anyone Monica might see in her daily life, although she could have invoked any number of poor people closer to home, from domestic workers in her own apartment to the homeless people one sees every day on New York streets. She also could have cast herself as privileged relative to those who are not poor but still have less than she does. Such a category would include, for example, most if not all the service workers she comes into contact with on a given day, including those who sell her food and clothes and educate her children.

Justin, who had assets over $10 million and a household income of about $400,000, made a similar interpretive move that classified those with less as those with much, much less. He reframed the comparison group when he said: "I think everyone, myself included, in this nation, is obscenely rich compared to other countries. I've seen a lot of the country. . . . The poorest guy in America's still one of the richest around. Still has a car, a house. You know, people in Africa, they don't. They never will have a car. So from that sense [I feel privileged]. But do I say and think daily, 'This guy walking down the street's poorer than me?' No." By focusing on basic needs, such as a house and a car, Justin interprets Americans as more similar to each other than they are to "people in Africa" and implies that differences above this basic standard are less important. All of these forms of recognizing advantage tend to spotlight only the radically disadvantaged, thus eliding the significant difference between those who are aspiring to the middle and those in the actual middle of the income distribution.

I noted previously that most upward-oriented interviewees described socializing with people of the same economic means. When they talked about exceptions to this tendency, they usually pointed to people they spent time with who had more, not less. Talia, whose husband earned about $500,000 annually in finance, said her friends were in the same financial situation as she was, except for a few "in a whole different stratosphere" of wealth. Alexis was a stay-at-home mother with a household income around $500,000 and assets over $5 million. Asked if her friends shared her lifestyle, Alexis told me, "I have a few friends who have, you know, quite a bit more money. But nothing too extravagant, like, movie star famous. But [most are], you know, similar. Still working hard, but have made enough money that they can have two homes." To "see" only the wealthier people when thinking about their social circle is another way of establishing themselves as "not really" wealthy. Alexis also contrasts herself and the majority of her friends with those who have more by referring to "still working hard"—that is, not having enough to stop working.

By the same token, several of those I interviewed also faced upward by suggesting that *real* affluence meant not having to think about money at all.[7] Because they did have to think about it, they were, implicitly or explicitly, not affluent. Maya told me, for example: "I don't feel like I can go do whatever I want to do at a store or something. I still think about all of my purchases. I still think about the children, how much money we spend on things." Talia, similarly, said she felt as if she and her husband were "fortunate, but [we] can't go off the rails." She said she hoped to be able to live a comfortable life if they saved enough, which she said was necessary because they would not be receiving money from their parents. As I show in chapter 3, most of my subjects did not chafe against these limits but rather used them to show that they were prudent as well as not "really" wealthy.

We might expect those oriented to others with the same as or more than they have to express feelings of covetousness or envy, to feel relative deprivation vis-à-vis those with more. But when I heard this kind of envious talk, which was relatively rare, it often seemed to come from anxiety and insecurity about their own financial situation rather than from a generalized materialism or status competition.[8] This feeling colored my respondents' sense of social advantage. Immediately after saying, "I feel like we're somewhat in the middle," Helen told me:

> I feel like we're well-off. I mean, I feel like—don't get me wrong. I feel like we do very well, and all of that. But I feel like we can't take it for granted, either. You know, because it's a slippery slope. You can easily slip into kind of being irresponsible with your money, or—not irresponsible, but just even in terms of borrowing to buy a house. . . . I mean, you know, all of the money we have, we made. Right? And I think it's just stressful, you know, the lifestyle we lead, we borrow to buy things. . . . And it's scary to live with that risk. And he's working now, and doing well. But, you know, the jobs are very intense. It's very up-or-out. If things don't go well, you can't really reduplicate your income.

Here Helen acknowledges her privilege very briefly, alluding vaguely to "all of that." Risk looms much larger in her account. Respondents like Helen, who depended on a single earner and had minimal inherited wealth, tended to be especially anxious. Several spoke of becoming more careful with money during the economic crisis that started in 2008.

Although the fear some of these interviewees expressed felt real to me, it also seemed to help deflect a sense of privilege that they might otherwise be uncomfortable with. I saw this link between denial of and discomfort with privilege most clearly in my conversations with two African American women. In approaching them for the interview, I used the word "affluent" explicitly. I had avoided this word previously because I imagined it would trigger people's sensitivity to talking about money. But Kelly, the friend who had promised to introduce me to the first interviewee, didn't think she would have any problem with this word. Kelly thought Pam (the interviewee)[9] and others in her circle were "proud" of their social status. She told me that when she had spent time with them they were always talking about their renovations and other elements of their lifestyle.

I thought I should follow Kelly's advice because she knew Pam and her friends quite well. I also thought "affluent" sounded better than "wealthy" and was less likely to provoke a negative response.[10] As it turned out, however, this was not such a good move. Pam brought up the issue of affluence—alluding to my email—before I had even turned on my digital recorder. Despite her household income of over half a million dollars, she said, "I don't feel affluent." When I asked why, she said, "Well, because affluent feels like, free of money worries, in a way. You know? And it's just, in New York, if you've gone down the path of saying, 'I'm going to educate my kids in private schools'— you know, theoretically, you're doing well. But it's a big commitment." Later Pam described herself as part of the "middle tier" at her child's private school. Describing a luxurious home where her daughter had gone for a play date, she said, "See, in this context, we don't feel affluent. At all."

In these comments Pam primarily described a feeling of financial insecurity and located herself in the middle. But eventually it became clear that she also felt uncomfortable with the *idea* of being affluent. She had been raised working-class, and her parents were active in fair housing and civil rights struggles. She attributed her discomfort with wealth to this background, saying, "It took me a while to shake this off. I mean, I think we grew up with this sense of distrust for rich people. So I had to work to get over that." At the end of the interview, she told me she and her husband had gotten into a fight about whether they were part of the 1 percent. Although their income put them well into this group, she was relieved to hear that the cutoff for the 1 percent in terms of *wealth* was beyond their assets of about $2 million. Pam's reaction highlights the way the cultural emphasis on and critique of "the 1 percent" can obscure privilege, as I noted in the introduction; if Pam does not have to think of herself as in this category, she can claim, at least to herself, that she is not privileged.

Around the same time I also interviewed Beverly, whose household income was about $2.5 million; she and her husband owned assets of several million dollars, plus two homes carrying only minimal mortgages. Yet she was so uncomfortable with my use of the word "affluent," she told me, that she had almost canceled the interview. She said, "'Affluent' is relative. . . . I have friends that just went away [on vacation]. . . . They went on a private plane. So it's a relative term. I mean, I have lots of friends that—most of my friends don't. But I'm just saying, there are those. You know. And so, I don't know if *affluent*'s the right word [to describe me]. *That's* affluence." As a way of not interpreting herself as affluent, Beverly keeps her eye on others who have more rather than on the reality that "most of [her] friends don't" have private planes. She also said, again invoking the local context, "Maybe in Denver, I might be considered affluent. But I don't know if in New York, *affluence* would be the word. That's my opinion."

Indeed it became clear that Beverly was quite uneasy with her social advantages. She first characterized herself as "uncomfortable talking about money. In any way, shape, or form." She recognized her discomfort with her own privilege in particular when she said, "But another uncomfortable thing is, when you talk about 1 percenters, we are in the 1 percent. End of story." Then, in a classic example of comparing oneself to those above, she went on, "The very, very bottom, probably, of the 1 percent. Like, the disparity between the bottom of the 1 percent and the top of the 1 percent is huge. So I can imagine why all the 99 percent thinks it's so much. You know? But there's a huge disparity between the top, and the people on top. So, it's not real. It's not real, that 'affluent' term. It's—it's—I mean, we're not struggling to eat. We're not struggling to go on vacation, we're not struggling to clothe our children. But it's not a real term." Beverly is working hard to get over her discomfort. She acknowledges her privilege but quickly discounts it, primarily by focusing on the gulf between herself and those above her. She portrays those with less as "struggling to eat." Like Monica's reference to the "trailer park" or Zoe's reference to the "underprivileged," this frame situates Beverly as not-poor rather than as rich.

In fact, Beverly explicitly identified two strategies for dealing with her discomfort vis-à-vis her more economically diverse African American community. On the one hand, she didn't talk about it. She told me, referring to her parents and siblings, "I tend not to talk to my family about . . . money. Because the money stuff is kind of outrageous. It's New York, too. And the amounts just sound outrageous and unfair. It sounds outrageous. I mean, how can I tell someone how much private school costs, when that might be [their] income? So, you try not to discuss those things."

On the other hand, she said (using the more distant second person "you"), "Because I'm uncomfortable about it, you have to be kind of unapologetic about [the fact that] there are going to be people that have some more means, and people that have less. And you can't be apologetic for it. You just can't. You still feel uncomfortable." In order to avoid being "apologetic," she has to rely on two ideas. The first is that there is an equivalence between those above her and those below, which puts her in the middle. The second is the idea (also articulated by Willa) that these inequalities are *immutable*, which implies that they don't have anything specific to do with her. This is just the way it is, which means there is nothing she can do about it, and she is absolved of any moral responsibility. (I discuss this viewpoint further in chapter 4.)

My unwise use of the word *affluence* ultimately led Pam and Beverly to describe fairly explicitly how their upward orientation is linked to a feeling of discomfort about privilege. Race may play a role here. The African Americans I spoke with had racially and economically diverse networks; their white friends were usually affluent, whereas their African American friends and family ran the gamut.[11] As I've mentioned and will discuss further, having a more diverse network seemed to be correlated with a greater awareness of privilege across my sample. Ties to African American friends and family in other classes, and also the sense of being a small minority among the wealthy, could provoke the discomfort that Beverly talks about. On the other hand, other African Americans in the sample described feeling proud of their upward mobility; and, as Kelly indicated, in conversations with their friends even Pam and others like her were quite comfortable talking about the trappings of their privileged lives. I suspect that they express different feelings at different moments, all of which can be "true."

In any case, I believe that many of the other people described in this section, regardless of race, would also have resisted explicitly describing themselves as "affluent"—let alone "wealthy" or "rich"—if I had used that language in recruiting them. For example, I suspected that Nicole, a photographer, had inherited wealth. But in the first half of our conversation, she repeatedly downplayed her affluence. She told me she struggled to pay her kids' private-school tuition, explained her mother's having an expensive home by saying she had had it forever, and talked about not being able to afford certain changes she'd have liked to make in her home renovation. She did not mention having an inheritance. After an hour or so, I just had to tell her I was confused and ask more directly about her financial situation than I normally would have at that point. Even after coming clean about her inheritance (about \$2.5 million), her household income (over \$400,000), and her home value (over \$2 million), she still tended to differentiate herself from people she knew—mostly other parents from her kids' school—who were "really" rich.

Nicole also framed her inheritance as her "nest egg," emphasizing that her family lived on her husband's salary. She told me, "I don't feel like we lead the life we do because of the family money, that the kids would not be able to go to private school without [it]. We could swing that." In reality, her parents *were* paying for the private school, and she and her husband did not have to save money, thanks to her inherited assets. But it was important to her not to "need" the inherited wealth to sustain their current lifestyle. She thus casts herself, as I discuss further in chapter 3, as "normal" vis-à-vis those with more rather than advantaged vis-à-vis those with less.

Moral anxieties around privilege and a desire to keep it unspoken also emerged when I asked these respondents about their political views, especially in the way they talked about President Obama's critiques of Wall Street. Several people I spoke with said they (and/or their partners) had voted for Obama in 2008 but were reluctant (or had refused) to do so again in 2012, less because they liked Romney than because they were angry at Obama. I initially imagined that this anger had to do with Obama's tax proposals (especially the proposal to let the Bush tax cuts for households earning over $250,000 expire), because such a change would have affected their incomes. But they talked mainly about the symbolic dimension of the proposal, indicating that Obama had transgressed by simply *talking about* inequality. Maya, for example, appreciated Obama's healthcare initiative. But, she said, "I think his economic policy and the ways that he talks about people that make a lot of money, I don't like that. I think it's wrong, and I think he's creating a divide." More than disagreeing with his tax proposals, she said she and her husband objected to "just the way Obama is talking about business. And almost making it like they're evil."

Marie said something similar about Bill de Blasio, who had recently been elected mayor of New York City when I interviewed her. She told me, "I don't love de Blasio so much. . . . I think he started his platform in a divisive way that says basically 'haves' and 'have-nots.' And then he made up an arbitrary number of haves versus have-nots. And you can't start a platform in a divisive way, in that way. I mean, I think that's a bad thing." By *talking about* division, Maya and Marie both suggest, politicians are *creating* division. In fact, of course, the division is already there. These wealthy people are trying not to acknowledge it because they don't want to be the moral bad guys, especially given that Wall Street is associated with massive economic collapse. But inequality is harder to avoid as it enters political discourse.

Overall, then, upward-oriented people situated themselves in the middle both directly and obliquely. They socialized with people like themselves, and they "saw" and compared themselves mainly to these people and those with more, a practice facilitated by the extreme wealth of a few in New York City. Comparing themselves to those above allowed these interviewees to position themselves closer to the morally legitimate "middle," as did casting those with less as extremely disadvantaged. They did not like to discuss money issues, but when they did, they often focused on anxieties or limits. The idea that society "will always be this way" also helped muffle their discomfort.

FACING DOWNWARD, RECOGNIZING PRIVILEGE

Like Keith and Karen, introduced at the start of the chapter, and Scott and Olivia, described in the introduction, many of those I interviewed did talk openly about themselves as privileged. They described conflicted feelings about their social advantages and about social inequality generally. Unlike those who aspired to the middle, these interviewees were usually either inheritors of wealth who worked in creative-class jobs or earners who were upwardly mobile (or, in a few cases, married to people in creative occupations). Partly for these reasons, as I discuss later, their social, professional, and familial networks were diverse economically, and sometimes racially. They were typically more liberal politically than upward-oriented people.

These interviewees recognized their privilege and were willing to talk about it much more openly than did those who faced upward. Nadine lived with her partner and their children primarily on income produced by her family's business. They also owned a large home and held about $7 million in additional assets. She said:

> It's always amazing to me. I know a lot of people with a lot of money who are not very generous. Or who don't think they have a lot of money. It's like, "You're kind of bitching about your situation. And you, like, have more money than 99 percent of people on the fucking planet." You know what I mean? . . . Especially [given] what's happened with this economy. It's, like, my brother, again, another case in point. He was complaining to me the other day that he can't buy a new house until he sells his house, and it's such a terrible position to be in, and he needs, like, more liquid assets. And they just have to get this new house, and it's three million dollars, and he can't, you know, afford it, unless they sell their house for two million, and how frustrating is that? I'm like, "Dude. I mean, I love you, and I know why it's frustrating to you. But let's have a little perspective."

Many people emphasized having freedom of choice in their lifestyles as a result of their privilege. Asked to characterize her lifestyle, Wendy, a corporate lawyer married to an economics professor, with a household income of about $500,000, said, "We live a very comfortable life, where we feel like we have the money to have whatever we need for us, for our family. We live in a really comfortable apartment in a location that we want to live in, and we haven't had to make any compromises around that." Gary, who had inherited wealth of over $10 million and worked as an academic, said, "I don't think we ever make a decision that's a trade-off with another decision." He also told me that he had been able to purchase his second home, over other prospective buyers, because he could pay cash, which "immediately got me the hook" with the seller. Then he spoke of spending time at the house:

> Let's say we go for the weekend. Or in the summer. Well, we go to the grocery store. And come home with three hundred dollars

of groceries. Not for caviar. But we're often going with friends, so there's four of us [in his family], and three or four others. You know, I don't walk down the aisle and compare the generic brand to the Green Giant brand. You know. Or the Bounty paper towels to the Pantry Pride paper towels. . . . That's a huge luxury, right? You're going to spend three hundred dollars on groceries for a weekend.

Gary is very aware of and forthright about these advantages. (Note, however, that he says his spending is "not for caviar," thereby casting himself as a reasonable consumer; I discuss this tendency in chapter 3.)

People who recognized their privilege also talked about freedom from fear as an advantage. Donovan, a nonprofit executive with both inherited and earned wealth, said, "It seems to me that one of the real benefits of having money is not having to worry about it! Not having to count pennies here and there. . . . I've never had to worry about food, clothing, paying for school. Enormously beneficial for a guy like me, who's—I'm a naturally anxious person. I just don't have a lot to be anxious about in my life." Echoing this sentiment, Eliana, who worked at a charitable foundation and owned about $9 million in family wealth, saw "safety from anxiety" as an aspect of privilege, "because most people's lives are deeply colored by anxiety over money."

Downward-oriented people seemed to have a larger space in their consciousness for others who worry about money, in both an abstract and a concrete sense. Janice, who worked in marketing part-time, had some inherited wealth and a household income of about $500,000, mostly from her partner's job in business. They had carried out a $700,000 renovation on their million-dollar house. Janice told me, "You know, it's a huge privilege to be able to buy a house in [this neighborhood] and renovate it. And just decide, like, what's here's ugly and I'm not going to live with it. I'm just going to make it my own. It feels like a huge privilege to be able to do that." She said, "I'm very aware that my kids' friends [from their public school] and my friends don't have this."

Linda, a professor and mother of two whose family had inherited wealth, said:

> There was a big article in the *New York Times* recently, and I showed my kids. . . . It was about people in Haiti making these kind of, like, crackers out of dirt. I don't know, it was just really horrible. So I always think about that, I just think about that a lot. Just, we have so much—I mean it's just crazy. . . . I go to the grocery store, I buy whatever I want. I don't look to see if the organic—I mean I do look, but it's like, I don't care that it's five dollars for organic raspberries. My kid likes raspberries, I'm gonna buy raspberries. I'm really aware that people are looking and rationing and paying attention, and I am not, in that realm.

These accounts make visible social others who have less, people who are "looking and rationing," as Linda said, who can't spend $300 on groceries, who can't afford to buy and renovate a home.

Penny, a part-time legal consultant, and her husband, who worked in management consulting, had a household income of about $3 million, which was far beyond what either of them had grown up with. Their young children attended a public school with an excellent reputation. Penny said: "You know, there's always someone in New York, especially—New York City, Manhattan—who has more than you do. And there's always a lot of people who have less. And going to a public school, you know, I mean, I would say we're on the higher end of having more [relative to the other parents]. And having an apartment like this. And when you see other people's apartments the kids go to school with, they're not as nice." Unlike those who situate themselves in the middle, Penny acknowledges that there are *more* people below her than above, even in New York, and that she is privileged relative to other parents in her kids' school. She followed this statement with a reflection on the desirability of this awareness, saying: "And it's a funny thing, but I think a good thing, perspective. I mean, I feel this way, perspective-wise, that— you know, I feel lucky, every day. That [her husband] has this great job, and he makes money, that we can do an apartment renovation, or this or that." The sentiment here is of gratitude that openly recognizes privilege rather than a euphemistic reference to it.

Downward-oriented people also mentioned the domestic workers in their homes much more frequently than upward-oriented people, and often expressed conflicted feelings about them. My conversation with Beatrice, a nonprofit executive with inherited wealth of about $3 million, focused largely on two decisions: one, whether to enroll her son in private school, and two, whether to buy a second home. One consideration, she said, was "Am I going to buy a house in [an affluent area] when this poor woman works in my house and takes care of and loves my child?" Teresa was a stay-at-home mother with two kids whose husband earned over $1 million annually in finance. She told me about her housekeeper, who had sent her own children back to her home country because she could not afford to keep them in the United States, and had also to leave Teresa's employ for full-time work. She said, "Who am I not to work and to have someone watch my kids, when she can't even afford to keep her kids here?" These struggles locate these women themselves and the workers they employ in larger structural relations of inequality, which contrasts strongly to Zoe's assertion that "we treat them very well," which takes these relations for granted.

Unlike upward-oriented respondents, who described their friends as having as much as or more than they, those who faced downward tended to talk about friends, acquaintances, and colleagues in a wide range of economic circumstances. For example, Danielle, a banker turned stay-at-home mother with inherited and earned wealth, said, "We have a huge range of friends that have a huge range of lifestyles." These diverse networks came about for a number of reasons. Some people had grown up middle-class or, in a few cases, working-class, and retained ties to family members and friends who had less. These were mostly earners, as we might expect, but a couple of inheritors had also spent part of their childhoods in much more economically constrained situations.[12] Those who worked in class-heterogeneous fields such as academia, nonprofits, and the arts, mainly inheritors, came into contact with more diverse groups of people in their jobs. Both inheritors and earners who tended to face downward had college friends or other longtime acquaintances with less. Like Janice and Penny, some of these parents had enrolled their children in public school, which further diversified their networks.

These relationships were not simply coincidental, however. Many downward-oriented people consciously sought out cross-class social relationships. Wendy said, "I think it's important, [in order] to stay grounded, to not just hang out with people who have the same means and the same backgrounds." To "stay grounded" is to remember the reality of one's situation relative to that of others; Wendy sees spending time only with people similar to her as a threat to that commitment. Eliana told me, describing her cross-class friendships and her political activism, "I've tried to not be just in my bubble."

Inhabiting privilege well meant creating more varied networks. Yet cross-class relationships also generated discomfort, as they forced disparities into the open. Speaking of the $180,000 he'd spent on furniture for his new house, Gary said, "My friends come out there and see all this stuff, and they're like, 'Oh. That's great, where'd you get that?' You can't say, 'I did this on a shoestring.' You know. It wasn't a shoestring." These affluent consumers also described feeling uncomfortable talking with friends about lifestyle choices, such as where to live and where to send their children to school. Wendy told me, "I wouldn't characterize this [her lifestyle and spending] in this way to a friend of mine as comfortably as [to you]. Like, I'm trying to be honest for your work. . . . Whereas I think it's—it's uncomfortable." When I asked why, she said her friends "are socially conscious people who are doing really wonderful things with their lives and don't probably have the means that we have and are having to make some of these harder choices." Beatrice made the same point when she told me, "My friends are facing the same problems that I'm facing [such as finding a school for children]; it's just that I have resources to deal with them that other people don't have." She continued, "I feel just some concern about, kind of, rubbing their faces in the fact that I have this wider range of choices." Ultimately, discomfort of this type might be one reason people end up with increasingly homogenous social worlds over time.

For upwardly mobile people, family of origin was a significant referent. Miriam, a banker earning over $1 million annually, said she currently spent social time with "probably mostly similar types of families in similar types of jobs." But, she added, "I make more money than my entire family put together." Miriam did not feel guilty about her wealth exactly, but she described money as "dirty," "soiled," and "tainted." She attributed this in part to her family, saying, "I mean maybe if all my siblings were, like, you know, doctors, lawyers, and bankers, yeah, then I probably wouldn't care. It would be sort of, 'This is what my family does.' But it's not what my family does. My family doesn't become a banker in New York City and make a shitload of money. Right? That's just weird." Miranda, who was married to an inheritor, said she would not talk with her brother about issues she struggled with related to her affluence. When I asked why, she said, "Because he works really hard, and I think . . . talking about how difficult it is to have a lot of money and [being] worried about your kids being raised feeling entitled seems really hard when [he's] trying to figure out whether or not [he] can afford something. You know what I mean?"

Again, these differences also led to silences about money in these relationships. Teresa said she loved her lifestyle. But, she said, "I do feel guilt. I feel like I have to downplay it when I talk to my brother and sister, definitely. . . . I didn't tell my sister I had a housekeeper for, I want to say, three years. I kept it like this big dark secret. I mean, I do like being able to get my parents nice things, and I definitely make a point of that and not thinking twice about getting my sister a wonderful present, but we never talk about how much this costs, how much our car costs, things like that, never, ever."

Both Teresa and Miriam had also grown up in politically progressive families. Miriam said, "I grew up in a family that [had] a very long tradition of workers' rights, you know? . . . So to be, like, 'The Man' to this extent is sort of weird." Teresa said, "My parents always said we wouldn't want a lot of money because there would be too much guilt involved. Like there's a million people who need money, and who are we to have that money? And their whole lives have been working towards giving back to the community, the world, and we never did have so much money. So there's that feeling. Like, when I was planning my wedding I called my parents to give them a preliminary budget, and they were like, 'Do you know how many people in the world that could feed?' So there is that type of guilt as well."

Upwardly mobile earners talked more about feeling privileged than did those earners who were not significantly wealthier now than they had been growing up. Raised middle-class, Penny talked about feeling guilty when she bought things for full price or shopped at fancy stores because she remembered shopping at the Burlington Coat Factory and "buying discount shoes" as a child. Her husband had been raised "working-class," in her words, but now earns $3 million annually. She told me: "[He] is an anomaly. Where he's in these meetings at work, and people are complaining 'cause they're [not being paid enough]. You know, 'That's not fair. I should make 2 million instead of 1.5.' And he's like, 'Do you know how lucky you are to be making this money?' You know. Like, he truly feels it, in his heart. Like, 'You're being ridiculous.'" Penny's husband invoked a point of reference outside the immediate world in which the other consultants seemed to live; he drew back to include more people in the scope of his vision.

Finally, as I have noted, most people who recognized their privilege openly were liberal Democrats. Some were "conservative progressives," as Gary characterized himself, or "pragmatic progressives," as Sara, an inheritor of over $10 million, put it (both were distinguishing themselves from radicals). A few had more of a "socialist vision," as Nadine put it; a real estate broker I interviewed characterized this type as "cashmere communists." Downward-oriented people never expressed any disillusion with Obama for bringing up economic disparities, and they were more likely to favor taxation of wealthy people. In fact, they often expressed affinity with

Occupy Wall Street, which was in the news around the time I conducted some of these interviews. Kevin, whose partner had significant inherited wealth, described himself as "liberal-left." He said, "I feel like in this whole sort of, like, conversation over the last four years or whatever, of the 99 percent, like, it's weird to be of the 1, or the 2, or the 3 percent when I feel like, 'No, *I'm* Occupy. That's me.' There's the weird paradox." These politics constitute another kind of awareness of and concern for those with less, who seem much more present in the imaginations of these interviewees than they do in the imaginations of those who aspire to the middle.

A few of the more progressive respondents also described their own social advantages as stemming from the same social forces that produce inequality and disadvantage. Eliana said, for example, "I am clearly personally benefitting from a system that aggregates toward inequality. And that allows a very, very, very, very small percentage of people to benefit. While the rest suffer, correspondingly. And so I feel that my wealth and poverty in the world have something to do with each other." This stance contrasts sharply with the idea of upward-oriented people that "there will always be people above, and people below," in two ways. First, these downward-oriented people believe that the "people above" and the "people below" are actually connected to each other by both economic relations and moral obligations. Second, they believe that structural change is possible. In their view, current social arrangements, especially of resource distribution, both could and should be different.

FLEXIBLE ORIENTATIONS

I have suggested that the class backgrounds, occupations, political views, and social networks of those I interviewed were related to a propensity to face upward or downward. But even these correlations (not causes in any case[13]) were not set in stone. As we have seen, Betsy was a management consultant and is now a stay-at-home mother. Her husband earns about $1 million per year. Her professional background is in the corporate world, where her husband also works. She is a social liberal but sometimes a fiscal conservative; she did not vote for president in the 2012 election because she disliked both candidates. So she is not especially progressive politically, which differentiates her from most of the downward-oriented inheritors. Nor has she experienced upward mobility, like most of the downward-oriented earners. And she does not appear to have especially diverse social networks. So we might expect her to offer a more upward-oriented discourse.

Indeed, Betsy strongly differentiated herself from people with significant wealth. She had been raised in New York in an affluent family (she mentioned that she had had a brokerage account "from birth"). But, she said, "The level of excess is totally different now than when I grew up in the city." She told me:

> In these private schools, there are a lot of very rich people. Like, millions and millions and billions of dollars. You go to their homes, they live in townhouses, you know, they're on full-floor—I mean, unbelievable. . . . I kind of have an inside joke with some of the moms that I know, that we're like, the "working class." You know? Because we actually really work. Not that these people haven't worked. But they have tons of money. We have been working very hard. And, like, we can't stop working and continue to lead a lifestyle that we are living. And so we are much more aware of what things cost, and how to buy—you know, how to use your money, where to put your resources.

In this upward-oriented move, Betsy differentiates herself and her friends from the "very rich," who not only have "tons of money" but don't have to work and don't have to worry. (Her joke about being "working class" invokes the legitimacy of wealth that comes from work, even though she no longer works for money herself, as I discuss in chapter 2.)

Yet Betsy also talked at length about her privilege relative to other people in general and in her life specifically. She said, of her home renovation:

My friends who . . . have different circumstances—I don't really like to talk about it [with them]. And I don't really like to, you know, discuss the headaches of my renovation. Like, it just seems wrong, and kind of gross to me, to talk about stuff like that. I'm not saying I'd hide it or anything. If someone asks me about it, sure, I'll talk about it. But I'm not out there with it, like it's the standard thing that everybody does. I realize that it's not. For us, we worked towards it. We wanted to do this. You know. And we were able to. It's not like—you know, we're—at the end of this, we're going to have to, like, rebuild the nest egg for a while. You know? And it's not without its risks and consequences. But, you know, I realize that—it's—you know, like, home ownership is really not a—reality for a lot of people. Most people. Especially in Manhattan! It's crazy.

Betsy still gestures toward others with more by emphasizing the effort she and her husband put in ("we worked towards it") and the fact that their resources are not unlimited (they'll have to "rebuild the nest egg for a while"). But she also signals an awareness of privilege. This awareness comes from her relationships with people who have less than she ("my friends"), as well as her capacity to imagine those people in a broader sense ("most people"). She mentions the challenge of talking about signs of privilege, such as renovations, with those who have less, and also the decision to avoid that talk. Betsy illuminates the fine line she has to walk between two unacceptable forms of managing privilege: being "gross" by mentioning it gratuitously and being disingenuous by "hiding it."

Betsy also talked about the circumstances of people working for her more than did most of the upward-oriented people. Her nanny had left her own young children in her home country. Betsy told me, "And I, like, could not get my head around it. . . . It made me feel bad in some way on a daily basis. . . . That was awful. It really—I loved her, but it made me feel really bad." Ultimately, Betsy was glad the nanny decided to return to her country of origin and sent her money for a period of time after she did so. Betsy described feeling conflicted again when she told me about a conversation she had had with the foreman of her apartment renovation. Betsy had recently decided not to keep a light fixture she thought was too big for the kitchen, though she had agonized about it because she did not want to act like "a princess." She recounted, of her relationship with the foreman, "You know, we talk about our kids, and one day I was like, 'Oh, what is your daughter doing for the summer?' And he was like, 'Oh, nothing.' And I was like, 'Oh, she's not going to camp?' He's like, 'Camp's too expensive.' Jesus Christ. You know? Like, we're talking about how I don't want my six hundred–dollar, five hundred–dollar lights. That makes me feel really bad. And I don't like that. So I feel like that's kind of—it makes me feel bad about myself." In this anecdote, again, Betsy recognizes not only her privilege vis-à-vis the worker but also the discomfort that arises from talking with people who are less advantaged than she is.

I think it is likely that at least some of the respondents I have called "upward-oriented" are more like Betsy in that they do see their privilege and feel some discomfort with it. They may minimize their unease not because they haven't thought about it but because they felt uncomfortable talking about it.[14] The African American respondents I described earlier, who resisted being called "affluent" yet ultimately recognized that they were affluent but uncomfortable with admitting it, exemplify this tendency as well. So it is hard to know what exactly the relation between *talking about* one's privilege and *thinking about* it might be and how this relationship might vary from person to person or depending on the situation. That is, some people might be more likely to talk about it to me than to a friend, while others might feel the opposite. The same person might also be more likely to talk about it at some moments than at others.

Therefore, although staying attuned to these patterned differences is generative, trying to classify people rigidly or permanently as having one orientation over another is ultimately futile. Instead, recognizing the *flexibility* of these interpretations is important because it highlights the interpretive work people do to situate themselves in a way they are comfortable with. Not talking about privilege takes it off the table as a basis for comparison. Talking about oneself as "in the middle" also takes it off the table, in a sense, by deflecting attention to those who have more.

We often imagine that wealthy people are operating in their own "bubble" with reference groups primarily composed of people "like them." We also often assume that it is "human nature" to compare oneself to people above. But I have shown in this chapter that these comparisons and reference groups vary. Furthermore, the bases of comparison—that is, what it means for other people to be sufficiently "like you" to compare yourself to them—are not somehow determined a priori. Instead, people make choices, though not always consciously, about which social others to keep in their consciousness, spend time with, and talk about.

As Eliana put it, "I feel that there's a myth of privilege. That [privileged] people are more out of touch than they really necessarily are. I don't think the privilege automatically puts the person out of touch. I feel like some of that is a set of choices and consciousness. And you can deal with difference. You can make it part of your life, that you deal with difference." Some of the privileged literally "deal with difference" more often, and sometimes more intentionally, than others—through their choices of work and peers and/or by virtue of their family backgrounds. Others, as I have suggested, avoid spending time with or even thinking about people who are different, at least partly because it is uncomfortable.

This chapter has analyzed how people locate themselves on a distributive continuum. Do they have a lot or a little, and relative to whom? But it has also shown that these self-locations have a moral dimension. The rest of this book investigates that dimension. Regardless of how they oriented themselves to others, or of how much they talked explicitly about their social advantages or acknowledged discomfort with their position, the people I interviewed *all* alluded to the importance of being morally worthy of their wealth. As I outlined in the introduction, upward- *and* downward-oriented people articulated a set of *similar* ideas about what it means to be a "good person" and avoid "entitlement": primarily, to work hard, consume reasonably, and give back. In talking about these imperatives, upward-oriented people do acknowledge their privilege, though often indirectly. Downward-oriented people symbolically mitigate their privilege, despite having recognized it explicitly, by appealing to these (middle-class) values.

I begin in chapter 2 with the first of these ideas: the moral imperative of hard work. As we have seen, some of my interviewees invoked "having to work" as a sign that they were not privileged, or at least not as much as some others. But whether or not they "had to" or did work for money, to interpret themselves as hard-working was crucial to their sense of worth.

2

WORKING HARD OR HARDLY WORKING?

PRODUCTIVITY AND MORAL WORTH

Paul was an executive in his mid-forties, earning about $500,000 annually, with two young children and a stay-at-home wife. I interviewed him in a bustling café as he stole an hour away from his midtown office. Our conversation focused primarily on the significant renovation he and his wife were carrying out on their home. Near the end of the interview I asked if he felt he "deserved" his lifestyle. I had started asking interviewees this question after I noticed that they often seemed to feel conflicted about their advantages. The question was ambiguous, I knew, perhaps even nonsensical. But I was interested in how they might interpret it and in the explicit justifications they might use to answer it.[1] Paul responded, without hesitation, "Absolutely. Damn right I fucking deserve it. . . . Where I am today, I've earned every dime on my own. No one's done it—I mean, my in-laws have helped, but I've done it. My job, my career, my [current employer] career, my [previous employer] career, this is all me. No one's helped me. It's been me. So I've earned every fucking dime, absolutely." Paul equates "deserving" with "earning" so completely that he responds almost as if my question was about whether he had earned his wealth. He also invokes independence and self-sufficiency, saying he did it "on my own." Although he alludes to having received help from his in-laws, he quickly turns away from this acknowledgement in order to maintain his self-interpretation as autonomous.

Paul strongly and repeatedly framed the basis of deservingness in general as work. When I asked, "And people who have less than you, do you think they deserve less?" he responded, "Some of them, absolutely. I mean, Occupy Wall Street, I mean, what have they done? They sat in a park doing nothing. You know?" Later, in talking about a pair of younger colleagues with whom he had shared some personal financial information, he said, "It's good, I think, because by seeing what they can work towards, it may drive them to work harder." But he wanted to make sure they didn't feel "entitled," by which he meant thinking "that they should be there already without working as hard." He insisted that his children would have paying jobs when they were in high school, saying "There's no doubt in my mind. One thousand percent."

This kind of orientation was exactly the one I had expected when I started my research. The idea of working hard on an equal playing field as the most desirable means to get ahead is the definition of the American Dream, which permeates American ideology and popular culture.[2] By the same token, other scholars have shown that privileged people often explain and justify their social advantages by alluding to their hard work.[3] My research both supports and challenges this idea. On the one hand, most of the people I interviewed, whether upward- or downward-oriented, echoed Paul's emphasis on working hard as one basis for deserving wealth. They valued self-reliance and independence and wanted to see themselves as productive rather than parasitic. And they cared deeply about instilling a work ethic in their children.

On the other hand, very few of them used this discourse as uniformly and as emphatically as Paul did. Talia, for example, was a stay-at-home mother whose family lived on her husband's $500,000 annual income from his job in finance. I met her for the interview at the apartment they were in the middle of renovating; she walked me through the rooms, describing how they were rearranging the space and showing me samples of the colors she was thinking about using on the walls. Later, as we continued the interview in a café, Talia told me she would never talk about "specific dollars" related to her renovation because it was "gauche" and because "you never know when it's going to go away. So don't brag about what you have." I took the opportunity to ask if she ever felt guilty about her privilege. She responded, "No. I mean because I don't feel like, I feel like we're good people and we don't—my husband works really hard. And you know, hopefully we'll be lucky enough to stay in this apartment and, you know—I don't—no, 'cause I think we give back a lot, too." When I then asked if she deserved it, she said, "Yeah. I mean I worked really hard and I, you know, I don't live a lifestyle that's like, so decadent." Talia mentions her own hard work, as we might expect, but she also mentions her husband's work, their moral status as "good people," the possibility of not keeping the apartment and the "luck" involved if they do, their prudent lifestyle, their disdain for bragging, and their "giving back" through charitable donations.

Most of the people I spoke to invoked this range of concepts, framing their own hard work as only one part of a constellation of morally worthy practices and affects. How they talked about work varied, however, according to the source of their money. Those who had earned all or most of their wealth drew relatively easily on the language of hard work and, sometimes, intelligence, to talk about their advantages. But most of them believed that hard work was not the only factor explaining their success or underpinning their worth. They spoke particularly of having been lucky. They also pointed to other kinds of behaviors and feelings required of them in order to be morally worthy, especially the need to be economically prudent in the face of risk.

Those who lived on wealth they had not earned—inheritors and stay-at-home mothers—could not draw so easily on ideas of themselves as hard workers. Inheritors felt uncomfortable, sometimes "guilty," about living on wealth they hadn't worked for and accumulated themselves. Stay-at-home mothers—all of whom were highly educated and had work experience—described mixed feelings about not earning their own money or "contributing" economically to the household. People in both categories emphasized their worthy, hard-working selfhood—even in the absence of paid work—by highlighting their own productivity, effort, and work ethic and by drawing boundaries against images of themselves as lazy or self-indulgent dilettantes. Most inheritors of wealth insisted on working for money even when they didn't need to. Stay-at-home mothers highlighted the work they did for their families, which I call the "labor of lifestyle." And they associated themselves with the hard work of others, including their spouses, parents, and themselves in earlier phases of life.

The struggles of these people show that "hard work" carries deep symbolic significance. They also demonstrate that not all forms of work are equal in symbolic value. It is much easier for paid, public employment to seem like "real work" and, therefore, to serve as an indicator of moral worth. This tendency draws on and reproduces a longstanding failure to see unpaid household labor (typically per-formed by women) as having economic value.[4] This kind of labor does have symbolic value, inasmuch as it is linked to the morally worthy work of mothering. However, much of the consumption work these women do does not seem to count as morally legiti-mate "hard work." Thus, as sociologist Arlene Kaplan Daniels argued thirty years ago, the notion of achieving merit through hard work is itself deeply gendered, inasmuch as unpaid work tends to be the (symbolic as well as actual) province of women.[5] As we will see in chapter 5, the "value" of this unpaid labor also becomes a site of tension in couples.

EARNING AS MORALLY WORTHY HARD WORK

Like Paul, most earners immediately reached for the idea of hard work when confronted with the question of the legitimacy of their wealth. For example, I asked Monica, the upward-oriented real es-tate agent, if she felt guilty about having more than others. She re-sponded, "I don't feel guilty. I mean, I work hard. My husband works hard, my kids work hard. I don't feel guilty." When I asked Betsy, the former consultant, if she felt she "deserved" her lifestyle, she told me she wanted to avoid "entitlement" but still emphasized hard work.

She said, "I think we worked hard for it. I don't think it was, like—I don't think we feel entitled to it. But I think we feel like, you know, especially for [her husband], he puts in a ton of hours. I actually think he's underpaid for the amount of time and energy and stress that is involved. . . . I don't know that I like the word *deserve*. But I feel like we've worked for it." Betsy is reluctant to say explicitly that she deserves her lifestyle exactly *because* she and her husband have worked hard for it, but she invokes the work itself as a legitimator.

Again like Paul, upwardly mobile earners alluded to their upward trajectory as evidence of hard work and intelligence and hence of merit. As we have seen, Miriam earned over $1 million per year as a banker. When I asked if she thought she deserved what she had, she said, "I think I work my ass off, so I think 'deserve' in that sense, I think I have earned what I have by a lot of hard work. . . . I don't feel that anything has been handed to me at all. I think that I worked hard for what I achieved in school, and I worked hard for what I've achieved professionally, and I still work hard."

Notably, Miriam also draws on the idea of self-sufficiency as a key dimension of achievement. As I described in chapter 1, Miriam was "downward-oriented," acutely conscious of her privilege relative to others, at least partly because of her class background and the political activism of her parents. In describing this tension she said, almost as if trying to convince herself, "But I don't think my father would think there's anything wrong with working hard and making money. It's sort of crazy, right? I mean, they gave us these opportunities, and [so] I was able to go to these schools and I'm able to make this money. And they gave me that, right?"

Warren, a private equity entrepreneur from what he called a "middle-class-slash-working-class" background, said that he felt "different" at his Ivy League college. But, he said, "the difference was empowering" because it was clear that he was there because of his intelligence, not his family history or connections. "The people who were around me . . . recognized that the fact that I didn't go to Andover makes me a little special. 'Cause it wasn't kind of like, quote-unquote 'handed to me.' . . . The fact that my father didn't go to college was, like, this kind of badge of honor, or talent. . . . It's like, 'Oh, I'm no legacy [admission]. I didn't go to private school. I'm just, you know, I'm actually smart.'"

By the same token, earners and former earners highlighted their self-sufficiency by distinguishing their earned wealth from money they might have inherited. Ursula responded to my question about whether she deserved her lifestyle by saying, "I don't know how to answer that. Over other people? Do I deserve it instead of somebody else? I feel like I worked hard. I mean, I don't think anything has just dropped in our laps. . . . I think we deserve what we have in the sense that we worked hard to get it. This is not something we've inherited." Frances was a stay-at-home mother married to a hedge fund director, with tens of millions in family assets. When I asked about how her parents saw her lifestyle, which was more lavish than theirs, she responded by emphasizing that her husband had earned the money that supported them. She said, "I think they're probably proud of [her husband]. You know, we're not living on his inheritance. We're living on money that he-we made. And I think they're very proud of his success. And so they're okay with it." By invoking "money that he-we made," Frances associates herself with the earning of the money, although her work had contributed little in monetary terms and she had long been a stay-at-home mother.[6] These women had been raised in upper-middle-class families, so they could not claim upward mobility as Miriam and Warren did, but they still focused on earned income rather than on financial and other advantages they might have received in their upbringings.

LUCK, HELP, AND STRUCTURAL ADVANTAGE

In speaking of poor people, Paul told me, "I don't feel the need every time I pass someone [asking for money] to give them money because I'm more fortunate. They don't do—some of them, not all of them, it's a stereotype—don't do shit. Others do some really good stuff and maybe, you know, whatever it is, play music—I mean I'd rather give money to someone who's on a subway working hard and playing music than someone who's sitting there literally doing nothing saying, 'I'm hungry.'" Stephanie, a stay-at-home mother married to an earner of about $500,000, told me, "Well, I mean, there's certainly people that work really, really hard, and just can't get ahead, or even buy a house. But then there's also a lot of fucking lazy people that are on the dole, that want to stay there. . . . They think that government should be taking care of everything." Both Paul and Stephanie strongly frame the basis of deservingness as work and frown on "dependency" on the state.

Paul and Stephanie also both acknowledge the fact that many people do work but still "can't get ahead"—but then they gloss over this fact, much as Paul also glossed over the help he had received from his in-laws. However, to my surprise, very few earners I interviewed skimmed over this contradiction so glibly. Even when they alluded to their own hard work as *one* reason for their success, many also saw themselves as having been "lucky." Wendy, the corporate lawyer, told me, "I don't know what I deserve, but I feel lucky that I have the opportunity to get paid what I do. Because there are people who work their asses off and they don't get paid a lot. For some it's because that's their choice, and for others it's because they just haven't had the opportunity. And I didn't deserve the opportunity, particularly, I was just lucky." Wendy challenges commonplace ideas about meritocracy—the notion that hard work means one deserves more—in two ways. First, she foregrounds the fact that many people work hard and do not get paid well rather than mentioning it perfunctorily and then turning away. Second, she points out that she did not especially "deserve" opportunities that led her to work in a high-paying job.

James, who worked in real estate, had accumulated over $3 million in assets. He echoed these themes when he said, "You just get lucky. . . . I was lucky to be born to a mom and a dad who gave a shit—I hit the lottery in so many ways." Like Wendy, James mentions others he knows who do work hard or are smart who haven't ended up where he has. He continued, "I think the mistake is if you start to think that your success means that you're smart. A lot of it's just luck. I mean a lot of it is, you know, if you get the opportunity, and there's no telling if you do, to jump on it. But there's guys who are, in my view, just as smart as me or smarter than me who have been in [this work] for the same amount of time as me and haven't made that money." He concluded, "And so it doesn't, and this is a view I've evolved to, but it doesn't make sense to feel guilty about it. I mean life is cruel, it just is. And sometimes it's—you know, I'm talking to you today, I could be dead of cancer next year. Who knows?"

Yet even as these earners may *explain* their success by talking about luck, it is hard work that *constitutes* them as morally worthy. James said, "I worked my ass off, but I got lucky. I wasn't gunning for any of this, it just happened. Again, I did work hard and I don't feel, like, undeserving or whatever, but I do feel lucky." James suggests that if he hadn't worked hard, he might be "undeserving." But given that he has, he can be both "lucky" and worthy.

To recognize that luck plays a role in success is to recognize that hard work is not the only factor. But to emphasize luck is also to obscure structural advantages that have likely also made a difference. "Luck" is arbitrary rather than the systematic result of having grown up in particular kinds of families, attended particular schools, developed certain skills and social networks, and so on.[7] While James acknowledges that having a certain kind of parents made a difference for him, his reference to the "lottery" and his ultimate conclusion that "life is cruel" suggest that there really isn't anything one can do to change the system. As Power et al. have noted, "The use of 'luck' as an explanation for success is significant because it signals an acknowledgement of the uneven distribution of opportunities at the same time as overlooking more structural explanations for that maldistribution."[8] Brown et al. refer to this interpretation as an "'individualization' of the systematic inequalities in education and life-chance."[9]

Notably, some of the partners of earners I interviewed did allude more or less explicitly to the ways in which the playing field is uneven. Lucy was a stay-at-home mother whose husband had earned many millions of dollars in private equity. Asked if she deserved her lifestyle, she said, "Nobody deserves it." I asked, "So you don't feel like you deserve it?" She responded, "No. Oh my gosh. Are you kidding me? No, absolutely not. I don't know what 'to deserve' means." She continued, "I think that there's a combination between intellect, hard work, and a lot, a lot, a lot of luck. Really, truly. So I think some people are unlucky and other people are lucky. And I also know a lot of very smart people who are trying, and it's not working." She went on, hesitatingly, "My husband works very, very hard. But the amount—it's a disproportionate amount. You know? And you—it's hard to—it's hard to defend that, I think, in truth. It really is. And so I can't—so I'm, you know, definitely sheepish about it. I'd say that I'm definitely sheepish about it." Lucy not only recognizes the luck involved in her husband's success but also the "disproportionate amount" of reward he receives relative to those in other kinds of work. She also recognizes and strongly dislikes the role of social networks, what she calls the "club mentality," in determining outcomes, saying that "what should matter" is "productivity and what you can produce, and a kind of personal hunger and all of those things."

Yet despite these critiques, Lucy and others I talked with still returned to the central narrative of hard work as legitimating.[10] Lucy described her husband as "self-made"—even as she acknowledged his class advantages. She said, alluding to his parents' having paid his elite college tuition, "His parents gave him every gift. And the gift to do whatever he wanted in an amazing school. But," she continued, "he didn't get rent checks from his parents. He didn't get spending money, discretionary spending at any point, you know? So he's very much self-made." Vera, who lived mainly on inherited wealth of over $1 million, was very progressive and had an extremely detailed critique of economic and racial inequality.[11] Yet she told me of her partner, who worked in finance and did not come from a privileged background: "I'm proud of his success. . . . [He] worked full-time as a short-order cook and went to college full-time. Like, he killed himself. He did it himself. I'm just, like, proud of him. . . . I mean, I know that being white helped. He looked, like, the right color. I know that. But he's also—he works his ass off and he's brilliant." These interpretations foreground work as the source of moral worth, minimizing even as they recognize particular kinds of unevenly distributed advantages.

In any case, most people in high-earning families were loath to talk about structural disadvantage. As I described in chapter 1, some of these interviewees felt affronted by Obama's talk of rolling back the Bush tax cuts for earners of more than $250,000 and saw politicians who talked about inequality as, in Marie's words, "creating division." Talia told me her husband was no longer supporting Obama. He thought, and she agreed, "that a lot of people in finance have been sort of cast as, like, the villain. I mean, there have been a lot of villainous people in finance that have done some really awful things. But [her husband] sent himself through business school." She also said that there should be "some recognition" of people who "have earned the money."

This reluctance to talk about structure extended to talking about white privilege. One African American stay-at-home mother told me that the African American men she knew who had elite business school degrees had not advanced as much as their white counterparts, which she believed was essentially due to institutional racism. But, she told me, "those are the kinds of things I don't want to say to my—like, I would never say that to my white friends, because their husbands do work really hard." To mention the obstacles her husband faces on the basis of race would be to challenge her white friends' legitimate entitlement on the basis of their husbands' hard work. For these respondents, a critique of structural imbalance feels like a personal critique.[12]

AFFECTS OF INDEPENDENCE: ANXIETY AND PRUDENCE

Earners were able to draw most easily on these discourses of hard work and individual self-sufficiency because they were the ones earning money. But the dark side of this provider role, especially among those who were the main or only earners in their families (usually but not always men) was a strong feeling of risk, and often anxiety, about money. James said, "My biggest fear is, I lose my job and someone gets sick. That's my biggest fear in the entire world probably. I lose my job, we don't have health coverage, and someone gets sick. . . . And all of a sudden that two million dollars [from a windfall] that's sitting out there, that I don't want to touch . . . it all gets paid to Sloan Kettering [cancer hospital] or, God forbid, you know?"

These earners did not tend to feel strapped on a daily basis but expressed a more general sense of insecurity about the future. They were especially aware of how much they needed to survive if a job was lost or something happened to them. James said that his wife was more laid-back about money and the future, whereas "I'm much more like, I'm on the iceberg with the gun looking for sharks and hoping it doesn't get too warm, you know what I mean?" Miriam said bluntly, "I'm very fixated on what will happen if I die, because I'm more supporting the family, right?" Several interviewees told me they worried about the cash cushion that they had in the bank. Penny said her husband "likes to sleep with a million dollars under his pillow, basically," because he did not trust the stock market.

Earners used various strategies of money management, coalescing around the idea of "prudence," to stave off these possibilities. Those who received bonuses often tried to save rather than spend them. Most had created 401k and college-fund accounts for their children, which they said they would not dip into. Some had bought large amounts of life insurance. They talked also about controlling their spending, as I discuss further in chapter 3, in order to avoid debt and put away for the future. When I interviewed Justin, a private equity entrepreneur, he and his wife had "downsized" their lifestyle, renting a less expensive and smaller home than they had previously lived in, despite having two children and a live-in nanny. They had started planning for decades into the future, hoping to be able to retire early. They had made these changes even before the

2008 economic crisis, because, in Justin's words, "My wife said, 'If one of us ever loses a job, like, I don't want to panic.' And we saw people buying houses that were too big, or whatever. Spending too much money. . . . Just, this light bulb went off." He told me, "I'm ready for the storm."

This self-protection in the face of risk is another example of the way anxiety can deflect a feeling of privilege, because it prevents people from feeling at ease financially. Even though Wendy had a "big cushion" of several million dollars and a household income of $500,000, she did not want to buy a home because she was concerned about losing her job. She was annoyed that she and her husband couldn't stick to the budget that they had carefully devised and was determined to figure out why they kept spending more than they had allocated and saving less, even though they faced no shortage. Betsy told me, "The last thing that I want to do, and I think my husband wants to do—we don't want to live beyond our means. We don't have any form of debt, other than our mortgage. Credit card debt—like, we don't do that. We spend what we have. And we like to have reserve. You know? Like, at the end of our last payment (on the renovation), we're probably in a slightly not-comfortable situation for us." Yet what she meant by "not-comfortable" was that if her husband lost his job (and hence his million-dollar income) they could live on their savings only for a year. The discomfort these interviewees feel is real, though the actual risk may be minimal. As I showed in chapter 1, worrying about money is another way to avoid feeling affluent.

Interviewees explicitly connected being prudent with money to having earned it. They said that the fact of having made the money themselves made them more careful with it, again contrasting it to inherited wealth. Lucy told me that when she and her husband had made a generous cash offer on their home, the seller had accepted it but then immediately tried to raise the price. Her husband was incensed and refused to pay, saying, as she recounted, "'Nobody gave me anything. And I worked hard for every penny I've got. I'm not just some guy with a trust fund running around [the neighborhood] who's going to, you know, just throw this extra money at you.'" Julia, a stay-at-home mother, told me, of her entrepreneur husband, "It makes us more want to hold onto it because he worked so hard to make it. I know he feels this way. He's like, 'I worked so hard for this money, I don't want to just spend it.' And so I think I've kind of picked up on that, too. He's worked really hard; I don't want to just spend his money that he's worked so hard for. Whereas I think if it was family money, [I'd be] like, 'Oh, well, this is like a gift from the gods. We have this amazing thing that somebody gave us; let's use it.'" Working hard and being prudent are twin processes that not only foster accumulation but also solidify its legitimacy.

Even when risk seemed remote, many people in earner families valued this self-disciplined ethic for its own sake and oriented themselves *affectively* toward prudence. Talia's husband was unlikely to lose his job, she told me. "But," she continued, "that's kind of the mindset that we prefer to have because, you know, like he always says . . . Don't get too comfortable. You always need to work hard and keep your nose down, and don't feel like you're entitled to anything, because that is not a good way to be. Especially in this economy, when there are really smart people out there who are unemployed." Again Talia acknowledges here that it is not only a question of intelligence or hard work, given that "really smart people" are unemployed. The "mindset" also governs feeling; although there isn't much risk, Talia wants to act as if there is, and even to *feel* as if she's not "entitled." She sees this as a smart way to orient herself to the vicissitudes of the economy. Emotional self-discipline complements material self-discipline.

Helen told me in detail about the obstacles her immigrant parents had overcome to succeed in the United States in what she called "one of those American Dream stories" (a story she had clearly told before). Later in the interview she contrasted herself and her husband with parents who let their children spend extravagantly. She said, "I feel like we have more of the values of, I think, my parents, who had to count every single penny. . . . And they got no gifts from their family. You know, moneywise, or anything. So they were very,

very self-made. So my mindset is from there." Having what Helen calls the "mindset" of hard-working, poor immigrants is the most important thing, thus again invoking a particular kind of deserving selfhood that is disconnected from actual material privilege.

INHERITORS, GUILT, AND LIVING UP TO PRIVILEGE

Not surprisingly, the inheritors I interviewed could not draw as easily on meritorious discourses of hard work, independence, and productivity, especially when they did not also have high-paying jobs.[13] As a consequence, in place of an affect or mindset of prudence in the face of risk, they were more likely to describe feeling uncomfortable or guilty about their wealth.[14] Ellen was a financial advisor to many people with inherited wealth and an inheritor herself. Her clients were often conflicted about not having earned their wealth. She told me, "We live in a culture of the American Dream. [Which] values work and values ingenuity and self-sufficiency. . . . You know, 'Go build your own company and be rich, and we're the land of opportunity.' But [with] inherited wealth, money comes in, and [they think], 'What did I do to get this money?'" Olivia, who, as we have seen, had grown up working-class and married an inheritor, made a similar point. She said, "I would say it's harder to grow up affluent, in a way. Because, while I had a lot of shame about where I came from, like, that's a badge of honor in American culture, to start from the bottom and climb your way up. . . . People look on you approvingly. Nobody's going to, like, pat you on the head and say, 'Good job,' when you're like, 'I grew up as a child of inherited wealth.'"

Beatrice, an inheritor of assets of about $3 million, echoed this characterization. She attributed her discomfort with her inherited wealth to the fact that it was "so disconnected from any sort of, like, morally supported form of earning. It's not like I worked hard to get it or was especially clever or whatever. It's like, my grandfather [made an investment many years ago that unexpectedly paid off]. *That's* why I am where I am. . . . So there's nothing about this story that has anything to do with a quality of my own that would make me feel a special kind of ownership over it. And maybe other people do. You know, people who've earned it themselves, not that that means that they deserve it, or actually even that they earned it, but that they got it through something that looks like labor." Beatrice is skeptical that earning money actually makes people more deserving. But the social legitimacy of labor, and the corresponding illegitimacy of inheriting, has nonetheless affected her feelings about her own wealth.

Sometimes this discomfort had to do with a failure of self-sufficiency specifically, signaling the shame of dependency. Caroline, who ran a small nonprofit, had grown up in a wealthy family and was now married to an architect who earned about $500,000. She told me she felt "guilty" about "siphoning off" some of her inheritance before she got married, at times when she didn't have enough free-lance work. She said, "It was just sort of shitty self-worth. . . . Like, why am I not capable of doing it on my own?" Vera primarily lived off the dividends from her assets of over $1 million, having lost her half-time consulting job, which had paid about $65,000. She told me, "I felt more proud of myself when I had a steady job." She felt uncomfortable allowing her high-earning partner to pay for house-hold labor, saying, "I feel like I need steady money in order to be able to do that. . . . If I were contributing steady earned income [to the household], it would put me in a morally different category."

Many inheritors were uncomfortable talking with others in their lives about having inherited wealth. Some used the metaphor of being "in the closet" to describe hiding their wealth and "coming out" to indicate being more open. They also described facing judgments from other people about their character and capacities based on stereotypes. Sara, who had inherited wealth of over $10 million, faced some stigma in her philanthropy-related job. She told me, "I feel like I have worked to overcome perceptions of, like, 'She just has this job because she's, you know, got family money.' Or 'She's not going to work that hard, because she's, you know, a little heiress,' or whatever the preconceptions are."

Most inheritors described feeling that they had to work for pay even when they did not actually need to. Sara worked in part because she did not want to "be a dilettante." She said her parents' message to her and her siblings had been "'You should work.' Very much like, 'You need to have a job.' . . . It definitely got drilled into us pretty early on that we were not to be, like, dilettantes." Her parents had said, "This money is to enable you to have a job that you like. [The money] is to enable you to plan for any, you know, medical issues. It's a fallback, but it's not what you should be banking on." Now, she told me, of herself and her husband, "I mean, we've run the numbers. We could afford to, you know, buy a house in Jackson Hole and be ski bums. Like, we'd feel kind of crappy about ourselves if we did that, you know?"

Eliana, an inheritor with over $5 million in assets (not including her home), told me, "A lot of guilt goes with the territory." I asked if she had enough money not to have to work. She responded, "Oh, yeah." She continued, "I've thought about it. But long enough to reject it, only. Because having a job is super-important. And I do think that's connected to the money. That's, like, part of my [being] normal thing. Is like, to hold a job. I'm a functioning member of society. . . . I think I'd be embarrassed if I didn't have a job. I think I'd be self-conscious about that." These responses illuminate the importance of *paid* work in constituting oneself as "a functioning member of society" as opposed to a dilettante. Eliana's reference to being "normal" also establishes having a paid job as required for belonging to a community.

Proving that they could earn money was especially important to inheritor men. Scott, as we have seen, came from an extremely wealthy family. He described himself as "high on the guilt-ometer." He had worked two jobs after college, even though he did not need the money, because "I wanted to earn more money. I wanted to be self-sufficient." Scott had worked on Wall Street for several years as well, which frustrated Olivia, because she didn't understand why he kept a job with such long hours when they had small children and they didn't need the money. When I interviewed him, he had initiated a business venture supporting nonprofits. He told me, "I got a check from that business over the summer. And I was so happy.

It was less than one-tenth of what I've put into the business so far. But I was like, 'Yes!' I mean, it was still a five-digit check. And I felt like, 'Okay, this is why I'm doing it.' Like, 'It actually can produce income.'" He added, "Also, somehow it's important to me to get recognition from my family, for the stuff I'm doing. . . . And so, I like the idea that I'm going to pull off a coup or two, to be able to trumpet it to them. I think that kind of equation is factoring in. . . . I really want to prove myself." Money he has earned is also symbolic currency, a way for Scott to show he is capable and not simply an incompetent inheritor who can only consume.

Donovan was an inheritor of over $10 million who had also worked in finance years before I interviewed him. He told me: "I've shown that I can actually earn a lot of money. In fact, I've shown that I can earn enough money to support my lifestyle. Now I choose not to do it, I think it would be obsessive to actually do it. But I think that's why I'm much more—I'm not conflicted about it. I think I'm pretty comfortable with this whole money thing at this point." Additionally, Donovan and Scott had both gone into independent entrepreneurial ventures linked to their political commitments, a choice Gary was also considering. I never heard women talk about earning a lot of money in the same way that men did, as proving themselves, although women did care about having a strong work ethic and contributing to their households.

In making and talking about these choices, these interviewees drew boundaries against nonworking inheritors ("dilettantes," in Sara's words). Willa, who worked in advertising and had both in-herited and earned wealth, positioned herself "in the middle," as we have seen. When I asked if she deserved her lifestyle, she said:

> I've worked hard for it. I mean, I was lucky enough to grow up with this lifestyle, so part of me is entitled enough to think that I deserve it. Just because I don't know anything different. You know, if you ask people who grew up in the projects, they think that that's where they're going to live for the rest of their life, just because they've always lived there. I've always lived in something

that looks similar to this. But at the same time, you see, as opposed to my—I have a deadbeat brother who thinks he should live this way. But he doesn't work. Or can't hold a job. And at the moment, he's not holding any job at all. And he doesn't do much to help society, or anything like that. And so, I'm like, "Well, then, why would you have this?" But my husband and I work hard.

Willa begins by alluding to her hard work. Then she pivots to a sense that she *should* have her lifestyle because she doesn't know anything different, almost suggesting that it is her destiny. As she invokes her "deadbeat brother," however, she makes it clear that the feeling of being "entitled" because of always having had the money is not enough to make her worthy of it. Work (or something to "help society") is also necessary.

Caroline emphasized her "work ethic mentality" and said she had always "worked hard," unlike people in her family who were layabouts. She said, "I mean, money ruins people. God, I've just seen it again and again and again. . . . One of my best friends in the world, daddy's princess, you know, never had to work. Quit every time a job got tough. Hates herself. She hates herself. She just feels like she's got no purpose in the world, and she spends all her time doing self-help stuff. Just wallowing in her 'What's wrong with me?'" The earning self, these stories indicate, is a healthy self as well as a deserving self.

Sometimes inheritors stretched the definition of work to cover other kinds of labor, linking themselves, by however tenuous a thread, to the legitimating discourse of work. As we have seen, Nicole preferred to think of herself as not privileged despite her several million dollars in inherited wealth. She told me she sometimes felt guilty because she did not feel stressed about money like some of her friends, but she immediately deflected by adding, "It's not like I'm rolling in it." I asked her if she had any self-consciousness about her large apartment when people she knew with less came over, because others I'd spoken with had mentioned this feeling. She responded, "I don't feel embarrassed. Because I did paint all the walls. I mean, now they've been repainted by professionals." She laughed. "I didn't do the best job in the world. But, I worked—you know, I put a lot of elbow grease into this. This was not, like, handed to me on a platter. I feel like we worked for it. Through, like, physical labor." Nicole interprets her having painted the walls and done other physical labor relevant to her renovation as the "hard work" necessary to legitimate her possession of the apartment.

These interviewees are not claiming that they have money *because* they work hard, since they know they would have it anyway. But work is how they make themselves worthy of their privilege.[15] Working hard means they are not illegitimately entitled. Many, though not all, work at jobs in the arts, nonprofits, or academia, which do not pay for their lifestyles. These inheritors enjoy their work and choose it freely. But it also seems as if they work as a way to legitimate spending their inherited money to support more comfortable lifestyles than their salaries would permit. Like spending reasonably, as we will see in chapter 3, requiring themselves to work is a way of setting limits on their own entitlements.

The earners I described earlier saw their earned money as precious, to be saved, while imagining that they would spend inherited money more freely. Inheritors reversed this "mental accounting": they felt they had to be restrained with the money they *didn't* earn, whereas they could spend that which they had earned.[16] Nicholas, an inheritor who also had a salaried job, said of the money he earned, "I feel a little bit more entitled to blow that money." Donovan, who was in a similar situation, told me, "I'm more willing to spend money I've made myself, on whatever I want to."

Inheritors described a sense of moral obligation to spend inherited money to help others rather than on themselves, which felt self-indulgent. Danielle had worked for years in finance but had become a stay-at-home mother. Both she and her husband had inherited wealth. She said:

Yeah, there's a lot of complicated feelings about spending money you didn't earn. Like the money we spent [to buy and renovate their primary home] we earned. That was money we had earned at our jobs. This money [for their second home] was entirely windfall [from their parents]. . . . And there's a lot of, you know, "Why didn't we build a school?" or "Why didn't we invest that money in some project that would help a lot of people?" Like, this is vanity money and we spent it in a way that makes us happy. Certainly there's lots of liberal guilt about how you do that, what you do with that. You know?

As we have seen, Olivia felt conflicted about having access to Scott's wealth because "I didn't do anything to deserve it. Like, I didn't earn it." Given this, she spent a lot of the money that was designated as hers (which I will say more about in chapter 5) on helping people in her extended family and social network who were much less well off. She loved playing tennis and wanted a tennis court at their house in Connecticut. But, she said, "As appealing as that is, because it is just completely about me, I don't know if I could ever really do it." She continued, "It is one of those things where it's just like, I want it. We have the land to do it. Like, why won't I just do it? Why won't I just invest the time and resources to do this thing that I love for its own sake? You know? [If] it's helping somebody, it's easy for me to spend money in that way. But it's much harder when it comes to just doing something that's sheerly for my pleasure." To spend "vanity money" on themselves and their own pleasure rather than on helping others feels morally wrong and induces guilt.

Over time, these inheritors often worked on themselves and their emotions, trying to feel less guilty or uneasy. Gary said, "I'm a lot more comfortable with it now than I was fifteen years ago, for sure. Fifteen years ago, I think I was totally uncomfortable with it. And hiding it." Like several others, Gary had spent years talking through these issues in therapy. Ironically, inheritors sometimes framed these feelings as *unproductive*. Janice said, "You know, I did some work on not feeling bad about it. It's not really productive to feel bad about it." Nadine said, "I still feel guilty about having money. I feel a lot less guilty than I did. Because I think guilt is unproductive." Caroline spoke with irritation about people who have money and feel ashamed about it, whom she saw as wallowing uselessly. "I just think it's unnecessary shame. Why be ashamed? Who does that help? . . . And you could be getting on with utilizing what you have to greater effect." Caroline suggests that feeling uncomfortable about having money prevents these inheritors from taking the worthy action of helping others and thus is a form of morally intolerable emotional self-indulgence—perhaps just as bad as the material self-indulgence the inheritors are conflicted about.

STAY-AT-HOME MOTHERS AND THE LABOR OF LIFESTYLE

Like inheritors, "stay-at-home mothers"—known as "SAHMs"—do not earn the money they live on. As recently as thirty or forty years ago, wealthy housewives' distance from paid labor was taken for granted; their primary role was to support their husbands, raise their children, and participate in the social and charitable organizations of their communities, as Susan Ostrander's aforementioned 1984 book *Women of the Upper Class* describes.[17] Although some of the women Ostrander interviewed wished they had had more choices, particularly the option to work for pay, the majority seemed relatively content with these narrow expectations and possibilities. But most of these women had been born before 1940 and had come of age before the second wave of the women's movement. Many had not attended or completed college, and very few had advanced degrees.

In contrast, the women I talked with had been born mostly in the late 1960s and the 1970s and are part of a generation of women expected to work for pay and educated to do so. A few of the eighteen nonworking or minimally working women I spoke with said they had always wanted to leave their jobs to take care of their children.[18] But most of them had felt some reluctance to give up their paid, professional, often quite lucrative jobs (and, as we have seen, many of them had earned advanced degrees that prepared them for these jobs). Several had not left paid work until their children were several years old, and most of them had left because their high-powered corporate jobs could not accommodate part-time or flexible schedules.[19] A few had stopped working when the 2008 economic crisis hit, as they were laid off or their jobs were otherwise affected. Others said that, next to the large sums their husbands were earning, their own salaries did not justify their staying in the workforce.

In the absence of paid work, these women turned to what I call the "labor of lifestyle." This work includes everything from basic household tasks such as cleaning and food preparation to child care and a wide variety of "consumption work,"[20] such as home renovation, vacation planning, and management of second (or third) homes. It also includes hiring and supervising paid workers in the home, such as nannies, housecleaners, tutors, and those involved in other projects, such as renovation. The labor of lifestyle also includes work on behalf of children, which goes far beyond simply feeding and clothing them to include choosing their schools, monitoring their progress, planning and implementing their leisure activities, and dealing with any health or disability issues. Many of the stay-at-home mothers also devoted significant amounts of time and energy to volunteer work, as I discuss further in chapter 4.

But this work is not typically recognized as economically or symbolically valuable in the same ways that paid work is. Although taking care of children is generally seen as morally worthy, household labor traditionally done by women has long been viewed as economically unproductive.[21] And consumption in general, historically and symbolically the province of women, is often associated with self-indulgence and the frittering away of money and time rather than being seen as necessary in order to reproduce families.[22] For both of these reasons, affluent women's labor may be especially undervalued because of the association of these tasks with wealth. It is hard to imagine taking care of a second home or planning a European vacation as "work." Thus, like inheritors, these women confront a stereotype of being dilettantes.[23] In fact, the risk is higher that others will judge them negatively because their "not working" status is more obvious than the inherited wealth of inheritors who have jobs.

I saw some of these judgments from working mothers about those who did not work for pay. Willa told me, of stay-at-home mothers: "It's amazing how you can fill the day with lots of things. . . . Renovations, decorators, going shopping, having lunch with your friends, going to the gym, going to Pilates, going to a masseuse, having acupuncture. I mean, there are a lot of ways you can fill your day. I find most of them to be quite vapid. Oh, you've got to get your hair blown out. That's another one." Lisa, an executive with a household income of $600,000, told me, "If we go to a party and the husbands are there, inevitably I'm talking to the husbands . . . [about] some kind of business thing. And the women—I can't really talk to them about that stuff. You're talking about your workout. They work out, like, five hours a day. Oh my God. I don't work out five hours a day! You know?"

Furthermore, staying at home goes against the culturally powerful idea that women can and should work for pay, as well as their own professional preparation and experience. Susan, a parenting therapist I interviewed, told me, "You have some people who are so wealthy in New York that they can stay home and they just take care of their kids, and that's great. But then they also feel so guilty that they're wasting their degrees. . . . They feel so 'less than.'" Later, she said, "They feel that they're not doing anything. That there's nothing productive that they're doing."

In the absence of paid jobs, the stay-at-home mothers I talked with tended to try to convince themselves (and me) that their activities legitimately counted as work and that their consumption was productive. To do this they needed to draw on multiple discourses of legitimate work—as mothers, especially—but also on allusions to their own busyness and productivity, as well as to their own paid work in the past and that of their husbands in the present. I found this among women of color as well as white women, despite historical variation in the relationship of women in these categories to paid work.[24]

Stephanie, as we have seen, was adamant that hard work was important and that poor people did not work hard enough. She and her husband had an annual income of about half a million dollars (plus her husband's significant equity in his business). They owned an apartment in New York City and two other properties, for a total value of about $8 million. Like Paul, quoted at the beginning of the chapter, Stephanie equated hard work with deservingness. When I asked, "Do you feel like you deserve the lifestyle that you have?" she immediately responded, "Hell, yeah. I work my ass off." She then continued:

> Other than having a wonderful place to escape on the weekends [her second home], I don't, like, spend my days going to get my hair done, and go shopping, and have lunch with my friends. Some days I feel like, what did I get done today? I feel like I never get anywhere. 'Cause I take my son to school in the morning. By the time I get home from that, it's 9:30. And then already, I'm leaving five hours later to go pick him up. And in between all that time, I'm cleaning the house, doing the laundry, going food shopping, dealing with stuff on the phone. . . . I don't indulge myself at all.

Stephanie elucidates her own hard work in the household while drawing strong boundaries against images of women who simply consume rather than producing anything. Again we see the rejection of self-indulgence, which she counterposes to morally legitimate productivity.

In particular, Stephanie emphasized her labor as a mother. She told me proudly that she had not hired a babysitter until her son was a year old, saying, "I had a kid because I wanted a kid, not so I could hand him over to somebody else." She spoke disparagingly of mothers she knew who "can't believe that they have to get through a weekend, because their nanny can't come." She highlighted her domestic (i.e., productive) labor, telling me, "I'm a big hit at school with the cookies. They're just all beautifully, intricately decorated." She also refused to purchase a Halloween costume for her child. She asked rhetorically, "What kind of mom am I if I buy you a costume?"

Stephanie devalues the commodification of both maternal labor (by denigrating paid child care) and goods like cookies and Halloween costumes; she thereby symbolically revalues her own unpaid labor, which cannot be done by anyone else and still have the same meaning.

Alexis was a stay-at-home mother with a second home in the Hamptons. When I asked if she felt she "deserved" her lifestyle, she responded, "Deserve? I don't feel guilty about it. I don't know if *deserve* is the right word, but I feel like, even though I'm not making money now, I was, like—I mean, I'm a smart person. I mean, I'm taking care of our children. Yeah, I don't feel, you know, guilty about that at all." Here Alexis reaches for several different legitimations. First, her *previous* paid work in finance, for which she had earned an MBA; second, her intelligence; and third, her care for the children. Like Stephanie, and unlike Paul, she needs to bring in multiple legitimations beyond paid work, though it is to paid work that she turns first.

Stephanie and Alexis were unusual among my interviewees in linking these discourses quite forcefully to their own entitlement. Other women I interviewed struggled more to cast their maternal and family labor as legitimate. I asked Ursula, for example, what she did on an "average" day, and then immediately clarified by asking what she had done the day before. She responded, "This is a very bad example, wouldn't you say? Both kids are in camp, and it's the middle of the summer. I feel like if I told you what I did yesterday it would be very— it would not be telling of a regular day." I answered, somewhat confused, "I don't know, would it? It depends on what it was." Ursula recounted, "I had nothing to do! So I went for a facial. I met a friend for lunch. I went shopping. And then I planned a dinner. My son came home [from camp], and I took him to the park. We played ball. . . . So he was back at 5 and we played from 5 to 6. And then we watched the Olympics! For three hours. But I do think it was—that's not my normal day."

Ursula was unwilling to describe this day, which had all the hallmarks of the "ladies-who-lunch" stereotype, as "average." When I asked her how she would describe a day when the kids were around, she emphasized a much more "laborious" day: "If [they are] in school I have a very different schedule. I take them to school. We leave the house at like 7:30 in the morning. I have to be dressed, I have to give them breakfast, I have no help at that time. . . . When I'm at school, I often volunteer for various [tasks]. . . . I spend a lot of time in the school. I come back, I have reams of paperwork that needs to get done. You know, the two homes, all the stuff that's going on in school. I manage other things like I just told you about the [kids' activities]." This day, as Ursula describes it, involves a lot of work, including volunteering, child-related tasks, and the labor of maintaining the family's two homes. Like Stephanie, Ursula represents the work of caring for children as especially legitimate—so her conception of herself as working hard is challenged when the children are not in school.

Like Ursula and Stephanie, other nonearning women drew boundaries against the ladies-who-lunch stereotype. Allison told me that after she worked out in the mornings, she spent her days paying bills, going grocery shopping, doing cleaning or household projects with her housekeeper, organizing the kids' schedules, and volunteering at three different organizations. She differentiated herself from the friends she worked out with by saying: "They don't even pay bills. They don't do anything to support their house. All they do is take care of their kids, and work out. [I do] all this stuff—like, I book all our family vacations. I do all this stuff. I manage, like, everything that comes to this house. These guys don't have to do all that. . . . Their husbands do all of it. [The mothers] just manage their kids' schedules, and their workout schedules." Allison further critiqued these friends for working out two or three times a day, having coffee, and then going shopping. (Although she accompanied them doing these activities, it was only "once or twice a month. But not, like, every day.") Like others I interviewed, Allison is working to draw distinctions that cast her own time as being spent in consumption that contributes to the household rather than consumption that is self-indulgent and unproductive.

Some women explicitly framed their labor, from child care to renovation, as a "job" or used other business analogies and economic equivalents. Several women told me they were "the CEO of the household." Maya's husband traveled a lot for work and did very little child care, even on the weekends. She said, "The way I've come to grips with it is, I have the nanny during the week, and so I can do my own things during the week. But that is balancing that with everything else. I feel like, when you put all of my stuff together, I kind of feel like I have a full-time job. Now of course, you know, I get to go to the gym and I get to do other fun things. But it just feels like [a job]." Maya acknowledges that her work is not like a job in that she can go to the gym and have fun. But she seems to dismiss this freedom, which contradicts the rest of her claim, even as she acknowledges it.

David, an interior designer I interviewed, worked with many affluent female clients in their forties. He said, "I see a lot in New York how . . . we're all raised with, like, 'Okay, women can do the same things that men can do.' But yet they might have been successful career people, but for whatever reason, they're not any more. Probably it's financial, they don't really need to work. But there's this desire to, like, make the house building and designing like their full-time job. . . . They really view it as their job. You know? So, say for instance, if you have a highly functioning woman who's had a career, gotten married, had the kids, and then now has four houses that they're redesigning or building one after the other, it really becomes like a job for them, because it takes so much time."

Assigning financial worth to this time and effort made it more like "real work." Danielle, the inheritor and former banker mentioned earlier who felt guilty about spending "vanity money," told me, "Earning your own money is validating. Somebody's paying you for what you're doing." Following this logic of validation, she and her husband had calculated "what it would cost to replace" her domestic labor. She said, "It's a sizable amount." She laughed. "You know, between babysitting, tutoring, housecleaning, cooking—what does that add up to in people hours? And it's not what I [earned before], but it's a bunch of money." In fact, Danielle had rearranged the family's investments to produce dividends, from which she paid herself a salary of $48,000 for this work, which she used for family and personal expenses.[25] She also spoke of her children jokingly as her "two very small clients" and made an analogy between the research she used to do as part of her work in finance and the research she had done for her renovation. Susan, the parenting therapist, told me that the women she worked with who were "in the best shape" emotionally were those "who really value what they're doing" (taking care of children). She said they felt best when "they're really feeling like 'What I do is worth *huge* amounts of money.'"

Some of these women associated themselves with paid labor in other ways. Some attached themselves symbolically to the hard work and upward mobility of others, especially husbands and immigrant parents. Lucy told me, "I grew up in an upper-middle-class family, absolutely. But my mother was an immigrant. She came with nothing.... My father paid for everything himself. He put himself through college. You know, like, my family was all about hard work and merit and hustle." Or, like Alexis, quoted previously, several women mentioned the paid work they had done in the past. Danielle said, "I think maybe because I had worked and I feel pretty confident about that, I don't really care when people ask me, 'What do you do?' I say 'I'm at home, I'm not working. I'm a retired banker.'" Helen, quoted previously as having the prudent "mindset" of her immigrant parents, also said, "And I feel like, you know, I worked for my money, so I know what that's like." Helen also suggests that *knowing what it is like* to work for money matters in terms of having the right "mindset" even when one no longer actually receives a salary. That is, one can have the deserving selfhood of hard work without actually doing such work.

PAID LABOR AND SELF-SUFFICIENCY

Framing the labor of lifestyle as a legitimate, time-consuming job raised questions for these women about what it meant to pay others to do household and child-related work. All the families in which one partner did not work for pay employed housecleaners, and interviewees seemed to take for granted that they would not do this kind of work themselves. But some women struggled over the choice to hire nannies, and most were conflicted about paying for other kinds of labor such as that of personal assistants, personal chefs, or night nurses. In some cases, as I have suggested, part of this ambivalence came from discomfort over class inequality with these workers. But many also felt that they should do this work themselves, especially when it came to mothering.

For example, Teresa commented, "You feel like you're not as perfect if you have help." She had had health problems when her daughter was an infant and had been convinced to hire a baby nurse. She told me, "I fought that one tooth and nail. You feel like you have to pay your dues. . . . I felt like, you know, who am I to have a night nurse? It felt like [I was] almost a failure as a woman." Like all the other women she knew who had hired baby nurses, she thought, "That's ridiculous; I should be able to do it myself." When her mother-in-law offered to help with the kids, Teresa resisted, thinking, as she put it, "I should be able to do it all. My house shouldn't be a mess, I shouldn't have clutter on the table, you know." This desire to "do it all" without help is another iteration of the value placed on self-sufficiency.

These mothers also described paid labor as facilitating their own unpaid work rather than as enabling them to avoid it.[26] For instance, Zoe said, "I have a nanny that helps me out. And she'll come, maybe take them out in the morning so I could go to the supermarket, or go do an errand, or [go to a] doctor's appointment, or whatever." Zoe indicates that the nanny is only allowing Zoe to complete essential household and personal tasks, not enabling her to indulge herself in other ways. These women also emphasized that the nanny would take care of one child while they took the other(s). Lucy said she spent nearly all her time with her kids. She qualified, "I do have a babysitter. But I've got three kids. . . . It doesn't happen that often that I'm not with at least one of them." Lucy and Zoe frame their use of time as productive even though it is unpaid, distancing themselves from the stereotype of unproductive dilettantes.

Alexis said, "It's not like we're sitting on the sidelines. You know. There's always dishes to be done, and laundry, and—you know. So, believe me, I know plenty of women do it all by themselves. And I know that I could, obviously, if I had to." But later in the interview she asked me if I thought she was a "total snob" for hiring a lot of child care. When I asked her to define *snob* she said, "Like, I don't know. Spoiled. That I'm not working now, and I have all this help." Her use of the words "snob" and "spoiled" implies that she is *illegitimately* using labor to which she should not be entitled. As we will see in chapter 5, this question also loomed in conflicts with her husband about how much paid labor was too much.

These stay-at-home mothers compared themselves to working mothers who could, they imagined, "do it all." Maya had hired a personal chef to come once a week to cook meals that the family would eat over the course of a few days. She told me, "The chef definitely feels like something I don't talk about a lot, because it's almost embarrassing. With the moms at school, I find it embarrassing. With our social circle [comprising primarily high-earning men married to stay-at-home women], I think it's fine. But with the moms at school [who worked for pay] it does feel a little silly, extravagant." She described friends with kids who also had jobs and/or who had no child care. Of one friend she said, "She does it all. She doesn't get time to exercise, her house might not be as immaculate as mine is, things like that. So I feel silly talking about being tired or being stressed given all the help I have. So I'm careful about that. Right? I mean I feel like with those folks, they're making it all happen, and to them [I'll] say, 'Oh, and I have this chef'? It's like, what the fuck?" Again, as I discussed in chapter 1, not talking about these issues with people in different situations is one strategy for avoiding discomfort with it.

Maya also felt that these women, as well as her old friends "from when I was working," would think that having "help" in the house when she was not working was "crazy." But, she immediately countered, as if to an imaginary critic, "None of my friends are 40 with [such young children]. They all had kids younger, and the husbands all came home [in the evening, to help with the kids]. Or if their husbands didn't come home they didn't expect a home-cooked meal. And my husband is quite picky about what he eats." Asserting the ways in which she is different from these other mothers legitimates Maya's "need" for the personal chef, as well as the full-time nanny, thereby assuaging her discomfort with it.

I did not speak to any heterosexual men who were "stay-at home dads" and spoke to only one father who did not work for pay. Richard was a gay man without a paying job, married to a financier. He did sometimes feel bad about not having paid work, telling me, "New York City's so much about work. And people define themselves through their work. You know, 'What do you do?' And sort of, 'I do this.' And having children doesn't seem to count. You know. It's like, 'Oh, fine. You have kids. But what do you *do*?'" However, in contrast to the women I spoke with, Richard expressed no conflict about hiring a full-time nanny and a baby nurse around the clock for their infant. He said, "I think we were just each honest with ourselves. We didn't want to give up a certain freedom, or certain involvements. . . . And also, having a woman's presence also [is good], right? So it just makes sense for us. And if we can afford it, it feels like a worthwhile thing to spend money on." Though Richard mentions the desire for a "woman's presence" in the baby's life, he does not describe having the nanny as allowing him to do more lifestyle work. Instead he feels comfortable using that time for his own "freedom" and "other involvements." Although the gendered expectation of paid work weighs on him, the gendered stigma associated with using paid labor does not.

RETURNING TO PAID WORK?

These conflicts about the value of unpaid labor also emerged when I asked them about returning to paid work. Again, these women were highly educated, and almost all had had lucrative jobs prior to or even after having children. Several liked earning their own money. Others spoke about the intellectual challenges of their jobs or said they missed the camaraderie of the workplace. Some wanted an identity beyond mothering.

But, most important in terms of the morally legitimate status of paid work, they wanted to be "productive" and to "contribute" to the household, which seemed to mean earning money. Julia, a mother of two married to an entrepreneur, said, "I keep wondering about [going back to work], just 'cause my kids are getting older. I'm like, well, I'm not going to be a housewife forever. It's not my personality to just have the kids go to school and still not do anything. I'm not the person that goes and gets my hair done and my nails. I just don't do that. . . . I'd want to be productive and bringing something in. And so I've really been trying to figure out what that next thing is going to be." Julia distances herself from the stereotype of the stay-at-home mother as the unproductive, self-indulgent consumer. While it feels legitimate to her to be taking care of her kids while they are small, she doesn't want to "not do anything" or to focus only on her appearance.

Although these women also try to value their unpaid labor symbolically, the idea of contributing *financially* is still powerful. As we will see in chapter 5, sometimes the value of the unpaid "contribution" becomes a bone of contention between husbands and stay-at-home wives. Yet despite these women's desire to contribute, the lack of economic necessity meant that their standards for paid work were high. They did not want work that was too time-consuming or inflexible. Most did not want to go back to reporting to a boss or serving demanding clients; some were not interested in returning to the corporate world. Some women said they would probably just continue to volunteer, which gave them the same social and intellectual rewards as work, without the money. Others imagined starting a business; a few talked about tutoring or otherwise working with kids. But it seemed unlikely that most would return to full-time paid work.

Here, again, the possibility of cultivating a hard-working self in the absence of actual paid work arose. Lucy was happy being at home with her small children, but she was thinking about the "next step." Partly, she wanted to work for pay because "I need another way to fulfill myself." And, she added, "there's also kind of just showing a work ethic, I think, to my kids." On the other hand, she thought she herself had a good work ethic even though her mother had not worked outside the home. She said, "I'm very committed. I'm a great worker. I'm loyal. You know, I get what it means to get up every day and do that. I totally get that. But my mother never worked. So I got that somehow in a house without my mother working." This notion leaves the door open for her not to work but still to be able to instill a solid work ethic in her children, which is a crucial part of being a good mother. Again, in a sense the mindset matters more than the work itself, because one's identity as a worker who "get[s] what it means to get up every day and do that" can be split off from one's actual work.

The idea of productive work looms large for these affluent New Yorkers. Some interviewees—those with a lot of earned wealth— use it as an empirical *explanation* of privilege ("I *have* what I have because I worked hard"). Many also recognize the role of luck, though rarely that of structural advantages. But, more important, hard work is a key element of *inhabiting* the worthy self for everyone I spoke with ("I *deserve* what I have because I work hard"). The most legitimate work is paid work, especially highly paid work, which is tied not only to effort but to individual self-sufficiency. Even the notion of being financially "at risk," while anxiety-producing, reinforces this idea of individual (usually male) responsibility.[27] The people I talked to who are more distant from paid work struggle with feelings of guilt, unworthiness, and dependency rather than anxiety. They create symbolic proximity to paid labor by alluding to work they have done in the past, that other people close to them do, or that they know how to do. To understand that work matters, to be able to work, and to be prudent can form part of a "mindset" of the deserving self even in the absence of paid work.

At the same time, to be hard-working is not the only feature of the deserving self. We have already seen here that the concept of hard work is twinned with that of prudence. Both are forms of disciplined—rather than self-indulgent—action. Together, these behaviors legitimate accumulation, not by indicating that one is chosen by God, as in the Protestant ethic, but by indicating that one is morally worthy. Chapter 3 develops the idea of prudence as it fits into a narrative of reasonable spending for earners, inheritors, and stay-at-home parents alike.

3

"A VERY EXPENSIVE ORDINARY LIFE"

CONFLICTED CONSUMPTION

Gary is a downward-oriented inheritor of wealth with assets of well over $10 million. He is an academic, and his wife runs her own small business; their young children attend a highly ranked public school. He and his wife own and have renovated both a brownstone in Brooklyn and a second home in upstate New York. Gary told me about an incident with the contractor on his renovation, who had ordered "one of those really fancy, big stoves." He continued:

> And so we said to him, "No, we're going to put in a regular stove." You know. Painted porcelain, whatever they are. I don't know. Part of that was, we're not going to [do] this big price thing. But part of it was very much about not ending up with the kitchen that looked like the luxury kitchen. You know, by the baseline comparative points of where our friends and colleagues live, the fact that our kitchen [is big], and it looks out on the yard, and it's lovely, it is already a really, really nice kitchen. But it's not a really nice kitchen that has really, really, like, top of the line [appliances]. I grew up with a stove. A regular stove. It gets hot. It still heats up the pots.

Gary went on, "It's almost like I can hear my grandmother, on my father's side, saying this kind of thing. She was a big influence, by the way. You know, the message of 'That big shot, Mr. Rockefeller, still has to get up in the morning and put his pants on.'" Gary invokes his grandmother as someone whose down-to-earth attitude influenced him to stay focused on function, to remember the basics rather than getting distracted by unnecessary bells and whistles.

Gary also told me that he and his wife and kids "have, by far, the most expensive ordinary life of everybody that we know." He continued, "You know, it's almost like we're making an effort to live, or appear to live, a pretty ordinary life. But, I mean, I'm sure our life costs ten times more than kids—not the kids in the projects. The other professional upper-middle-class families whose kids [are in school with ours]." In talking about the expenses of this life, he mentioned his mother-in-law's nursing home costs, amounting to over $200,000 per year, and summer camp for his kids, which had cost over $20,000. Asked to elaborate on what he meant by an "ordinary life," Gary said, "Ordinary in the sense of, we don't own a car. . . . That we expect the kids to clean their dishes. We don't go to Vail at every chance to ski. Probably even more important than that is a deep commitment to be part of the community. [My wife] has often served as a class parent at school. I do nonprofit board work. Which you could say is the provenance of privilege. Or you could say it's an avenue of commitment to community. Or both."

Gary was especially thoughtful and straightforward about both his privilege and his family's consumption. But, although they might have left off the word "expensive," most of those I interviewed were, to use his words, "making an effort to live, or appear to live, a pretty ordinary life": a life focused locally on kids, homes, and family time.[1] Regardless of whether they faced up or down in terms of the self-positioning that I described in chapter 1, these affluent consumers shared the desire to see their consumption as "normal" and reasonable rather than as excessive or materialistic. They also described themselves as obeying the imperative of prudence paired with hard work that we saw in the previous chapter by setting limits on consumption. They talked about making most decisions on the basis of family and children's needs—basic needs they framed as common to all, regardless of class. And they expressed discomfort with visibility and display. All my respondents criticized ostentation, drawing strong boundaries against showing wealth, just as they drew boundaries against talking about it.

Thus my interviewees construct themselves as worthy people not only because of their hard work but also because of their consumption choices. Their discourses tie the "worth" of the spending to the moral "worth" of the person.[2] In framing their consumption in these ways, my interviewees symbolically situate themselves as part of the morally upstanding American middle class. Here they "aspire to the middle" not in the *distributional* sense I discussed in chapter 1—how they locate themselves in relation to others—but rather in the *affective* sense of having the habits and desires of the middle class. Many struggle with what exactly it means to live reasonably, and nearly all describe becoming comfortable spending more money over time. But regardless of what their lifestyles actually look like, they try to preserve their self-definition as "ordinary" consumers.

REASONABLE CONSUMPTION AND BASIC NEEDS

One way my respondents maintained this sense of ordinariness was to associate their expenditures with family life, children's needs, and having a "normal" lifestyle. As Olivia told me, "I think we're normal people, we buy normal things. We do normal things." Talia, as we have seen, is a stay-at-home mother whose husband earns about $500,000 per year in finance. She told me, "We have a pretty normal existence." Asked what that meant, she responded, "Just like, it's not—I don't know. Like dinners at home with the family. The kids eat, we give them their bath, we read stories. It's not like we're out at, like, Balthazar. . . . Out in [our summer rental] our life is really very—it's very much like any other kid who lives in the suburbs. And you know, [in the city] we walk to school every morning. And you know, it's fun. It's like a real neighborhood existence." By contrasting herself to those who dine at (fancy) Balthazar and alluding to family dinners and walking to school, Talia implies that she and her family are the same as any other family. Being "normal" thus comes to mean sharing priorities common to the (implicitly "middle-class") majority rather than consuming luxury goods or experiences.

Nadine and her partner, who lived primarily on Nadine's family wealth, had lost money in the economic crisis, and their renovation had cost much more than they had expected. As a result, they had had to re-evaluate their spending, which they lowered from around $19,000 per month to $16,000. When I asked what they had eliminated, Nadine said, "Just, like, anything extra. I mean, there wasn't that much extra. It sounds ridiculous [to say that], because sixteen thousand a month is so much. But, like, most of that is, like, house, school, child care, bills. I mean, things that are sort of fixed." Nadine uses the word "ridiculous" to show she recognizes that $16,000 is a lot of money, but she immediately justifies these "fixed" expenditures by framing them as the basic essentials of family living—a very expensive ordinary life.

Similarly, in conversations specifically about homebuying and renovation, respondents typically referred to wanting light, space, room for kids, accommodations for visiting parents, or a layout that suited their family's habits. For example, Maya, the stay-at-home mother who described her work as a "job," said of her house hunt: "View was not important. Light was important, space was important, being near a park was important." She also wanted a summer house "because we don't have a back yard" in the city. Chaz, a corporate lawyer, told me he and his wife had chosen their $3 million apartment because it had quiet bedrooms so their young children could sleep, was near a park so the kids could play, and was in a building with a doorman for safety. Ursula's renovation had combined three prewar apartments; she emphasized family needs when she explained the combination by saying the original New York City apartments were "not built for families."

When I asked one respondent with a household income of about $2 million if she had done anything extravagant in their home renovation, she responded, "I mean, this is how pathetic this answer's going to be. The fact that we have two sets of washer-dryers. That was my big, like, go crazy moment. Yeah. Of course, we did not need to have two." When she showed me the second laundry room, she said, "This is my extravagance." It is not entirely clear whether she thinks her choice is "pathetic" because it implies she values domestic duties or because it is not extreme enough to be considered "extravagant." But either way, the assertion denies *illegitimate* excess by connecting it to an ordinary need.

By the same token, many of those I talked with asserted that they would be fine living with less. Talia, whose renovation had combined two apartments in Manhattan, said, "I don't have needs that would require—like, I just want to have food on the table for my kids." Alexis said, "I mean, if [her husband] said to me, 'We can't have the two houses anymore, we can't afford this, we have to make some changes,' then we would. You know. I hate to see him feeling stressed." Kate, Nadine's partner, told me, "If all this were to go away tomorrow, I don't think I'd actually be—maybe I'm wrong; check back with me if something happens—but I don't think I'd be totally crushed. I think I'd be like, "Oh, well, we have to change things a lot and dig up that tuna casserole recipe and move on."

Thus something about not "really" needing the more comfortable aspects of an affluent lifestyle makes having the lifestyle more legitimate. This is another aspect of the legitimately privileged self in which, if privilege is not required, it becomes more acceptable. It is related to denying a *feeling* of entitlement, as I discussed in the previous chapter, and alludes to a capacity to work if necessary. The "real" self that is elucidated here is not dependent on this affluent lifestyle.

LIMITS AND PRUDENCE

We have seen that some of these consumers invoked the wealth of the New York City super-rich to cast themselves as "in the middle" and asserted, "In New York City, we're not wealthy." Similarly, many attributed the large amounts they spent (which they often called "ridiculous" or "crazy") to the high cost of living in the city, implying that they didn't have much choice. They lamented that family members who lived in other cities or suburban areas did not understand life in New York and thus thought them more privileged or extravagant than they actually were. Nicole, as we have seen, was an upward-oriented photographer with a household income of about $400,000 and assets of about $2.5 million. She told me: "What I say to [my husband] is like, 'You can't talk about what we pay for things to your family outside of the city. 'Cause they will not understand. They'll think that we are the craziest people in the world. And we're not. We're, like, totally normal people. But, like, no one should be paying this much money for anything. You know? So, just don't tell them.'" She was incensed that her husband's ascetic parents thought she was "a consumer" (which clearly had a negative connotation) because she felt they were judging her as a spendthrift for using money in ways that were necessary in New York, including paying her mortgage, condo fees, and private-school tuition.

My respondents also emphasized the minimalist or frugal elements of their consumption. Nadine said, "I don't shop, you know? I wear the same stuff pretty much every day. I wear the same pair of shoes every day." Several women mentioned buying clothing at inexpensive stores such as Target, Kohl's, and Costco or at discount outlets. Other respondents gleefully recounted bargains they had picked up. Wendy, a corporate lawyer, had snagged a used $1,000 stroller for $100, which she "felt good" about; Beatrice, a nonprofit executive, had gotten a $20,000 dining table for $6,000. They told me about buying a used car or driving the same car for many years. Stephanie emphasized to me that she bought her clothes at outlets such as Zara and H&M; she also recounted in detail the ways she had saved money on her home renovation. David, an interior designer whose clients were of the same class as my respondents, told me, "Always, for every job, I always throw in Ikea and Crate and Barrel pieces. They love that. It makes them feel better." I asked, "Because it makes them feel like they're economizing?" He replied, "Yes." In contrast to this talk of bargains, none of my respondents *ever* highlighted the price of something because it was high.

These specific consumer choices are linked to my respondents' broader framing of themselves as economically prudent, which I described in chapter 2. Nicole said, "We don't take fancy vacations. We're pretty frugal about, kind of, everything. You know? We don't buy stuff." Paul described his wife as "the woman who will price check, and this is not an exaggeration, Target versus Costco. It's what she does. And so while she comes from money and likes nice things, she's very prudent about what she [spends]." Chaz, the corporate lawyer, said of the renovation he and his wife had done, "I'm sure there's people that want to put gold plating on their ceiling, but they're not going to get that in return [when they sell] the apartment. I mean, we wanted to do whatever we think we could do within reason. And we absolutely did not have an unlimited budget, to do whatever we wanted in the apartment. I think it was within reason. And there was plenty of things that we thought we wanted to do, and decided, "Forget it." Those who had bought high-end stoves, ovens, and refrigerators in kitchen renovation often described these as being necessary for resale value, even when they had no plans to sell the property.

Willa, who had both inherited wealth and annual household earnings of about $2 million, told me proudly that her architect had said she was one of his only clients "who keeps to a strict budget." She said, "I feel we're in a very comfortable position, where we do what we want. But we don't live extravagantly—certainly don't live beyond our means, at all. . . . I mean, particularly now that [her husband's job is uncertain], like, we're just kind of stockpiling a lot of things, and, like, not going on vacation, and not doing big stuff." Yet she continued by recognizing that this practice primarily reinforced a mindset of prudence rather than actually making much of a difference in their financial situation. "But I mean, the reality is, like—the percentage that we would spend of what we have is relatively small. But it's just the perception, I think, to us, of like, you know, this is not the time to go on vacation."

The "mindset" of prudence establishes limits on consumption; like the mindset of hard work, it characterizes a disciplined self.

Some earners felt critical of others in their lives who could not get their spending under control, thus failing to enact such discipline. For example, Justin, the finance entrepreneur, described himself as "highly organized" in his personal finances. He contrasted himself to his spendthrift sister, to whom he had often lent money. He said, "I have this feeling, like, if I wrote a check for one million dollars and gave it to my sister, it would be gone. She would need one point five. Like, it would never—she's insatiable. A lot of people are." In contrast, he said, "I'm a disciplined person."

They also reacted negatively when it seemed that others might be judging *them* for spending too much. As I mentioned in chapter 1, Karen feared that her neighbors and friends might think it was "too profligate" that she and her husband were renovating. Speaking of one neighbor who had asked them how they could afford to do it, she described his habit of spending a lot on eating out and entertainment as a way of explaining why she might have saved more money. She also added defensively, "I mean, they have more stuff at their garage sale than we have in our house."

To women, spending on themselves was morally suspect, especially in terms of clothing, accessories, and body labor. They tended to highlight doing their own nails and their own hair, and they tended to pay for services such as spider vein removal, Botox injections, or Invisalign orthodontics with their own money, not funds from the family coffers. Sometimes they kept these expenditures secret from their husbands, marking them as illegitimate. Miriam, for example, said she didn't want her husband to know what she spent on having her hair cut and colored, although he had tried to find out. She spent "more than I should," she said, adding that he would be "shocked" if he knew how much. The reasonableness of these needs was sometimes a source of conflict between nonearning women and their husbands, as I show in chapter 5.

The only consistently legitimate exception to the rule of frugality was spending on children. In keeping with their emphasis on family, my respondents almost universally spoke of kids' needs as worth spending money on. Wendy, who generally watched her spending closely, had hired a full-time nanny for her daughter when she went back to work. She said that daycare was "a much cheaper option, but we felt strongly that having a nanny would be better for her, and we just felt like it's safer and we were more comfortable with it. . . . When she was a tiny baby it was just hard to imagine not having a one-on-one situation where someone could always be picking her up and holding her, when she was really little. And I think that children who don't have a one-on-one caregiver at that age probably turn out perfectly fine, but I really wasn't willing to take the risk for my kid, since we had the money to have someone just focus on her." Many moms took for granted that they would buy organic food for children, although they often said the cost was "ridiculous," such as the $300–$600 per week that Zoe told me she spent at the grocery store. The fact that they are shopping for their children justifies the spending of money they would not want to say they had spent on themselves.

Richard was one of the few respondents who acknowledged the allusion to family needs as a form of justification. He said that the reason for the renovation he and his husband had done to their home was that they had a baby on the way, and then he immediately referred to that claim as a "story." I asked him why, and he responded:

> I think, in order to undertake a big renovation, I think for just me and [his husband], it didn't feel somehow justified. Like, I felt the need to justify. Which I think is sort of a personality tic of mine. . . . But you know, in terms of undertaking renovation, the expense and the strain involved. And the stress. I kind of felt like we should have a good reason to do it. A good reason for ourselves, and also a good reason for the world, kind of. I mean, sure, we could have done all this just for me and [him]. But it kind of would have been like, "Well, we don't really need to do it." So I think the kid provided the need, and the justification, and then it became the story, in the sense of, like, we're doing this for, you know, our child.

Richard's allusion to "a good reason"—for himself and his husband and for "the world"—highlights the internal desire to justify the expenditure of renovation. Richard interprets it as particular to him ("a personality tic"), but in fact many of my respondents seemed to share this desire, even when they did not recognize it as explicitly, and to assuage it with reference to family.

Both these gendered ideas about women's spending on themselves and the greater legitimacy of children's needs are clear examples of "earmarking"—putting certain monies into particular, morally loaded categories.[3] Another category my respondents created was the notion of the "treat" or exceptional spending—often associated with travel. Olivia described her three-week honeymoon as "very luxurious." She said, "That was a real, like—whoo! You know. But again, it was our honeymoon. We sort of felt entitled to do that. Or, I wouldn't even say we felt entitled. But it felt okay. We could kind of rationalize it, I guess." Justin described himself as "price-insensitive" on travel. He said, "I want the best hotel room, on the best island. I don't do it all the time. But when I go, I want to go to the top place." He said he might spend $500 or $1,000 a night on a hotel. "When I'm on vacation, you know, it's rare. So I want it to be just blockbuster. But I don't spend a lot of money on clothes or a watch. Like, this watch [indicating his watch] is thirty dollars, but I'll spend ten thousand on a one-week vacation." Ursula described her husband as spending a lot on vacations, which gave her "sticker shock." But, he told her, "'You know what, I don't want to think about it. I said in my mind this is how much this vacation is going to cost. And I don't need to come [in] under.'" Luxury spending is categorized as *exceptional*. Thus these consumers don't have to "think about it" or include it in their otherwise disciplined spending choices; it stands outside their self-conception as prudent.

MATERIALISM, OSTENTATION, AND DISPLAY

When my interviewees talked about their own expenditures as "reasonable," of course, they were always implicitly indicating what kind of spending is "unreasonable." As the previous examples suggest, they construct unreasonable consumption as materialistic, self-indulgent, unnecessary, and excessive. Nadine told me, "The way that I grew up, husbands rewarded wives with, like, new jewelry, new car. That whole thing. And I always thought that was sort of hideous and horrible, and why would you spend ten thousand dollars on a piece of jewelry? And why would you buy a new car for eighty thousand? And I still think that."

Many of my respondents were critical of consumers who seem to make purchases based on their economic value rather than on their exceptional, experiential value. Nicholas, an inheritor, described his reaction to a hotel his wife had suggested for their vacation:

> It's like fifteen hundred dollars a night, and you know, like, they massage your toes before you go to bed, whatever it is. And my crass response is, "You've got to be a fucking asshole to do this." They've got to be an asshole to spend that much money and think that, like, there's some value [to it]—it just seems so senseless to blow that money, other than a lack of imagination or this sense that makes you feel like [part of] a group of people who do that.

Danielle, who prided herself on planning cheap vacations, said, "I judge people who have very fancy vacations. . . . Like you didn't imagine it, or you didn't figure it out or something. You just plugged in." Valuing uniqueness and individual customization, these interviewees also draw a strong boundary against an excessive focus on spending for its own sake.

Maya was more upward-oriented than Danielle or Nicholas, and she didn't value this kind of unique experience as much. Yet she also critiqued materialism, explicitly using the language of "values," when she talked about choosing a private school for her daughter: "[Where] economic diversity comes into play, it might not even be that it comes into play, but it's in the way people—it's in the values. We do not want a school where everyone comes in private driven cars, where the children are all dressed out of Jacadi and where all the moms carry Chanel bags. Right? We want to be in a place where none of that shit matters." Maya slides from talking about "economic diversity"—presumably referring to people with different amounts of monetary resources—to talking about consumption choices. She values not exposure to significant economic difference but rather a particular way of inhabiting privilege. The indictment of materialism is a moral indictment as well—but it refers to a particular *use* of money rather than to the possession of it.

Closely connected to materialism is ostentation, the *making visible* of wealth, as Maya's example suggests. These consumers drew especially strong boundaries against this kind of display. Penny told me, "One of the reasons we're not in the suburbs, I feel like there's a lot of show of wealth. . . . I just, kind of, reject a lot of that." One of the wealthiest women I talked with lived in a house in the suburbs worth over $12 million. She was appalled by the excesses of her neighbors, who lived in what she called a "McMansion." She told me of her first visit there, lowering her voice, "The gates opened up to this *huuuge* house. And the play set—like, we don't have a play set. But, like, a play set in the backyard was, I'm not going to kid you, bigger than this whole room. It was something you would see out of—I don't know. It was like bigger than a school's play yard." She differentiated her own preference by saying, "So there's some things, like, flashy for the sake of flash, or big for the sake of big. Something small in a special, personal way would feel more impressive to me, or nicer to me. Or more interesting—maybe the right word is *interesting*—to me, than something that's just scale for the sake of size."

Alice is the stay-at-home wife of a corporate lawyer with whom she owns outright at least $8 million worth of real estate, including their home and a country house. She said, "When I think about [our] homes—I mean, when you add it all up, it's a lot of value and real estate. But the people who go and buy, like, twenty-million-dollar homes in the Hamptons or whatever. I just have a hard time with that. Or these humongous houses. I don't know that that would ever be something that I could see as part of our lifestyle." For Alice the problem is not "a lot of value and real estate" but rather "these humongous houses," which are both unnecessary and showy.

Drawing boundaries against ostentation and against spending for its own sake is a way for my subjects to distinguish themselves from the "bad rich" who spend illegitimately. They appeal to distinction, demonstrating high cultural capital—the knowledge that smaller is more "interesting," that generic expensive vacations are unsophisticated, and that "flash" is gauche.[4] But to distance themselves from wealthy people with less refined taste is also to situate themselves in the middle. For example, Miriam, the investment banker, lived in a $2.3 million home in Brooklyn, which she and her husband had spent $600,000 to renovate. She said, "I mean, obviously I think we have a large apartment by a lot of New York standards, but, you know, it's not got pillars and a curved driveway." "Pillars and a curved driveway" are rarely seen in New York City; they are an iconic image of wealth in the social imaginary, just as the trailer park described in chapter 1 is an iconic image of poverty. Invoking these comparisons, whether to imaginary rich people or to their actual McMansion-dwelling neighbors, my respondents situated themselves in the symbolically-middle, legitimate space of reasonableness.

In making these comparisons, my interviewees subordinated *having* to *showing*. That is, having is acceptable as long as it is not shown (or shown off) in particular ways. Yet they faced the possibility of *seeming* to "show off" in relation to people with less, including coworkers, family, friends, other parents, and household workers. That is, although my respondents did not find their own choices ostentatious, people with less might certainly see them as such. And the signs of wealth that marked their consumption, even when it wasn't "flashy," could create distance between them and their friends, peers, and family. They therefore tried to minimize the visibility of the choices they had made—hiding or downplaying them—especially when it came to their homes. As we saw in the introduction, Scott and Olivia were conflicted about inviting others to their expensive apartment (Scott said, "We don't want that 'Wow'"). Eliana, an inheritor with a large brownstone, told me she was sometimes uncomfortable when her son brought his friends over, especially one friend "who lives in the projects."

Miranda lives in a five-story brownstone with her inheritor husband and two young children. They had installed an elevator in their home as part of a gut renovation. She explained that they had put it in partly so older family members could visit them (a "basic" need) and so they could locate the guest room where they wanted it instead of on a lower floor. She also mentioned that the elevator was "not that expensive" because they were renovating anyway. Sensing that she might feel embarrassed about it, I asked, "Are people like, 'Oh my God, you have an elevator'?" She responded, "Yeah, it seems a little—yeah. That's why I have that little line, 'You know what? If you're doing that much work, an elevator isn't that expensive.'" The denial that it is expensive serves to minimize any sense that the respondent and her husband are extravagant (though of course "expensive" is a relative term). She also said, with a laugh, "I don't usually tell people I have an elevator." Asked why not, she said, "The house is really big on its own, and it's a full brownstone, and I realize that it's an enormous luxury to have in New York. So I don't need to be like (snotty tone), 'And, *the elevator.*'" Notable here is not only the justification itself but her *awareness* of this self-protecting rhetoric, similar to Richard's admitting that he told a "story" about his child in order to justify his renovation. Downward-oriented people were especially conflicted about this kind of display. As I argued in chapter 1, the discomfort caused by difference, which makes inequality visible, can become a motive for people to seek more homogenous environments and social circles.

Beatrice invoked another kind of social interlocutor—domestic workers—when she spoke of hiding purchases from her children's nanny: "Oh, you know, I mean it's just uncomfortable for me for her to know what I spend on things. . . . If I buy something, if I buy, like, clothes in the store, I take the tag off. I mean, we're not talking about—I take the tag off of my Levi's jeans. I mean, it's not like it's a mink coat or something. I take the label off our six-dollar bread. . . . I think again, for me, it's a choices thing—the choices that I have are obscene. Six-dollar bread is obscene." David, the interior designer, confirmed that this practice was common. During renovations, he said, "Things come in with big price tags on them. They all have to be removed, or Sharpied over, so the housekeepers and [staff] don't see them." He attributed this practice to shame about what he called "the obscene level of wealth" of a very small number of people. Such attempts at invisibility are curious because of course domestic workers in these households know that their employers are wealthy, even if they do not know exactly how much their bread costs. So the removal of this evidence would seem to be a way to obscure the conflict from themselves rather than to hide any meaningful information from their employees.

Beatrice told me she would not take the tags off the bread if a friend were coming over, even one who did not have much money. Instead, she said, "It's about the extremity of the inequality, and the fact that I know that she [the nanny] struggles." Despite her conflict about the nanny, Beatrice was not conflicted about inequality with her housekeeper, Elena, because Elena worked for another, wealthier, employer. She said, "It depends on who I'm thinking about it in relation to. I think that that's actually really key to my feelings about the money. Elena works for one of the richest women anywhere. And so I feel somehow, whatever we have is puny compared to what Mrs. [X] has. So I don't worry nearly as much about what Elena thinks." Again, Beatrice follows a logic of middleness, comparing herself both to the housekeeper and to Mrs. [X]. And even as she describes feeling bad about it, Beatrice signals that her consumption is reasonable ("not a mink coat or something").

DEFINING LEGITIMATE NEEDS

Nearly all those I interviewed wanted to be "normal," nonostentatious consumers. But many, especially the wealthiest, described grappling with questions of what exactly reasonable consumption consisted of. For example, Sara, mentioned in chapter 2 as not wanting to be a "dilettante," had inherited wealth of over $10 million. She and her husband, who worked in finance, were struggling to determine a level of lifestyle spending they felt comfortable with. She said:

And so the question of, like, what is our limit? I mean, we've now run the long-term projections. Okay, if we spend X percent for a year, like, what does that leave us in ten, twenty, thirty years? And is remaining where we are today [financially] okay with us? Especially considering that our kids already have trust funds. So, yeah. That's the question for us. Like, what is [the limit]—because that limit is somewhat arbitrary. I mean, it's not arbitrary, but it's deciding, you know, when I retire, do I want to have fifteen million or twenty-three million dollars, depending on how much I let myself spend now. It's like, you know, what am I going to do with fifteen million versus twenty-three million dollars when I'm 65?

Beyond these big-picture questions of how much to spend or to save, respondents worried about everyday spending choices. Scott and Olivia, as we saw earlier, struggled over "what it is okay to spend and not spend," in Olivia's words. Olivia described a conflict she felt when buying a new minivan about whether to get the model that included an interior vacuum cleaner (she called it "every mother's dream"). This model cost $10,000 more, even though she did not want any of the other features that came with it ("It comes with a giant DVD thing. We've never had a DVD in the car. We're philo-sophically opposed to watching TV in the car"). She said,

And so, you know, like, part of me was like, "I really want that vacuum, and we're not, we're not going to miss ten thou—" I mean, it's terrible to say. But it's the truth. We're not going to miss ten thousand dollars. And we're going to have this car for another ten years. Like, we don't buy a car every three years or five years or whatever. So the vacuum would really make me happy. Ten thousand dollars, amortized over a bunch of years. But then in the end, I was like, no. You know. All right. We're going to live without the vacuum.

In the end, Olivia said, it did not feel right to either of them to spend $10,000 on a vacuum—even though, as she points out, they can easily spare the money. Notably, Olivia feels that "it's terrible to say" that they won't miss $10,000, which she seems to have admitted by mistake—a sign of the transgressiveness of this kind of explicit acknowledgement.

Nicholas, who hated the idea of a hotel where "they massage your toes," told me he did not face material limits. Yet he created small hardships for himself to save money, such as not staying in a hotel on the beach on a beach vacation. His style differed from that of his wife, who was more comfortable spending money. Nicholas neatly summed up the difference between them when he said, "All of her questions [about spending] are like, "Can we afford it?" And I'm always like, "It's not a question of can we afford it. The question is, do we need it?" He continued, "I'm fearful of the slippery slope towards needing more, feeling like you need more and more in order to be satisfied. It just seems preposterous to me." He described furnishing their home after the renovation: "Do you just buy a chair for eight hundred dollars or two thousand dollars or three thousand dollars? Do I get an extra thousand dollars' worth of comfort and beauty from this more expensive chair?"

We often imagine that people have fairly clear desires, constrained only by their ability to pay. But the accounts of these consumers show that their desires do not always exist independent of these limits.

These questions of need and want were clearly also moral ones, which linked spending, again, to "values." Lucy told me she and her husband had agreed that each of them could have "one veto" once their renovation was finished—that is, to choose one thing to change or get rid of just because they didn't like it. They had come up with this policy after living for ten years with a sofa they hated. To get rid of it, they felt, would have been "wasteful," but the decision was "based on principle," she said, "it wasn't financially driven." The "waste" was a moral issue rather than an economic one. Lucy tied this to her feeling that buying things for the house that weren't only functional was self-indulgent; she asked rhetorically, "Do I really need another sofa because this one doesn't please me?" Their agreement to give themselves a veto was essentially a free pass to not feel guilty if they ended up wanting to alter something without a "legitimate" reason—but the fact that they only got one apiece meant they would not allow themselves to make constant changes. She said, "I feel really hypocritical when I talk about [these issues], because I—here I have this stuff, and this house, and all these other things. It feels very hypocritical. But at the same time, I'm trying to be kind of mindful about it. I will buy nice things, but I don't want to just turn them over for the sake [of novelty]. . . . Hopefully, I'm buying these things, I'm buying them with care, because I hope to live with them for a long time. And maybe pass them on in some way."

In talking about these moral dilemmas, some people alluded more explicitly to the context of inequality in which they were making choices and to the fact that most people do not have these options. Nadine, for example, first framed her spending as reasonable relative to her assets, saying, "Starting five years ago, it was like, wow. You know, we have all this friggin' money. We sold [some assets]. We were getting fourteen thousand a month from [family sources]. And I have, like, just all this money in investments. Like, I don't know, a million dollars. And I'm like, "Well, I guess I can buy this leather coat for five hundred dollars. I mean, I really love the coat." I asked, "What's the part of you that's saying, 'Okay, that's true, but I still shouldn't do it?'" She responded, "Well, I don't actually believe that [some] people should have that much money and other people shouldn't." Nadine is trapped between evaluating her desire in relation to her vast resources, which makes it seem reasonable, and linking it to the limited resources of others, in which case it seems excessive. It is not clear that *not* buying the coat would be a better moral choice, particularly, but she still feels hesitant about it.

As Nadine's comment indicates, these consumption choices can be thought of in different ways depending on the alternatives to which they are compared. Many people I spoke with used these kinds of comparisons to situate their own spending decisions. Ellen, a progressive financial advisor who is also wealthy,[5] spoke of "coming to terms with the dichotomy of being an activist interested in improving the world and having a comfortable life." She continued, "And, can I, short of, you know, taking a vow of poverty, sleep at night, and say, 'I am improving my corner of the world.'" Notably, Ellen compares her lifestyle to a *minimal* standard of existence associated with religious asceticism (a vow of poverty), which has a contemporary valence of unreasonable sacrifice as well as extreme self-deprivation. Even as she's explicitly acknowledging this dilemma of how to live while also wanting to "improve the world," this comparison locates her consumption in a middle ground between absolute self-denial and excess.

Even people with fewer resources (relatively speaking) struggled with these limits and talked about them in moral ways. For example, as we have seen, Keith and Karen were among the less wealthy in my sample. They felt anxious about money, especially because of recent expenses for their kids, such as for tutoring, and for their ongoing renovation. Keith said: "This is the classic debate. It's been a horrible day, it's 10:00, the kids are finally down, we're fried. All I want is an eight-dollar burrito. Am I bad person for ordering and getting an eight-dollar burrito delivered? It's like, we make three hundred fucking thousand dollars a year. I can't get an eight-dollar burrito? You know? I'm not going to Momofuku or something." Nicole told me, "There are things I feel guilty about. I feel like I take too many cabs, for sure. And when I'm in a cab, I'm like, 'Oh, [my husband's] going to see that I took a cab.' But he doesn't give me grief for it. I just feel guilty. Because I know it's stupid, and I should get in the subway instead of taking a cab. Or I feel lazy. But that is the luxury of my life, is taking a cab." Both these speakers feel morally conflicted about small purchases such as a burrito and a cab ride. Yet while they recognize these conflicts, they make comparisons that cast them in a good light: the burrito is explicitly compared to the expensive dinner at trendy Momofuku, and the taxi ride (like the second washer-dryer) is implicitly compared to some other kind of "luxury" that presumably would be more *truly* luxurious.

On the rare occasions that they talked about coveting expensive items, my interviewees tended immediately to dismiss these longings as "ridiculous." For example, Willa explained why she is always on the lookout for a new property to purchase and renovate: "It would be to get a townhouse with a bigger living room. To be able to have bigger parties. I mean, and this is such a stupid thing. Because the reality is, like, I should listen to myself. Because why am I buying a house—or an apartment, whatever it might be—for the three times a year that we have a huge party? Like, we, in this house, cannot have a huge party. Is that the worst thing? No. Like, do the children have bedrooms and a bathroom? Yes. Like, we're fine. We're fine." Willa believes her desire for more space is unreasonable; she tries to talk herself out of it, alluding to the basic needs of the children, but she can't quite "listen to" herself.[6] Nicole had already combined two apartments in her renovation, but she told me, "I've got this pipe dream of taking over [a third adjacent apartment] someday. Which would be ridiculous. I mean, that would just be too much space." Asked why she wanted it, she talked about the possibility of her children's having their own area away from where grownups would be socializing. Although this is a "legitimate" use of the space, her comment—the characterization of her "pipe dream" as "ridiculous"—still manifests a deep ambivalence between what she wants and what she thinks she should want.

James, the real estate entrepreneur with assets of over $3 million, told me about a conflict he felt after seeing a colleague's large house: "I'm just, like, looking at this place, feeling like, wow, my house is so small. And then thinking, 'That's a ridiculous statement you just made to yourself. What's wrong with you?'" I asked, "Did it make you feel bad, like 'I should have a bigger house'?" He responded, "Well, I felt that instinct, and I checked it. And I turned around and [said to myself], 'That's crazy. That's a road to nowhere. That kind of mindset is a road to nowhere.' . . . You have to consciously check it because [having] money does it to you, or to me." James suggests that desire and envy can quickly get out of control, which will also diminish his sense of his own achievements.

Alexis, as we have seen, was a stay-at-home mother with a household income of around $500,000 and assets of over $5 million. She was one of a few female respondents who talked about desiring the more stereotypical accoutrements of upper-class femininity, such as expensive shoes and handbags. She described her most recent purchase and the negotiations with her husband and with herself that made it acceptable:

> I just bought a very expensive handbag. That I feel guilty about. I'm, like, smiling because I love it so much. But, you know, I know I didn't need it. And we first talked about it, and [her husband] was like, "Come on, you don't need it." And I was like, "You're right. You're right. This is silly, silly, silly." And then, like, a month later—you know. For, like, Mother's Day, he was like, "Why don't you get it?" And I was like, "No, no, I don't need it." But then I was like, "Oh, wait a second!" [She laughed.] So of course I did. But yes, I do feel a little—you know, a little guilty about that.

In this and many other examples, Alexis's husband disciplined her desires, initially encouraging her to forego the $2,000 bag. But by deeming it a Mother's Day gift, they placed it in the exceptional, and acceptable, category of a "treat." Alexis also asserted again that she loved the bag and that it had "spoken to" her, establishing it as personally satisfying through uniqueness rather than as the result of a blindly consumerist impulse.

Maya, the stay-at-home mother married to the corporate lawyer, demonstrated deeper ambivalence about what she needed to be happy. On the one hand, as noted previously, she did not want her kids to be educated in an environment where people cared too much about Chanel handbags and fancy clothes. She also told me, about one friend who spends whatever she wants, that "I pass judgment and think that's really crazy to spend that much money." On the other hand, she actually did want these items herself; she wished that her husband, whose annual income was about $2 million, was more free with money so she could buy them. She told me he drew "stricter lines in the sand" than her friends' husbands. She said, "'It's my birthday, buy me that handbag!' Like, what's the big deal? Right.

But it is 'No, that bag is too expensive. I am not buying it.' Flat out." Notably, she frames the handbag as a potential birthday "treat." (As we will see in chapter 5, other husbands of stay-at-home mothers likewise try to corral their wives' spending.)

In the face of this refusal, Maya makes an effort to tamp down her desire, reminding herself that she has the basics and should be satisfied with them:

> Sometimes I wonder why doesn't my husband feel more comfortable with us doing a little bit of that kind of stuff [such as spending a lot on a handbag]. But I always come back to the fact that I live a very comfortable life. I do not want for anything significant. And so I'm grateful for what I have. And maybe I don't have that Chanel bag or maybe I didn't get to buy that Prada dress or I don't have that house in the Hamptons, but I've got this [home] and I've got two healthy kids and I've got a great marriage, and I'm very grateful for that. So. You know, I mean the mind wanders, yes it wanders. But it doesn't—it's nothing that kind of bothers me that much.

Maya works to convince herself to feel not only satisfied with what she has but also grateful for it, even when in fact she does not feel that it is enough. As I show in chapter 4, the feeling of gratitude is another aspect of the legitimately entitled self.

In modifying her feelings, Maya formulates what she does have—a home, healthy children, and love—as essential and what she doesn't have—Prada, Chanel, the Hamptons house—as insignificant. This antimaterialist formulation makes sense, of course, and I don't think it is intentionally strategic. But the idea that she doesn't "want for anything significant" erases the extreme difference between her "basic" existence and that of most people. This upward-oriented move helps her establish herself as "in the middle."

Penny, the very part-time legal consultant whose husband's income was around $3 million per year, was one of the few respondents who did *not* describe struggling to define her needs. She saw herself as drawing clear limits against unnecessary spending while not sacrificing comfort. She said, "Our car is twelve years old. Could we buy a new car? We could totally buy a new car. Could we buy, even—friends of [her husband] have—like, a friggin' Lamborghini. Like, we could actually buy a Lamborghini. Like—ugh!" But, she said, their car had only 60,000 miles on it. "So why would we buy a new car? So, I don't think either one of us is driven by that. I think we're pushing it away a little bit. But at the same time, when we look at the summer houses, when we want to buy, we're not going to buy a crappy house just to make a point. So it's a balance." Although Penny and her husband were willing to pay $1,300 per night for two rooms on a family vacation, they refused to fly first class (though sometimes they would spend more for the "middle" category of seats). She also counterposed their spending to that of several friends who spent more, including a couple who spent $250,000 on their daughter's wedding. By comparing her choices to theirs, she places herself in a more moderate category. The idea of "balance" also connotes middleness by referring to a middle ground between excess and self-deprivation.

SOCIAL OTHERS AND LUXURY CREEP

Regardless of their struggles, almost all my respondents described becoming acclimated over time to making more expensive consumer choices. Maya said that she would not spend $1,000 on a dress, but added that "the number of hundreds I would spend seems to go up all the time, right?" Nadine said, "I didn't want to be one of those rich people that just spends money without thinking about it. But I will say that there was a period where my thinking about what was reasonable became very different than what it was, like, you know, in 1992. So, over the span of ten years, what I [had] considered a luxury or extravagant or whatever didn't seem as extravagant." Eliana, whose inherited wealth totaled about $9 million and who believed deeply in economic and racial justice, said she felt like a hypocrite, because "I don't think I fully live out all my values, I guess I would say. I used to say I was gonna be a revolutionary, and then I had that first massage."

Beatrice identified this phenomenon as "luxury creep":

> Well, there's definitely been luxury creep in my life. I just feel comfortable spending more money on more things. There's luxury creep within categories that look like necessities. So, like, I spend more and more money on clothes. . . . We spend a *lot* of money on wine. . . . We've recently had a big leap in the amount of money that we spend on bottles of wine, like fifteen or twenty-five dollars. So we would have bought wine before, and considered it, like, a life necessity, but it's the luxury creep aspect of it that's changed.

Beatrice went on to associate luxury creep with her peer group, saying, "It's a very insidious thing, you know, because it's much less conscious than, like, 'keeping up with the Joneses' kind of conspicuous consumption, that competitive consumption thing. It's really about this, like—I mean for me, it's just like this vague sense of what's normal."

We often imagine that consumption is motivated by status competition.[7] And a few of my respondents did indicate that they had fears about status in the conventional sense, as when James worried that his house wasn't big enough. Another example came from Bruno, who had decided to give up a lucrative job to pursue a lower-paying career in a field he loved and live primarily on his wife's salary of over $500,000. He readily admitted that he had always cared about having the "right stuff," meaning material goods such as clothing and technology. He described having had to give these up with his career change and to accept that he would not have a country house, as his peers (whom he called "my Joneses") did.

On the other hand, however, most people I talked with distanced themselves from the idea of status competition. Willa, for example, told me about a family member who had suggested she have guests over to "show off" her renovated home, an idea she rejected out of hand. She said, "I didn't do this [renovation] to make people feel good or bad about—like, this is our house. I've provided a home for our family that totally meets our needs. I'm not making a statement about how much money we do or do not have. I don't care about stuff like that."

A few women who explicitly recognized feeling competitive about consumption described these feelings as having to do with fears about not fitting in with the group.[8] One stay-at-home mother talked about worrying that she would not have the right clothes for social events attached to her husband's work. Confessing that it was because of "insecurity," she said, "I like to feel like I look amongst the best in a room." Another stay-at-home mother talked about worrying that her home renovation would be judged by her neighbors, saying that "consumption is my job." She admitted that she would imagine that her home was "nice enough" only if it appeared in a magazine. These women see (and fear) their consumption choices as reflections of themselves, to be judged by others, rather than as practices of competitive one-upmanship.

Beatrice's idea of luxury creep further challenges this simple idea of competitive consumption, replacing it with common consumption. Rather than compete with her peers, she looks to them for signals about what she should be doing. Other interviewees referred to a similar dynamic. Asked what established her "normal," Grace, a nonprofit consultant married to an inheritor, said, "I think I see probably a lot of the parents of [my daughter's] friends and stuff, like, what [they] do. And probably my normal social group that I've hung out with since college." Karen talked about increasing her spending partly as a function of being "surrounded by people who are all doing the same stuff."

Getting used to rising levels of spending and new lifestyles was not always easy. Interviewees who had grown up with significantly less than they have now tended to be especially uncomfortable with particular kinds of consumption. Talking about his live-in nanny, for example, Justin recounted, "In the beginning, I was, I guess, hesitant. It was, like, a status I never had. I never had anyone working in my house. I mean, I cleaned my toilets, growing up. So it was kind of like, hmm. Now you have, like, a servant. It's kind of a weird thing for me." Nathan, a money manager with an income of around $350,000 who came from a working-class background, said, "When I do something that is associated with high wealth, I get a little bit of an out-of-body experience. A little bit of looking down on myself, saying, 'That's weird that you're doing that,' like, 'What are *you* doing?'"[9] Karen told me, referring specifically to discomfort with self-indulgence, "I grew up without a lot of money, and I always felt kind of uncomfortable about the idea of having money and spending it on yourself."

Sometimes past influences clashed especially sharply with present ones in establishing what was "reasonable" to spend. Maya described, on the one hand, the restraining influence of her husband and the norms of family and old friends. As noted, she told me that spending more than $1,000 on a dress would feel "very uncomfortable." When I asked why, she responded,

> I know, isn't that silly? I don't know what it is. I think—I was on my own until I was 34. And I made money, and I spent my own money. And so I had what I thought was insane [to spend] then. And it's changed a little, but not that much actually, even though I'm now married to [her husband] and we have so much more. . . . And if I do talk to him about it, like, "Can you believe that handbag so-and-so bought cost three thousand dollars?" We're both like, "That seems crazy." My family thinks it, my mother thinks it. So part of it is from my family and, like, what we think is normal and not normal. Part of it is from when I worked and my friends from my [working] life, and so it's kind of, you know, a combination of all of that.

These influences from earlier in her life have shaped what she thinks is "normal and not normal."

But people in Maya's immediate social circle, whom she described as her current "reference points," are more affluent and spend more freely than she. She described how this group of wealthy people affected her sense of what was acceptable to spend, saying, "Look, I think renting the [summer] house is really extravagant. But again, in our social circle everyone *owns* a house. And renting, they're like, 'Why are you only doing it for a month? Why aren't you doing it for two months?' And every now and then I feel, like, things that I buy for myself, I feel extravagant about. But relative again to my friends, it's not, and that's what kind of makes me feel like it's okay." Maya was mostly upward-oriented, as I showed in chapter 1, in that she explicitly compared herself to those in her current social network, who tended to have more, and to those above them. But the diversity of her experience has shaped her sense of "reasonable" consumption.

This increase in spending also corresponds to a particular life stage. Some earners talked about leaving behind their more spendthrift habits of clothes shopping or partying in order to focus on the future, especially once they started a family. But, at the same time, most talked about the increase in (certain kinds of) spending associated with family life. Gary said, of the transition to buying a home, moving to Brooklyn from Manhattan, and having kids, that it "absolutely shifted us into a category of consumerism, of spending, that is exponentially more than it used to be." In some ways these are objective changes, as owning and renovating property and purchasing child care and education are more expensive than sleeping on a futon in a shared apartment, as many had done in their twenties. (Ursula said, with disbelief, of herself and her graduate school roommate, "We brought furniture in from the *street*!")

But having children also changed their *ideas* about how much is acceptable to spend. Olivia said, for example, "I think when we first were together, I sort of joined Scott undercover, I would say. Just because I felt really uncomfortable with unearned privilege, basically. And he did, too. And I would say that we've grown more and more comfortable. I think our children, having a family, has really pushed that." Asked for specifics, she said, "I mean, we moved from this somewhat ratty apartment to a giant place. And for me, the way I could rationalize that is just, we knew we would have more than one child. We wanted to stay in the city, but we wanted to be comfortable. And we wanted it to be comfortable for our child. We never would have moved to a place like that if it were just the two of us." As I described in the introduction, Olivia was even planning another renovation on their current apartment, despite the trauma of their earlier experience, to increase closet space, modify bathrooms, and redo the kitchen. She saw this decision as part of getting over her ambivalence once and for all, saying, "If we're going to live there, like, let's really live there." Yet she also represented this effort as one made primarily to meet the children's needs, which she saw as reasonable, asserting, "I don't think having a closet in your room is over the top."

Paid consumption experts also help their clients become acclimated to certain levels of spending. Interior designers, architects, personal assistants and concierges, and other service providers often both shape clients' taste and approve their consumption.[10] One woman with a household income of over $2 million told me that she had been too intimidated to shop at Barneys until she needed a dress for a special occasion, when she had sought out a personal shopper whom she loved. She kept going back to him, and *he* had "slowly upped" the amount she was willing to spend. Now, she said, "I'll go to Barneys, I'll spend five thousand. Which used to be one thousand, or two." So the personal shopper has made her feel comfortable both in the store and with the spending. When I interviewed Regina, an interior designer who had been in the business for over thirty years, she made a similar point, commenting that "using me gives clients permission to spend money." She compared her job, from a client's point of view, to "going shopping with a friend who says, 'You *have to* buy that dress,'" thereby both encouraging and legitimating the purchase.

David, the interior designer, recounted of one client, "I was [suggesting] a desk that was maybe, like, five thousand dollars, or whatever. But he ended up spending thirty-five thousand on a desk. And he was a little conflicted about it. But I said to him, 'You know, if there's any place you're going to spend a lot of money, it may as

well be your desk. I mean, it's like, what you do. It's your work.'"
Thus David offers a discourse of need to his client that allows him to
think of ever-higher levels of spending as legitimate.[11]

Noticing that he seemed to be actively legitimating this purchase, I asked, "Do you feel like you have to do that regularly? Kind
of make it okay for them to spend money that they want to spend,
but that they feel conflicted about?" He responded, "Some people
yes, and some people no." Referring to clients who had not been
born with wealth and felt uncomfortable with it, he continued,
"Sometimes it's the more new-money [people]. The 'shame' people.
They're a little conflicted about that. They think it's all just a little
weird. Because, you know, they're first-timers. It's their first time
using a designer. It's their first big foray into, like, the big life, you
know? Other clients of mine who are maybe divorced women, or
this and that, are just kind of used to it. They're just like [breezily],
'I pay five thousand here, ten thousand here.'" As David points out,
the experience of doing these expensive projects, such as renovation, helps these consumers get used to spending money. Indeed,
people I interviewed who had done more than one renovation described the first one as the hardest.

THE ORDINARY, DISCIPLINED SELF

My interviewees told me they spent anywhere from $120,000 to
$800,000 per year, usually without sticking to or even drawing up a
budget.[12] But they interpret their consumption as basic and family-
oriented and draw boundaries against excess, materialism, and ostentation. They work to suppress unruly desires. They frame "ridiculous" expenditures as special "treats" or situate them in relation to
the choices of others who spend more, not less. Therefore they can
continue to see themselves as living an "ordinary" life, even as their
spending ratchets inexorably upward. As I described in chapter 2,
the desire to be ordinary and reasonable further illuminates their
wish to be morally worthy, complementing the desire to be productive, and thus legitimately entitled.

It might be tempting to read these interpretations solely as justifications of spending that is "really" motivated by status competition or materialism. And there are likely more elements of status consumption in these spending habits than my interviewees were willing to recognize in talking with me. But status is not their only motivation or the only dimension along which they relate to others. Certainly their repeated negative characterizations of those who spend more suggest that Veblenian conspicuous consumption is not at work. Although we see some evidence of the more Bourdieuian idea that they seek distinction—which can be indicated by consuming less or differently—the story remains more complicated. These accounts are marked by deep ambivalence about legitimate needs. Consumption is at least sometimes driven by fears of being judged by others and a wish to fit in with peer groups. And these groups help the wealthy to define what kind of lifestyle is "normal," not only to set parameters for competition.

Indeed, in their allusions to basic needs and "normal" lifestyles, these consumers are trying to *avoid* seeming different. By eschewing the most visible and morally transgressive elite lifestyles—those of "real" housewives or wolves of Wall Street—they can almost be seen as *not* wealthy (a word many would never use to describe themselves) because they don't occupy the symbolic space of wealth. Instead, they move to occupy the moral legitimacy of the middle class. This idea of the disciplined, hard-working, "normal" self thus begins to split off from particular practices of consumption. If one can claim to have the right affect—to be an ordinary person with the "mindset" of working hard and spending with care—the fact that one has so much more than others comes not to matter. Yet, as I show in chapter 4, sometimes the morally worthy self also has to acknowledge privilege.

4

"GIVING BACK," AWARENESS, AND IDENTITY

Frances, as we have seen, is a stay-at-home mother with three children and assets in the tens of millions. Asked if she deserved her lifestyle, she responded, "I couldn't say that I deserve this, no. . . . I don't know that anybody does. I mean, the amount of money that—once you have money and can invest that money, the returns get so much bigger over time. There just is such a disparity. You know, when you look at how much money CEOs are paid in America—do they deserve that? Absolutely not. But is that what the market bears? Yes. Do I think that the government should be taxing them? Like, I don't agree that they should necessarily have to—I mean, I understand we pay slightly higher tax. But should our tax rate be 75 percent, and everyone else's 5? I think that's wrong. Because I do believe in a market economy. But I definitely am aware that it's insane how much more money—I mean, the fact that I don't have a budget, or don't think about—I recognize that that's incredibly privileged and foreign to most people. And, I don't know, I hope that by us giving back and doing volunteer work, you know, we help to spread it back around."

Nadine, her partner, and their two kids lived primarily on wealth that came from Nadine's family. Nadine told me, as we saw in chapter 2, "I still feel guilty about having money. I feel a lot less guilty than I did. Because I think guilt is, like, unproductive. You know what I mean?" She continued, "I mean, I'm lucky I have it. I should be happy. I should try and do something with it. I should try and give back in whatever way I can. I feel like we've done that in a whole series of ways, through [paid] work for ten years, for both of us. And through creating a gift fund, and giving back. And just trying to be really generous in the world. . . . I mean, there's a difference between guilt and, like, being aware, and conscious, and having a conscience."

In many ways, Frances and Nadine are very different. Frances is politically conservative and lives mainly on wealth her husband accumulated through paid work. Her belief in the "market economy" helps her justify the earnings of CEOs and, by extension, her own household income, even though she doesn't think anyone "deserves" the kind of wealth she has. She is opposed to paying higher taxes. Nadine is a progressive inheritor, with more conflicts about having money and a more critical view of inequality, who says she'd be happy to pay higher taxes. But both articulate the same key condition for deserving their wealth: "giving back."

In fact, nearly all my respondents alluded to giving back in their implicit and explicit descriptions of worthy personhood.[1] This obligation constitutes the third dimension of the legitimately entitled self, along with working hard and consuming prudently. But in contrast to these imperatives, giving back might acknowledge privilege more explicitly, because one must receive something in order to owe something. Implicit and explicit allusions to "middleness" become more difficult. This chapter looks at how my interviewees understood giving back and at the extent to which their understandings and practices involved recognizing privilege.

"Giving back" is a fairly general, and generic, cultural value in the United States, one not limited to wealthy people. The concept had various meanings for my respondents. For some it meant "contributing" in a general sense (echoing the emphasis on contribution we saw in chapter 2). Justin said, for example, "I feel a sense of an obligation to society, just to contribute. Not necessarily financially. Just to add something, instead of taking it away." Some parents also described raising children as a contribution to society.

Such descriptions do not link giving back to having privilege. But some of those I spoke with did make this connection. Caroline had grown up in a wealthy family and inherited several hundred thousand dollars. She said, "I think [money] comes with responsibility! We have opportunities other people don't have. So that's great! Take advantage of it!" I asked, "What exactly is the responsibility?" She responded, "To contribute. I mean, everyone has to figure out their own way, right? What are you good at, and what calls to you. . . . Generally, to be part of the solution and not part of the problem." Her idea of giving back had to do with a nonprofit she had started to support community development. Some others I talked with—like Nadine in the opening vignette—similarly saw paid work in socially responsible occupations as their way of "giving back" and compensating for their privilege.

Beyond allusions to work and parenting, two central aspects of giving back stood out across my interviewees' accounts: first, traditional philanthropy and volunteerism, and, second, "awareness" of privilege. Asked what "giving back" meant, Sara, the inheritor, described both facets: "I guess it means different things to me in different ways. I mean, on a very basic level, just being a good—sort of, giving back financially. Giving of your time. Very traditional, basic, like, volunteering kind of stuff." She hesitated, and then continued: "More broadly, I would [say] having a consciousness about, particularly, you know, class issues and wealth and money. . . . So I guess what I mean by 'giving back' is, like, just some awareness. . . . Some recognition." Both of these elements also appear in Frances's and Nadine's accounts.

As I'll show, the practices and affects associated with awareness and philanthropy fall along a continuum of public recognition of privilege. Awareness recognizes privilege very explicitly, but it is internal, and therefore essentially private. In interaction with others, being "aware" means not making other people feel bad about having less or treating them differently. This imperative is a variation on the Golden Rule, to treat others as you want to be treated, which is a prominent cultural norm in the United States (and elsewhere). But this reciprocity usually means treating everyone the same. Thus the transmutation from private awareness to public egalitarianism *silences* difference rather than acknowledging it. Although the social norm of equal, reciprocal treatment serves to avoid shaming those who have less by not drawing attention to their status, its function of obscuring difference also serves to mitigate discomfort in those with more.[2]

Traditional practices of philanthropy and volunteering, however, are likely to be more public acknowledgements of advantage. Many of the people I spoke with gave away significant amounts of money and time and saw philanthropy and volunteering as important aspects of their identities. But here, too, they recognized privilege in different ways and with varying degrees of public visibility. People in more upward-oriented earner families, especially stay-at-home mothers, tended to be relatively public about their philanthropy and volunteerism, which was taken for granted in their communities, even though they tended to talk *with me* less freely about their social position. In contrast, inheritors, especially the more "downward-oriented," were often very generous philanthropically, but they described having to come to terms with their identities as wealthy people in order to develop a philanthropic practice. That is, even though they recognized their privilege more openly in conversation with me, their very consciousness of privilege made them more conflicted about public philanthropy. Very few practiced the traditional volunteering of the stay-at-home mothers. Finally, a significant proportion of my interviewees, in contrast to both these groups, gave away relatively small amounts of money and did not see charitable work as central to their identities, although it seemed possible that they would become more philanthropically active in the future.

I also ask in this chapter whether it is possible, or desirable, from the perspective of these interviewees, to use giving back to challenge structural arrangements that ultimately benefit them. Sociologists have tended to question the motivations and functions of philanthropy and volunteerism, often arguing that these actions both depend on and justify class privilege and that philanthropy essentially reproduces class divisions.[3] People I interviewed in the more traditional group bear out this skepticism, as they tend to focus their giving and volunteering either on their own communities, especially their children's schools, or on organizations that help the very poor (thereby ameliorating the worst effects of capitalist inequality rather than changing the system). However, donors I interviewed who are more politically critical articulate a sense of helplessness about challenging the conditions of their own privilege. They are attuned to and frustrated by the limits of their own capacity to make meaningful change.

AWARENESS AND APPRECIATION

To begin with, then, my interviewees often invoked "awareness" as a responsibility of privilege. This concept meant, first, not taking their advantages for granted. When I asked Frances, for example, "Has it been hard for you to get used to being more well-off than you were growing up?," she said, "I hope I'm never used to it. . . . I would never want to take any of this for granted." Penny told me she and her husband were a bit torn about buying a second home rather than renting, as they had been in the summer. The house they really wanted cost $5 million, which they found "ridiculous"; they had seen another place they liked, but they weren't sure the owners would sell it. She said, "These are amazing problems to have. I never want to lose sight of that." To become "used to" or "lose sight of" privilege means somehow to become embedded in it, perhaps to have it become too much of one's identity.

Awareness not only entails *knowing* intellectually that one is privileged but also *feeling* lucky, appreciative, and grateful. Gary told me that he and his wife shared "fundamental values," including "that you should never forget the privilege that you have, and be aware. Thankful." Nicole told me she sometimes talked with her cousins about her extended family's advantaged financial situation. She said, "I mean, we're incredibly grateful. To be able to go to [her prestigious college], without having to work your ass off? It's like, that is huge. And I knew it at the time. I know it now. Like, knowing more people who, like, had to work their butts off. Or who have student loans. I mean, all that kind of stuff is just such a big deal. So, we are, all of us, incredibly grateful."

Nicholas articulated the moral imperative of appreciation very explicitly. He told me, of his Manhattan townhouse, "I sit around and I appreciate it. . . . I go, 'Wow. I don't deserve it. This is amazing. Like, nobody deserves this. No one should feel entitled to such luxury.' Not like, 'I'm worthless, I don't deserve it.' Like, generally speaking, how dare anyone feel entitled to such space and light and wonderfulness? . . . I feel super, super lucky." He also said, "A pox on anyone who would feel entitled to such things and not feel appreciative of them." Though he doesn't think anyone deserves what he has, Nicholas clearly suggests that to feel entitled rather than grateful is to be *especially* undeserving. Penny told me, "I don't think the money has changed us, in our core, that dramatically. I think we still think, 'Oh my God. This is so crazy.' Like, we don't feel entitled, at all." Again, maintaining this distance between one's core self and one's privilege serves somehow to keep illegitimate entitlement at bay. This affective stance also echoes the desire not to "need" this lifestyle, which I explored in chapter 3.

The people I talked with also contrasted themselves more explicitly with wealthy people who did not express this kind of mindfulness about privilege. As I mentioned in chapter 1, Betsy and her friends jokingly referred to themselves as the "working class" because their lifestyles depended on continued earnings and hard work. She also distinguished her level of awareness from theirs. She said, of her friends, "I feel like that group of people cares more about groundedness. And understanding that [ours] is an outlier situation. This is not how the vast majority of the people of the world live." As we have seen, the notion of "groundedness" implies some kind of symbolic link to the reality of those with less.

My interviewees also tied consciousness of privilege to thoughtful, prudent spending of the sort I discussed in chapter 3. Nadine, for example, said, "When you have more money, it's tempting to stop thinking about it. And to be like, 'Well, boy. [I have], like, millions of dollars. So I don't really need to think about this, and this handbag's nice. Why do I need to torture myself over whether or not I should get it?'" But, she said, "I still think that it's really important to kind of interrogate every—especially every expensive—thing you're doing. Like, is this really worth it?" Warren told me that his financial caution came partly from his working-class upbringing. He added, "I also think it's important not to piss away money. Because we have a lot of money. And people don't have money. And you've got to, sort of, act respectfully and responsibly with it." To act "respectfully" with money appears to mean being both prudent with it and aware of those with less, and thus constitutes a moral obligation.

Wendy, the corporate lawyer, similarly connected an awareness of privilege to her consumption decisions. She described herself and her husband as "struggling with how we feel about the type of money we're spending, and trying to be conscious about it, like, careful, and be grounded and have the right values—you know, recognize how lucky we are—but also not live life with a hair shirt." Here "conscious" connotes both prudent ("careful") and "grounded," with the "right values." Wendy also explicitly contrasts her awareness of "how lucky we are" with the behavioral practice of "not living life with a hair shirt." That is, *thinking about* being fortunate is like the compromise point between a lack of awareness and concretely giving up enough to cause discomfort.[4]

In some cases, awareness intensified and began to feel like conflict. A few of my subjects seemed almost to "torture" themselves, to use Nadine's word. But, perhaps counterintuitively, experiencing this internal struggle sometimes seemed to help them feel better about their privilege. As we have seen, Beatrice had inherited wealth from her family, and she was struggling to decide whether to buy a second home and whether to send her child to private school. She and her husband could afford it, though it would have meant spending some of her inherited wealth rather than living on their combined income of about $250,000. Having grown up around people she thought cared only about money, Beatrice strongly disliked this orientation. Living on their income was important, she said, because

"I feel like it's a commitment to the life choices we've made." By "life choices" she mainly meant her choice to work in a nonprofit, which she characterized as a decision "not to make my life about the earning of money."

Beatrice added, "I feel like it was like an ethical commitment, to choose the kind of career that I chose, and that suddenly giving myself freewheeling access to this [the private school and the second home], without some sort of wrestling with it, is a little bit of a betrayal to my ethic." I asked, "If you had chosen to be an investment banker, then it seems like you would think it would be more legitimate to have this money . . ." She interrupted me, saying, "Yes, you know why? Because I'd be an asshole." I responded, "So does it make you an asshole to spend the money that you do have without conflict?" After a long pause, she responded, "Yes, I think it does. I think that that's what I'm concerned about." I asked, "Are you concerned that other people think that, or just you think that?" "No," she said, "it's really mostly what I think." Beatrice seems to feel that her entitlement to spend this money rests on "wrestling with" these decisions—on imagining that she might make a different choice—which means she is not taking her advantages for granted. The struggle itself is a moral obligation. But ultimately she and her husband did send their child to private school, and they did buy the second home.

Eliana also wanted to distance herself from people with money and was glad when it seemed that others in her social and professional circles couldn't tell she was wealthy. In explaining why, she said, "I have class hatred, too. . . . I believe, like, a lot of totally knee-jerk things. Like, that a lot of those people are, you know, total assholes. . . . So I can't completely align with the rich, because I also have that antagonism." Eliana had "spent a year in deep agony" about putting her daughter in private school. Speaking of that decision, she said, "Part of it was just like, I'm going to be in self-hatred all the time. Because I'm going to go pick her up at school. I'm going to line up with the other white mothers on the street, and I'm going to hate that I am indistinguishable from them. It's, like, an affront to my pretensions of uniqueness, or inhabiting it in a particular way, or whatever." I asked her if it made her "feel better, to be, like, 'Well, at least I'm conflicted about it.'" She responded, "Yes! Yeah. It does." She described having the conflict as "a moral appeasement to self."

In the end, she told me, "I decided I'm going to have to accept that these are really very deep contradictions. And I feel, in a lot of ways, like, just a completely thoroughgoing hypocrite all the time. But I also feel like it's not un-thought-through." "Thinking it through" partially alleviates the sense of hypocrisy that Eliana describes, though she is also trying to accept these contradictions (an issue to which I return at the end of the chapter).

It's also striking that Eliana recognizes her "pretensions of uniqueness, or inhabiting it in a particular way." This recognition shows how deeply her sense of occupying her privilege appropriately depends on not being like rich "assholes" in terms of her lifestyle choices, although she may be exactly like them in terms of her economic situation. And even when the choices these women make—to send a child to public school, to buy a second home—*are* the same as the choices "rich assholes" make, having struggled emotionally with the decision is a way of differentiating themselves from people they believe have an illegitimate sense of entitlement.

RECIPROCITY, EQUALITY, AND EFFACEMENT

The people I talked with translated this broad imperative of "awareness" into their interactions with others. But being aware of difference, ironically, meant acting as if it didn't exist. That is, these interactions were largely governed by norms of civility that *effaced* class difference. First, a norm of silence prevailed, as I have already pointed out. Many respondents told me they avoided discussing certain issues, such as the hassles and costs of home renovation, when talking with people who had less. Talia said, as noted, "You don't want to brag" about your advantages. Others didn't want to be "stuck up." Maya told me she tried to be careful about what kinds of clothes she brought on "girls' weekends" with old friends who had less than she.

Second, my interviewees emphasized the importance of treating other people well, meaning with kindness, respect, and gratitude. As we will see in chapter 6, parents repeatedly stressed how important it was to inculcate this value in their children. The Golden Rule—"Do unto others as you would have them do unto you"—mandates this norm of reciprocity. The norm applies regardless of the class position of the other person. Like not talking about money, "being nice" *obscures* class difference by treating everyone the same. It presumes equivalence, and therefore equality. Furthermore, to be nice to others is to demonstrate that one does not *feel* entitled in the negative sense. Alexis made this connection most explicitly in speaking of restaurant servers, saying: "I'm always appreciative. I don't feel, like, entitled to service." To appreciate the work of others is to recognize a responsibility (a form of awareness) and to demonstrate the proper unentitled affect.

Again, those I interviewed drew boundaries against wealthy people who transgressed these norms by being rude or unappreciative, and they praised those who were "nice." Stephanie told me, for example, "Well, once summer hits [in the Hamptons], I can't stand— like, we don't go out to dinner. We don't really leave the house, other than going to the beach. Because the people are just awful, you know—too much money, spoiled. They hate locals. They're rude to people that work in restaurants and everything, because they're locals." Linda articulated the importance of being a nice person in order to occupy wealth legitimately when she described a wealthy friend, saying, "He's a really nice guy. He's really, really, really rich. I mean, I have a lot of questions about the values in our society that enable him to be so rich and others to not be, but he's a nice person. His child is a great kid." Linda's friend (and Linda herself, though she is less wealthy) can thus distance themselves from the "values in our society" that lead to this kind of wealth by adhering to another set of values about behavior, which indicates that they are a certain kind of people.[5]

The service providers I interviewed likewise differentiated among wealthy people on the basis of behavior, prizing reciprocal and friendly interactions. When I asked what it was like to work for wealthy people, many of these service professionals responded by telling me how "nice" their clients were. They were adamant that they would not work with people who didn't respect them. Annie, a personal concierge, told me, "If they're not going to treat me properly, I'm not going to take it. I'll walk out, away from the situation. You know, simply because you're paying me to do the job doesn't mean that you should have any right to treat me any less than you would anybody else." David, the interior designer, put it more concisely, saying simply, "I don't work with assholes." Regina, a long-time interior designer, differentiated among wealthy people on the basis of character, saying, "I don't work for terrible people. There are a whole bunch of rich people out there who are so—their character is so bad. They are so greedy. And, well, you know what's happened to this country [in the economic crisis]. And I don't decorate for those people. The people who I work for are really, really kinder, gentler, caring about other people." By making these distinctions, these interviewees set up a requirement that clients be "good people" in order to deserve the service providers' services (and, by extension, broader entitlements as well). Being caring and kind is the basis of legitimate entitlement.[6]

Some service providers believed that their clients tried to mitigate their discomfort with economic disparity by being nice. For example, Robert, a real estate broker, said many of his clients were conflicted about money. When I asked how he saw these conflicts, he invoked reciprocity repeatedly in his response: "Basic things. Are they on time for the appointment? Do they apologize? How do they treat the doorman?" Robert, who is African American, also said that he saw the conflict in the way his black clients would greet workers. "If you're black, and you're here looking at a three-million-dollar apartment, and there's some black guys on the job site, and you say, 'Hi,' [you're showing] a certain guilt that '[I'm] a shithead, and I'm looking at a three million dollar apartment.' So you try to equalize it."

Reciprocity suggests that everyone is entitled to the same recognition of personhood ("I treat everyone the same") regardless of material resources. It thus denies that having fewer resources makes a meaningful difference. Monica explicitly distanced moral worth from having money, saying, "I don't know what my friends make a year. I don't really care what they make a year. I don't need to know. I just need to know that they're nice people. Nice to me. And they have good kids. . . . Those are the values that are important to me." She creates silence about difference by denying that money matters, elevating the ideals of "niceness" and good personhood instead. In the main, awareness and treating others as equal go together—the private affect recognizes difference, but the public interaction insists on equality.

At the same time, many of my subjects also talked about being generous financially to people in their own lives—a practice that does acknowledge their advantages relative to these more intimate others. Many gave money on a regular basis to their family members, especially parents, but sometimes also to siblings or extended family. They also talked about being generous on an everyday level. Alice said, of her family and old friends who had less than she, "For them, my thought process is always sort of, 'What can I do? What dinner can I buy? What trip can I have somebody tag along on?' Because most of that group of people in my family or friends circle are not in a position to be able to do things that they necessarily want to do, or buy the things that they want to buy." Gary said, "We have an ethos of trying to share it. So we'll lend our house to somebody. We're the host of the class party." Others also shared their homes in various ways.

Unlike "niceness" that obscures class difference, these efforts sometimes caused tension, precisely because this kind of generosity between friends and even family members exposes inequality. Scott, for example, spoke of the strangeness created for Olivia when she went back to her working-class family of origin with what he called her "infinity checkbook." This kind of exchange also breaks the taboo on talking about or even acknowledging financial differences. Nadine said, "You've got to start where you live. Who you are. You know what I mean? Like, you can think about feeding, like, starving people in Ethiopia. But if you're fucking miserly in your everyday life, you know? Then that's a problem." Part of her rule was to "take people out to dinner, unless it's really awkward and they don't feel like being taken out to dinner. Because I think class is a big reality, and people get—I totally understand it—defensive about being taken out, or it feels weird." She told me a story about a recent encounter with a friend with whom she had planned to have dinner, but he couldn't afford it and was uncomfortable with allowing her to pay, so they ended up having a drink instead. Other respondents also described this discomfort, and some complained that even their parents or siblings resisted taking money from them.

Several people also talked about trying to be fair employers of domestic workers. Sara said, "I mean, the most stressful part for me of employing a child care provider at home has been being a good employer for them." She emphasized paying more than her friends did and asking less of household workers. Janice told me she paid her nanny twenty dollars per hour, above the going rate in New York of fifteen dollars or so. She said, "That's a political thing for me, and a social justice thing. . . . I want to pay well for that work, and treat whoever's doing it well." One respondent sent money to her former nanny for years after the nanny returned to her country of origin; another "helped" her nanny financially when someone in her family had health problems. As I have already mentioned, Zoe wanted to treat her domestic employees well, saying, "If I don't give my clothing or anything that we're giving away to the church, I give it to them. They're very happy with how they're paid. Days that I give them off. I like to keep them happy." Zoe explicitly compensates for her advantages over her nanny and housekeeper (and their access to her lifestyle) by treating them generously. These choices also expose class asymmetries between workers and employers but seem to create less tension in these relationships than in relationships with family and friends, likely because these differences are more taken for granted.

In talking about the workers who were renovating her apartment, Betsy said she felt uncomfortable with their having less. I asked, "And what do you do with that?" She responded with significant hesitation and atypical inarticulacy, perhaps because my question implied that there was something she should "do" beyond feeling uncomfortable. She said, "Well, my—I mean, the way that I deal with it, is that I—I talk to them. I want to know, like—if they want to tell me. I treat them like I would treat anybody else. And—but I'm aware that that's—you know, that that—that—that—they're making very little money in a week, and doing a really hard job. You know?" I asked, "Do you think there's anything that you can do about that, in some way?" She said, "Well, I'm tipping them all. You know? I don't know whether that's standard or not. But no. There's nothing I can do about it. I plan to write them all a thank-you note and give them a tip. You know? Because, whatever they can do with it, that's extra money that can make them happier, then I'm more than willing to do it, and they deserve it." I said, "And beyond that, I mean, in terms of kind of inequality generally. I mean, do you feel like there's anything that you can do, or can be done?" She said, "Personally? I mean, no. No—Not right—not—not—not now. For me, not now. But I feel badly about it, and I'm aware of it, and—I just—am aware of, like, not making people feel worse, or uncomfortable around that. You know? Understanding it." Betsy describes not only her own awareness, but also two forms of interaction with these workers, which stand in tension: treating them as equals (which denies difference) and tipping them (which acknowledges difference). But she frames these as an inadequate solution to the structural problem of inequality, as I discuss later.

GIVING MONEY AND TIME

The traditional way to "give back," of course, is with charitable contributions and volunteer labor. Nearly all my interviewees said these forms of giving were important in principle, and nearly all said they gave some money away. But not all were equally active or identified with giving. The amounts they donated varied widely, from a couple of thousand dollars annually to over half a million, though very few gave more than 5 percent of their income.[7] The recipients of their money and time also spanned a wide range, although their alma maters and their children's schools were by far the organizations they mentioned most often.[8] The vast majority also gave at least something to causes that mirrored their own interests or those of their children. Lawyers gave to legal aid; artists gave to arts organizations; parents gave to groups their children participated in; people with certain illnesses in their families donated to cure those illnesses. African American respondents gave to racial empowerment groups or volunteered with Jack and Jill (a social organization for the black middle class and above) or in African American communities in other ways.[9] Women of color volunteered on the diversity committees of their children's schools. Some women gave to women's and girls' rights groups; gay people gave to gay rights groups. They participated in neighborhood groups or served on their condo or co-op boards.

People for whom charitable work is a significant part of their identities fall into two broad groups. The first comprises philanthropists and volunteers in a fairly traditional model, who seem relatively comfortable occupying public roles. Some people with this orientation identify strongly as community philanthropists and volunteers. Others take on a similar role but to a lesser extent, partly because they have younger children but also because they identify less as wealthy. The people in the second group, composed mainly of liberal and progressive inheritors, tend to donate large amounts of money, but they feel torn about developing public identities as philanthropists. They are more likely to work full-time and hence less likely to volunteer large amounts of time, although many serve on at least one board. The rest of the sample comprises people who are less involved in this kind of charitable work, although most imagine it will become a bigger part of their lives in the future.

Traditional Public Philanthropy and Volunteerism

Many people in families with male earners and stay-at-home wives saw charitable giving and volunteerism as quite important to their identities. I typically interviewed the wives in these families, who reminded me of the wealthy women that scholars such as Susan Ostrander have written about, in that it was part of their lifestyle and their sense of social obligation to give away money and do volunteer work.[10] Some spoke of having grown up in families with traditions of charity and volunteering. One woman told me, "My dad was always a big volunteer. And believes very much in giving back. And so, that's definitely been instilled in us." The idea of noblesse oblige that implicitly governs this giving tends to be unapologetically public, and my interviewees did not express ambivalence about it. These givers are often photographed at charitable galas and luncheons, and at least a few have been recognized in their communities for their philanthropic or volunteer efforts.

Some women, especially the wealthiest, were prominent community volunteers, spending a few hours a day on this work in busy times. They and their husbands often sat on the boards of at least one organization. Several women I interviewed had run major fundraising drives for organizations they supported. Their families gave away tens or hundreds of thousands of dollars each year; a few had set up family foundations. These women did not express conflicts about taking on public identities as volunteers and philanthropists, which is the norm in these communities. Except for the very wealthiest, who are downward-oriented because it is nearly impossible not to be, as I have discussed, the people in this group tended to face upward, comparing themselves to others like them or those who had more.

Beyond their own and their children's schools, these women had strong and ongoing commitments to particular organizations, such as a local hospital or religious or civic organizations. Several in the suburbs belonged to the Junior League. They also gave to causes associated with extremely poor people, such as foster care, homelessness, or food pantries. One mother, who was active in her children's school as well as in an antihunger organization, told me she and her husband gave away money because "we realize how lucky we are" and because she wanted to distribute the money before her death ("I just would rather do it, and see people being able to enjoy that money"). She signaled the twin concerns of the "less fortunate" and her own community when she said, "In the end, I think we give money because we want to improve the lives of other people, either less fortunate than us or our kids, I guess, to some [extent]." In this sense, the practice of people in this group was consistent with research indicating that wealthy people often give primarily in ways that both benefit and reproduce their own communities and community institutions and that, when they give to recipients outside these communities, it is often to mitigate the most pernicious effects of capitalism and curb more radical alternatives.[11]

Some of these women spoke of their volunteer work as satisfying in the same ways their jobs had been, and they did not express a desire to return to paid work. When talking about what she would do once her children were older, I asked Frances if it would matter whether she got paid. She responded, "No, because I don't need the money. And no, because for the moment, at least, all my volunteer work is done with a lot of other pretty smart, highly motivated people. So I'm still in an environment that I think would be somewhat equivalent to an environment where I was getting paid." Like a few of the other women I interviewed, Frances seemed well on her way to developing a career in philanthropy, though she (like most people) would probably not identify it as such.[12]

Some stay-at-home mothers, many of whom had young children, seemed to me less actively involved with philanthropy in the broad sense as a key source of their identities. Many of their husbands sat on boards of arts or poverty-alleviation organizations. Such work struck me in several cases as something that was expected of the husbands in their professional capacity. But the women themselves rarely described particular philanthropic interests of their own—possibly because they did not feel that the money was theirs, as we will see in chapter 5. They gave primarily to educational institutions they were connected to and to causes espoused by their friends. While many volunteered—sometimes quite extensively—at their children's schools, they did not describe wanting to volunteer in other organizations. Sometimes their volunteering felt perfunctory.[13]

Rather than talking about improving the community, these women tended to be more focused on their nuclear families' needs.

Penny, for example, had participated enthusiastically in fundraising at her kids' school. But, she said, "Other charity stuff, I feel like I just haven't been engaged in anything else. Like, if someone came to me, or I was to seek out something, I feel like that could be a next thing. But I don't have time. Or the interest, right now. Like, thank God, no one's been really sick. I haven't done a cancer thing, or this or that." Penny seems to imply that she would only be motivated to become more active in philanthropy if she were to have a reason that came very close to her own life or her family.

Indeed, it seemed to me that these women's identities were not so tied to this kind of charitable and community work largely because they did not consider themselves to have the responsibilities of noblesse oblige and community building of the kind Ostrander talked about. In contrast to most women in the suburbs, whose environments featured a set of clearly defined local institutions, the women in the city were less likely to see themselves as part of a cohesive, singular community of wealthy people. This tendency may be partly due to the characteristics of the group of people I talked with, including their willingness to define themselves as wealthy.[14] But it also illuminates the diversity of wealthy microcultures in and around the city.

The lack of identification with philanthropy among these women also seems linked to the strong focus on family at this stage of life, as I discuss later. Several women planned to volunteer more when their children were older. Maya said, for example, "I'm not giving enough of my time right now" because her children were so young. She asserted, "My goal longer term is to do a lot more philanthropic stuff" rather than go back to a paid job. This vision indicates that these women may become more like those who have deeper identity commitments to philanthropic work.

Ambivalent Identities

The other group of people who tended to take their philanthropy very seriously were downward-oriented liberals and progressives, who usually (though not always) had both inherited wealth and paying jobs. Some gave away amounts in the hundreds of thousands of dollars; others gave less, but all spoke of themselves as having a philanthropic responsibility. Like more traditional givers, some described having been raised in households where philanthropy was emphasized. Eliana, for example, had been trained from an early age to give away money. She said, "My parents gave us a book called *Robin Hood Was Right* [a progressive guide to philanthropy]. That was our first thing. They're like, 'Here's two hundred dollars. What are you going to do?' So they gave us to understand that that was just, like, not optional. . . . It was like, you know, the Eleventh Commandment." But in contrast to those who took volunteerism and philanthropy more for granted, these donors were less comfortable with giving a public face to these activities. This distinction was connected to other variations in their giving habits.

First, they volunteered less of their time than more traditional givers. Several served on the boards of nonprofit organizations and/ or participated in the philanthropy of their family foundations. But they did not speak often of devoting time to their children's schools or other organizations. This is largely, I believe, because their professional obligations meant they had less free time. Many worked for nonprofits, so they were paid for labor they might otherwise have volunteered, and some interpreted this paid work as their "contribution." But they also did not typically belong to communities where traditional public volunteering (usually by stay-at-home mothers) was the norm.

They also tended to give to different kinds of causes. Like traditional givers, these donors usually gave to their own and their children's schools.[15] But, whereas more traditional givers also favored local institutions and civic organizations that were more middle-of-the-road politically, these givers tended to support organizations advocating reproductive rights; local and international health and human rights organizations; small arts organizations; and anti-poverty organizations. The most progressive gave to organizations that were more critical of economic and racial inequality.

Progressive herself, Sara and her husband, who worked in finance, mostly socialized with people from the corporate world, who were more politically conservative. She described trying to raise money from these friends for a progressive women's organization whose board she had recently joined: "I'm trying to think about, like, how are my friends going to, you know, get [the organization's] work for social change and social-justice feminism. A lot of people are going to be like, 'What? They did, huh?' And frankly, I think a lot of my friends haven't really thought of charitable giving beyond, you know, an alma mater. I would say, for the most part, my friends' giving is probably focused on their schools."

These givers also differed from more traditional ones in that they were or had been more conflicted about recognizing themselves as wealthy people, which had affected their giving habits. They tended to describe developing a philanthropic practice over time as they came to terms with their identities. Gary said that, for many years, "I literally gave five hundred dollars to hundreds of organizations. I exaggerate not. Hundreds of organizations." He had done this, he said, "To stay below the radar. To not draw attention that I was giving a lot of money." He did not want to be pegged as a potential donor, an issue many of the wealthier people I talked with mentioned, because it meant managing more requests for money. But giving his money away also tapped into Gary's conflicts about having the money to begin with. Yet he had largely overcome these conflicts, saying, "Another transom I've crossed is a readiness to give in bigger amounts that definitely can draw attention."

Experts I interviewed who worked in the world of progressive or alternative philanthropy also identified difficulty in giving money away as a paradoxical consequence of feeling troubled about wealth. Diane, a financial advisor for affluent progressives, told me that people who were more conflicted about their wealth were actually much harder for fundraisers to deal with because they were less straightforward about how much they wanted to give and to whom, and they were not good at saying no. She said, "They often give misleading cues to the fundraisers, you know, it's like, 'Would you like to give?'

'Well, I'm not quite sure, I need to check with . . .' You know, they can't say no. They won't say, 'I've got my strategic giving plan, and I'm sorry but I don't give to animals, I do give to women, so [I won't donate to you],' you know?" Such people, she said, "waste a lot of energy in indecision, or between their desires and their 'shoulds' and 'oughts,' and would be a lot more liberated and probably a lot easier for fundraisers to deal with if they could just be clear about who they are." Diane means they should be clear about who they are in terms of what they are willing to give, but in order to have this clarity they must also be clear about who they are as wealthy people. She said, "People who are clear are at peace, and they're just easier to deal with and they have an easier time living their lives." Ironically, then, discomfort about being wealthy in the first place can *prevent* philanthropic "giving back."

Often these conflicts had to do with acting publicly, "coming out" as having wealth. As we have seen, Olivia said she wanted to be especially generous with her money because, she acknowledged, "I didn't earn it." She wanted to use these resources "to help somebody out [who's] in need. It's to equalize." She gave money to people in her extended family, and she and Scott contributed hundreds of thousands of dollars every few years to a donor-advised fund.[16] But she was torn about developing an identity as a philanthropist, largely because she was uncomfortable identifying as a wealthy person. Speaking of her desire to be "normal," she said, "I mean, that's a big reason why I don't think I've grabbed the philanthropy bull by the horns." She felt their charitable giving was "haphazard," directed toward "obvious things like our kids' schools." She said she could imagine becoming more directed and consistent. "I know that a lot of the good deeds in the world wouldn't have happened if people with money hadn't supported them. So I know that. But, like, having that be my identity, [I'm] just not comfortable at all with that. I'm just not comfortable. And the vast majority of things we do anonymously."

Kevin was conflicted about the wealth he had access to through his partner, including their large home, mostly because he agreed with political critiques of inequality (*"I'm* Occupy"). He also feared judgment from progressive peers, a fear that testifies to the diversity of his network. But he described getting used to this identity after hosting an event for some activists, saying, "There are moments of clarity to me where [I think], 'You know what, we *are* the people with the big house, and money has given us the possibility of, not just, like, buying fancy things for ourselves but kind of creating space where other things that I think are important can happen.' So I have moments of kind of like, 'Yes, let's have all those activists into our home.' Because there's no other easy space to gather and this will be comfortable and we'll do a thing and that'll be useful." Here Kevin overcomes his reluctance to make his privilege visible to other progressives, which then allows him to make a contribution he might have otherwise avoided. It also seems to be a step on the road to becoming more comfortable in this identity.

Minimal Givers

Regardless of their politics, the rest of the people I talked with—about half the sample—did not describe philanthropy or volunteering as a significant part of their identity. Nearly all said they would like to give more or felt that they "should" do so. They certainly believed that "giving back" in this way was desirable. But philanthropy was not a significant priority for them, and they did not seem especially committed to particular causes. Asked if he gave away money, Justin said, "To charity? Some. I'd like to give away more. But, yeah. . . . You know, different fundraisers come up. You know, someone has a fundraiser. This disaster stuff. Like, Haiti, I'm probably going to give some money to the Red Cross." Like Justin, most gave away just a few thousand dollars a year, often to friends who asked for their own charitable causes. Others gave to a variety of causes to which they sometimes had personal ties, including reproductive rights, the arts, education, and health. Some gave to international organizations doing humanitarian work.

Future Philanthropic Identities

Many people I talked with also imagined becoming more involved in philanthropy in the future. Some of the wealthiest envisioned consolidating a more coherent philanthropic identity. For example, Lucy and her earner husband were giving away $250,000 per year, but they felt this was not enough. She said, "It should be a much greater percentage of what we earn on an annual basis. Like, it should be more in the millions of dollars, to our point of view." Lucy was also unsatisfied with the causes to which they were giving. She felt that, rather than developing a coherent plan, she and her husband tended to give to friends who asked for money for their pet projects. She told me:

> Right now, it's pretty pathetic. I think we donate a decent amount of money to our schools. And the only reason for that is because we don't feel like we've been able to get our act together enough to actually give in a thoughtful way. We give to people when they ask, and not because we feel like it's aligned with what our values are. I think what we have decided is that we'd like to go kind of strong and deep in a particular area, and not kind of all over the place. . . . But the challenge for us has been finding organizations that we feel are well run, whether we know enough about, to feel like we can really, like, channel a lot of money that way. Because it takes time and energy to do that. And we just haven't had the time and energy to research all the organizations that we feel like are worthwhile. So we end up getting lazy.

Similarly, Nicholas consistently set aside 5 percent of his income to give away, which went into a donor-advised fund, but he did not always disburse the money from the fund in a timely manner. He said, "I'm really bad at choosing where it goes. But I put the same, you know, 5 percent every year [into the fund]. I don't give it out as fast as I put it in. And that's an issue." A former staff member with Resource Generation, an organization for young people with wealth, told me: "One of the big ways that class privilege plays out is per-fectionism. So, the sense of 'I have to come up with the perfect plan and do it right.'"[17] These donors expressed a strong commitment to giving away money but lacked clear priorities for it and had not developed consistent positions.

As noted previously, some potential givers described having kids as impeding their engaging in volunteer work or philanthropy. Chaz, for example, told me he and his wife had not given "significantly" to charitable causes. But, he said, "I'd say that it's tough for it to be, like, a focus of ours now. Just, life with little kids. I think hopefully it will become more of a focus in the future for both of us. But right now, with three [small children], we're just trying not to drown." Janice told me, "I am very aware of being at a time in my life that's very sort of inward-focused because I have little kids. I'm not as politically active as I used to be in social justice causes. I mean, I'm trying to give money to support them. But I'm not as involved."

Beyond the time commitments, having kids also shaped potential donors' thinking about what it meant to have enough. Karen said, "When I was like, a teenager, I always thought, like, as soon as I had enough money to just meet my basic needs, I would just give the rest away. Like, how can you see people who don't have enough and do anything luxurious? I mean this partly comes from the mother that I was raised by, who actually does live that way. But [my husband and I] were just talking about how your values change when you have kids, and you want to amass something to give to them."

Other people also mentioned postponing giving until after they had accumulated more assets. Donovan already had over $10 million; he gave away about $100,000 per year and also directed some of his family foundation's giving. He told me, "My attitude is . . . I think I'm a pretty good investor. So I feel like I'm playing for a longer term. So I haven't been willing to make very large [philanthropic] commitments because it's going to reduce my flexibility, and that's something I'll be looking at as I get older. So probably in the next decade I'll be looking at doing this more seriously."[18] Several people who currently gave away very little were also those most focused on amassing wealth to protect against risk in an unpredictable market, and they imagined that they might give more in the future.

Paying Taxes as Giving Back

Some people I spoke with spontaneously connected charitable giving to taxes.[19] James, for example, gave away about $2,000 per year (less than 1 percent of his income, let alone his $3 million in assets). He said, without my raising the question of taxes, "Yeah, we don't give a lot of money straight away. I do pay a shitload of federal income tax. It's seemingly endless." James seems not to see a difference between taxes and charitable contributions, but most of the rest of those I interviewed did. The more politically conservative people tended to distinguish taxes from philanthropy on the basis of who controls the ultimate destination of the money. In the quote at the beginning of the chapter, for example, Frances explicitly distinguishes philanthropic giving from paying taxes. That is, she denies that she has an obligation to pay more taxes, despite the unequal returns to assets she identifies, but she believes she does have an obligation to give her own money voluntarily to causes she chooses. Describing a similar logic, Alice said, of her husband: "It's interesting. Because, like I said, he's very generous. Very philanthropic. But he wants to decide what to do with his money. He doesn't want the government to decide what to do with his money. . . . He thinks the private sector can do a better job with certain things."

By the same token, high earners were usually opposed to higher taxes, which seemed to take away their rightfully earned money. Paul, as we have seen, was adamant about the value of hard work as the basis for entitlement. He said that, with higher taxes "they're taking more of my money that I've earned." One stay-at-home mother and her husband (with an annual income of about $500,000) had voted for Romney, partly because, she said of her husband: "He's one of these people that is being pegged as, you know, 'You don't pay your fair share. You're not paying your fair share.' It's like, all his money goes [to taxes]! And that's part of it, too, that's very upsetting for him. Because it's like, there's no incentive for him to make more money because they just take more of it. And hand it out." Even some of the more liberal or downward-oriented people had become increasingly antitax over time. Penny told me her husband, who earned about $3 million per year, had "become more of a Republican, because of taxes." She laughed. "So, as he's made more, he has to give half of it away or more. He's like, 'Oh my God. How is that possible? I don't get that. I work so hard, now I have to give half of it away. Like, really?'"

Women who stayed at home were sometimes more conflicted about this, consistent with their distance from paid work. Lucy's husband hated the idea of raising taxes on high earners. But she was ambivalent: "I think I feel a little bit more conflicted about it, I have to say. I don't think anybody wants to be taxed more. I do think that taxes support good projects and good programs. I guess I'm more conflicted about it than he is. I really am." Though Alice's husband did not trust the state to use "his" money well, Alice herself was more pro-tax, arguing that "not everyone is going to" give away what her husband would give.

In contrast, downward-oriented people tended to see taxes as a form of giving back analogous to charitable giving, especially when they were inheritors and hence less connected to discourses of earning. Nadine herself mused, "I wish more rich people felt like it was their job to give back, you know? Everyone I know feels like, 'Oh, it's so heinous how much we get taxed.' Because I know people in that top income bracket. And it is pretty brutal. I mean, you know, you basically—I mean, it's like, the death tax is . . . it's like, more than a third.[20] Well over a third, right? Forty percent. But I just feel like, 'Yeah. Okay, that makes sense to me.' You know, it kind of sucks come tax time, and sometimes it hurts. But what do you expect, you know? You have more, you give more. I just feel like, that's common sense, to me. I don't understand people who feel like that's not."

As this stance suggests, these downward-oriented people were also less suspicious of the state. Danielle, who described herself as "pretty far left," said, "I think socially the government has an obligation to people, and that if you have more, you should give more, and you should pay more taxes. And I think that as a culture we can't spread it equally, so we need the government to do it largely for us." Miriam likewise defended the government's role when she said, "I actually totally believe in taxes. I think that I should pay more taxes.... Sometimes I get really annoyed with people in the city who are always, like, complaining about taxes and complaining about the subway and this or that. I'm like, you know what, the subway's pretty fucking awesome. It's really amazing. There's problems with this and that, but mostly it runs, and it takes you from here to there, and it's fast, and it's, you know, reasonably clean. It's efficient. And someone has to pay for all this shit, right? So you buy your tokens and there's city subsidies and all this stuff. Someone needs to plow your streets. I totally believe in taxes, and I don't—I'm fine with paying more taxes."

Specific tax policies did shape charitable giving, however, even for more liberal people. Talia said, "I mean, we donate to like, public radio. We give to our alma maters. I would say probably ten to twenty [thousand dollars per year]. And again, the tax benefit is also nice." Nadine said, suggesting that the amount of her and her partner's charitable giving was determined by the desire to avoid taxes, "Our charitable gift fund offsets capital gains [tax]. So there are years we've given away twenty thousand, and there's years we've given away five." Tax preparation also influenced the timing of giving, as some people made annual charitable contributions when they were thinking about their taxes. Wendy justified her fairly small donations with reference to the *lack* of a tax benefit. She told me, "We do [give money away], but I struggle with that, it's not enough, like, given what we have, I think I'm probably supposed to be giving away more.... Part of it is, is like, I don't get any benefit from our taxes, which pisses me off. Like, somehow—and I don't understand taxes well enough—but we would have to give away a lot more in order for it to be above a minimum where we start to get some credit for the itemized deductions."

Tax policy also shaped decisions about transferring money in families with multigenerational wealth. Even progressives, who advocated higher taxes for the wealthy in general, took advantage of rules permitting untaxed annual gifts under a certain amount from older generations to younger ones as a way to minimize estate taxes when the older relatives die. Similarly, grandparents often paid for the private schools of their grandchildren (this was common in the families of those I interviewed) as a way of passing on wealth without paying taxes. Sara, who otherwise believed in paying taxes, called this practice "just good estate planning."

GIVING BACK OR GIVING UP?

Most of the people I talked with resembled wealthy people who have been studied by other researchers, for whom giving back does not challenge structural inequalities in any way. These are people who mostly have faith in the system, as Frances asserts in the opening quote ("I do believe in a market economy"). They acknowledge disparity but take it as given—beyond the control, and thus the responsibility, of the beneficiary. Monica told me, "I don't ever feel guilt [about people with less]. Because I didn't necessarily personally put them there." She also recounted, of a lesson she had learned from her mother,

> I remember [when I was] growing up, and I was saying to my friend, "Oh, I can't believe this, people live on the side of the highway." My mother was like, "Well, they can't afford to live in the suburbs. That's what they can have. And they're happy about it, that's what they have." And that has always stuck with me. You know? It's like, you do the best you can do, and it's going to be better than some, and it's going to be less than others. But it's good. And someone's going to have it better than you, and somebody's going to have it worse than you. Just have what you have.

Warren commented, "You know, I'm not like, 'People shouldn't get help.' Like, 'No welfare.' You're dealing with a society where no one has figured out how to deal with scarce resources, and no one has quite figured out the best way to allocate things. And so yes, you're in a situation where you're enjoying more than, you know, the less fortunate in our society. But it seems like that's part of the system we're living in, so why not enjoy it if you can?" For these donors, giving time and money often ends up *consolidating* their privileged position, especially because their philanthropy supports institutions that benefit them, such as schools.

But many downward-oriented people I spoke with, like Nadine, critiqued the system from which they benefit. Their giving reflected these critiques, as they often supported organizations advocating gender, race, and economic justice. They knew such giving was unlikely to lead to major change, but it was not clear what else they could do to challenge inequality.[21] Miriam said, "Is the division of income in society fucked up? Absolutely. And do we value the wrong things? Absolutely. So you know, what I get [paid] is ridiculous. And then, if you think about, like, a teacher or people who are like giving a ton—a firefighter, right—I mean, they're not making anywhere near as much. . . . And you know, that is crazy. But where I feel most guilty is sort of with regard to people who just really aren't getting by." For this reason, she said, she mostly donated to organizations in New York that served people struggling to survive. "But," she continued, "I definitely feel guilty, and I try to assuage some of that by giving. But I don't know what else I can do."

When Kate, Nadine's partner, mentioned "giving back," I said, "A lot of people say that, and I'm never exactly sure what it means. Give back what, and to whom?" In response, she first invoked awareness. She said, "Well, I think for me what I mean is that I do know that it's extraordinarily random and lucky that I am in this situation. I didn't earn the money that is coming to my house, and the money that pays for my mortgage comes from somebody who works and [bought the family company's product]. . . . So the money that's paying my mortgage is somebody else's salary, and I am aware of that." Kate continued, "So in the larger system I think the whole thing is quite unfair, that because we have assets we have income, and that we don't have to work. You know, I realize that. And there's nobody to give that back to, unless we sort of get rid of capitalism, you know? But I do think that we have an obligation to support charities and be charitable. To sort of not, I don't know, not spend our money on frivolous things and to give money to people and causes that we think need it."

Kate's answer outlines the structural problem she and Nadine face—that their possession of assets allows them economic freedom and that those assets come directly from the earnings of people who do have to work. But, she says, "there's nobody to give that back to" under our current system. There is no such thing as "giving back" that actually solves the structural problem. Instead Kate highlights all the aspects of legitimate privilege I have described—earning, not spending frivolously, being "charitable," and being aware. For the most part, these progressives "give up" on making systemic change. As individuals, this is the best they can do.[22]

Or is it? One thing they could do would be to take "giving back" to an extreme by giving all their money away and/or devoting all their time to activism.[23] Giving it all away was an option a few of the most progressive people had considered but ultimately discounted. Gary said, "I've learned a lot about humility in the last ten years. And part of my humility is to think that I could give away all my money, and it wouldn't make a dent in the world. It just wouldn't. For five minutes, it might change the life of one organization." He also alluded to appreciating the "benefits to financial security" for his family. He said, "In the case of my family, I don't feel I have the right to make decisions about poverty, or well-being, for my kids and their kids. Because I had the privilege of making the choice. I don't feel I have the privilege of making the choice for them." Others who had contemplated this option (or giving away larger amounts than they did) also referred to the long-term consequences for their own children and grandchildren.

Needing to protect against risk was important as well. Vera, who did not have children and lived a frugal lifestyle, felt very guilty about her inherited wealth. But when I asked if she had considered giving it away, she responded, "Well, I'm scared in this country. Because you have one illness, it's gone. You know, you can't count on—so I give *some* away. I feel like, one illness, I'd be done. So I'm trying to preserve myself." She contrasted the United States unfavorably to European welfare states, which guaranteed at least that "everybody eats."

Eliana believed that she could have used her privilege to the advantage of others if she had become a "superactivist," perhaps in education. She said, "So, if I were to give my whole life to that, I maybe could make a little impact on education, in some way, in some city. Never mind all the other things I also think are really important. So I couldn't fix everything. But I could give everything I have to fixing. Instead of giving a lot of what I have to making sure my child is, you know, especially privileged." But, she said, she had made a number of decisions along the course of her life, including having children, that steered her away from that possibility. And she was unwilling to give up certain comforts (recall that she had joked, "I was gonna be a revolutionary, and then I had that first massage"). Finally, she commented, "the older I get, the more and more discouraged I get, about making an individual difference."

For the younger inheritors I interviewed,[24] who did not have children and who were active in extremely progressive circles, these possibilities were less remote. Yvette was an activist in her early thirties who had recently inherited over $10 million dollars. She had almost immediately given away about a quarter of the total and was thinking seriously about giving away most of the rest. She said, "I think my idea continues to be, give the majority of it away, and do the best I can at thinking about 'In this world, what piece am I going to keep as a safety net?'" She was critical of social messages about potential risk that made people feel they had to hoard their assets, and she was trying to figure out a way to feel secure while also learning to develop and rely on a broader community. She worked full-time in a nonprofit for very low pay and hoped to live on her salary. But I wondered how this might change if she decided to have children.

John, a young activist with wealth who did not have children yet but hoped to, differentiated between charitable "giving" and "redistributing," which meant giving more of one's wealth away. He called this a "real debate among progressives and radicals." John had decided that rather than giving away a radical proportion of his wealth, he would use his philanthropic access to influence more progressive change. He said, "I think that using the access and the privilege that I have to be able to say things in circles that other people can't get into is actually very valuable. My friends and peers who are doing grassroots community organizing who can't get into conversations with communities of wealth, I can on their behalf. As long as I keep the conversation [connected] with them, not saying only what I'm thinking up in my head but what we're developing together, that's actually a valuable thing to do. And," he concluded, "it also lets me still have money and go travel and have a nice house." Ultimately, John said, "What I often say is that if you choose not to give everything away, you're choosing to have some level of discomfort on an ongoing basis. If you have belief in equity and equality but choose to have a lifestyle with wealth in it."

Giving back, like working hard and consuming prudently, involves emotion, disposition, and behavior. It means feeling aware and appreciative, being "nice" to others, and, to different extents, giving time and money. These practices and affects are publicly visible to varying degrees. Awareness in particular is private—it keeps privilege visible to the privileged individual herself without necessarily making it visible to others. Actually donating time and money is often, though not always, more public. The publicness of my interviewees' identities as wealthy people affects how they choose to contribute.

Regardless of how they give back, the people I interviewed do not "give up" anything of material significance; their giving, even in large amounts, does not diminish their own comforts. An architect I interviewed described a wealthy liberal couple who were his clients: "They're the kind of people that don't pass a homeless person without giving him ten dollars. They just feel guilty about having so much, in a world where people don't. They're politically active, and this and that and the other thing. And ultimately, yeah, it doesn't stop them from buying an Armani outfit. . . . They don't deprive themselves of anything, either. They're not flying coach." On the other hand, it is not clear that their giving up more would be morally better.

And "giving back," in whatever form it takes, ultimately does not lead to broad structural transformation. For most of the people I talked with, this kind of change was not the goal; "giving back" was a less conflicted, more taken-for-granted part of their identities as good people. For those who would have wanted more radical change, it was frustrating not to be able to make it. But ultimately they accepted these limits—an acceptance facilitated by becoming parents and the slow ratcheting up of "needs."

The legitimately entitled self—hardworking, reasonably consuming, and contributing—is always acting in and constituted by relationships with other people, especially in families. The next two chapters address how these issues of disposition and worth played out in relations with partners and children.

5

LABOR, SPENDING, AND ENTITLEMENT IN COUPLES

On a muggy day in June 2013, I drove out to the Hamptons to conduct two interviews, both with stay-at-home mothers. My conversation with the first interviewee, Alexis, began with a discussion of the $400,000 cosmetic renovation she and her husband had done on their summer house. The renovation had been his idea, because he thought it would add value to their home while also making it more pleasant to live in. She had been more inclined to live with the house as it was and wait a few years until they could buy something bigger and better. But he'd prevailed, and she had ultimately spent many months both planning and supervising the renovation.

Alexis loved to shop; as we saw in chapter 3, she was enthralled with a handbag her husband had bought her as a Mother's Day "treat." But her passion for shopping caused conflict with her husband, who tried to rein in her spending. She said, "I wish I could be better at saving more money. That's the one thing we really fight about. And, like, the credit card bills." She admitted sheepishly that her husband was right, saying, "I do have a shopping problem." She was less inclined to agree, however, when her husband gave her a hard time about having "too much" paid labor—a nanny in the mornings and sometimes a babysitter in the evenings. He didn't understand how much work it was to deal with the kids while he was in the city during the week, and she wanted time to get her "own stuff" done. She confessed that she sometimes hired a babysitter without telling him.

Stephanie, the second woman I interviewed that day, was a stay-at-home mother married to an architect. Like Alexis, she fretted over constraints her husband put on her consumption. She complained that he would buy gourmet food and wine for his friends but give her a hard time for spending on what she saw as necessities for their child and household. She protested that she didn't spend any money on herself, and she went into detail about how she had saved money renovating their summer home. She also thought her husband failed to understand how much work she did not only taking care of their son but managing their real estate, which included a Manhattan apartment, a summer home on Long Island, and a rental property. Also like Alexis, Stephanie said she had had more control over money when she was earning it herself.

Driving home to Brooklyn along the tree-lined Southern State Parkway, I thought about the emotions around spending that these women had described, including anxiety, frustration, denial, and desire. I considered the power struggles over the control of money that they were clearly engaged in with their husbands, Alexis in a more muted way, Stephanie more overtly. I felt compassion for them, because their husbands criticized them for being too consumerist while seeming to diminish their household, renovation, and child-related labor. As a feminist scholar of domestic work, I knew that this tendency to devalue the unpaid household labor that women typically do is common, regardless of social class. Later, when I listened to the interviews, I heard myself taking their sides as they described these disputes, as I would with a friend. I agreed that Alexis needed more babysitting and sympathized with Stephanie's difficulties in talking about money with her husband.

The greenery of the parkway gave way to the Long Island Expressway and eventually to the run-down streets of eastern Brooklyn, lined with dilapidated brick low-rise buildings. Still musing about these women, I stopped at a red light and noticed a long line of eighty or a hundred people, primarily men but also some women and children, stretched along a building and around the corner. As far as I could tell, all were people of color. I realized the building was a church. A large sign outside proclaimed "Hot Food Wednesday Nights." It was Wednesday night.

What struck me at that moment was how much I had forgotten about the broader context of inequality that had brought me to this project. In feeling sympathy for Stephanie and Alexis, I had started to see their situations through their eyes, which distracted me from something I would usually have been obsessed with: their social advantages over others, the expensive renovation, the three properties, and the many other comforts that they and their families enjoyed. That is, the relations of distribution in the household—these wives' conflicts with and sense of subordination to their husbands—had deflected my attention from relations of distribution more broadly— their privileged lives relative to those of the vast majority of the population.[1] To put it another way: my feeling of gender solidarity with them had obscured their class position.

Ultimately I came to believe that these tensions with their partners also made it harder for Stephanie and Alexis *themselves* to see and *feel* their own privilege. Conflicts over money created a sense of scarcity within these intimate relationships and loomed much larger in their daily experience than did their advantages over abstract others with less. I realized, too, that these challenges from their husbands were also refusals to recognize the legitimate entitlement of their wives. Stephanie and Alexis were trying to establish their labor as productive and their consumption as reasonable—that is, they were trying to interpret themselves as good people, morally worthy of their privilege. But their husbands' failure to support these interpretations made it hard for them to constitute themselves as deserving.

In this chapter I explore how money, time, labor, and recognition become objects of negotiation and discord within wealthy couples. I focus especially on how couples constructed the relationship between earning or otherwise providing money and being entitled to spend it, how they valued unpaid household and lifestyle labor, and how they understood what it meant to contribute to family life. An extensive scholarly literature on the control of money in couples analyzes the relationship of each partner's income to marital power and control over various aspects of the couple's life (including decision making, money, fertility, and sexuality).[2] An equally vast body of research explores the division of household labor and its relation to gender identity.[3] My primary interest and contribution here is to link class to gender by looking at how entitlement *within* these relationships, which are influenced by gendered beliefs about the value of paid and unpaid labor and the control of money, relates to my interviewees' larger sense of entitlement *outside* them.

CONFLICTS AND CONTRIBUTIONS

As I started hearing stories about arguments or tensions over finances, I initially imagined that perhaps one reason interviewees might clash over money would have to do with whether they shared a spending style—that is, ideas about what kinds of needs were reasonable and how much it was appropriate to spend to meet these needs. And indeed some people believed that their lack of conflict came from agreeing on these priorities. As Penny told me, "We don't have a conflict over [spending]. We're both similar about it." Some indicated that class background and upbringing played a role in spending styles. Danielle described herself and her husband as "skinflints," saying they shared the same outlook; she explained, "I think part of it is, we basically had incredibly similar upbringings about money."

I surmised that a lack of financial constraint would also foster a harmonious relationship around money, and some people did mention this freedom in their descriptions. For example, Janice said, of her partner, "There aren't big things where we disagree. And it may be partially a function of not really having the stress or worry about it. I mean, I think it is. Like, we don't have to stress about it. So, if [her partner] wants to spend more money on a coat than I would ever spend, it's not taking away from something else. And I'm aware of that."

But I soon realized that both spending priorities and having "enough" to meet their needs were matters of interpretation between the members of the couple. Penny said, "I think having money and not having to worry about it totally alleviates the conflict, in a way." Yet she went on to say, "Although there are plenty of people with money who spend a lot and who have conflict." As Penny's comment highlights, it is not an absolute amount of money but rather a particular understanding of needs relative to assets that fosters ease or anxiety. I came to see that many of the members of the couples I interviewed had different spending styles but still described minimal conflict over spending; others had enough money to buy whatever they wanted but still disagreed with their partners about it. I also realized that how people spent time, as well as money, was often an issue and usually had to do with the valuation of unpaid labor.

In the end, I found that clashes over money and time in these relationships primarily stemmed from *interpretations* of how each member of the couple was contributing to the family's lifestyle relative to their entitlements. Because money itself is a recognized form of contribution, those who brought money into the relationship—through either earning or inheritance—were likely to feel entitled to spend it. Those who had not brought the money to the relationship were more conflicted. But these entitlements were not set in stone simply by the balance in monetary contributions. What mattered most were the ways both parties to the relationship recognized and valued each other's contributions and their needs.[4]

In turn, these valuations were influenced by deeply gendered ideas about the value of certain kinds of labor and time. As feminist theorists have long pointed out, household "consumption" is also "production" (and reproduction) of both humans and lifestyles.[5] Yet the men in my study did not always recognize the labor of lifestyle as productive work, despite the women's desire that it should count as such, as we saw in chapter 2. The men were more likely to be bringing home the proverbial bacon, so they were more automatically able to draw on ideas about legitimate, productive (paid) labor. In contrast, stay-at-home mothers sometimes struggled to legitimate their own unpaid labor—including consumption work—as productive, prudent, and family-related. Stay-at-home mothers also sometimes felt uncomfortable spending money they had not earned.[6] They depended on their husbands to help them cast their labor as worthy, but, as the stories of Stephanie and Alexis showed, this recognition was not always forthcoming.

When the women I talked with had access to their own money, through either inheritance or their own paid work, they required less of this kind of recognition. But when they brought in more money than their husbands, they went out of their way to recognize their husbands' contributions—often more than the men did those of their wives. Female inheritors talked about (and tried to assuage) the conflicts their husbands felt about not being the primary providers more than male inheritors did. Likewise, women who significantly out-earned their husbands described having to compensate for their husbands' feelings of inadequacy. Yet such women retained primary responsibility for their homes overall, as did all women in dual-earner couples. Notably, I did not see much variation by race in these accounts.

DIVISIONS OF LABOR AND RECOGNITION IN SINGLE-EARNER FAMILIES

Heterosexual couples composed of male earners and stay-at-home mothers (or very low-earning wives relative to the husbands[7]) usually observed a strict division of household, family, and lifestyle labor in which the women did much more of it than the men. The men were providers, bringing all or nearly all of the money into the household by working outside it. The women were consumers, responsible for nearly every aspect of the home and the children's lives. Husbands who worked in finance or the corporate world rarely spent time with their children during the week thanks to long hours and, in some cases, punishing travel schedules.

The male earners and female "consumers" I interviewed seemed to take this division of labor for granted. Only one woman complained to me that her husband spent too little time with their children. In fact, several went out of their way to recognize their husbands for spending any time at all with the kids. These women took the demands of their husbands' jobs in finance, business, and law for granted, comparing the men to others in their fields who did less, not to what they might otherwise have wanted. Alexis, for example, told me that her husband was a great father; he had gotten up with her for night feedings and never had a problem changing a diaper, unlike some of his colleagues. Teresa called her husband a "very hands-on dad," relative to other men he worked with, because he tried to get home on weekday evenings in time to put the kids to bed.

The men were usually in charge of family money management, planning, and control.[8] Even when women I interviewed were tasked with paying the bills, they often did not have a broader sense of what their families' assets were or how they were organized. Julia, for example, told me, speaking of her husband, "We have a couple of different accounts. And he's always juggling, 'Okay, pay this out of this account. Pay this out of this [other] account.' He does all that." Several women told me, sometimes sheepishly, that they did not understand how much money there was or how it was invested.[9]

In home renovation specifically, the men were almost always identified as having cared primarily about the money, while the women were much more likely to have concerned themselves with logistics.[10] As Susannah, a mother of two married to an executive, said of her husband, "Budget, budget, budget. That's all he cares about." Grace said of the renovation she and her husband had done, "He watched the numbers much more than I did." Husbands and wives usually made big decisions together, such as who the architect and contractor would be and what changes would be made to the space. But once the projects were off the ground, the women ordinarily managed the renovations on a daily basis, while the men attended occasional meetings with architects and/or contractors. David, the interior designer, said of the female clients he worked with on renovations, "It's like these women are on salary for their husbands."

The women were also typically, though not exclusively, in charge of the aesthetics of renovation. Many described confronting the vast array of possibilities about everything from faucets to light fixtures, tiles to paint colors, as they spent hours surfing the Internet or roaming around Manhattan's Decoration and Design Building and other retail outlets. After the women had narrowed down the options, their husbands would help choose from among the available alternatives. Some men cared a lot about one or two issues, lobbying for a particular kind of shower or asserting control over the design of a home office.[11] But, for the most part, the woman's preferences drove the changes. In talking about a meeting his wife had asked him to attend with an interior designer, Paul said, "I don't care about any of this. I care about the budget. Honestly. I sat for three hours; I couldn't even bear to go any longer."

When the division of labor was not clear enough, it could lead to conflict. Talia's description of the process with her husband was fairly typical: "I was in charge of getting bids and managing that whole process at the beginning. And he would ask a lot of questions. And I kind of felt like I was back at [my old job], with the boss I hated second-guessing every single thing. And my biggest irritation was that—I was like, 'If you're going to let me manage this process, you can't be gone and then come in and ask all these questions.' You know what I mean? So there were a few bumps in the road at the beginning. But eventually we decided, 'Okay, you [the husband] are in charge of the money part, you keep track of the invoices and, you know.' He's just very good at looking through an invoice and finding any discrepancies. And I'm in charge of, basically, making sure the trains are moving and keeping things going."

In these households, the husbands would often review monthly expenditures (even if the wives actually paid the bills), thus essentially monitoring and potentially disciplining their wives. The women were highly attuned to this possibility. Ursula said, "I mean, every now and then [when reviewing the bills] he'll be like, 'Oh gosh, what happened this month?' You know, like, 'What are you doing?' I'll be like, 'You know, that's the camp for the two kids for the summer.' And then it's like, 'Oh, okay.' If I'd said it was, you know, the cocktail dress that I couldn't resist, it would probably be like, 'Gosh, are you serious?' But it was the camp for the two kids for the summer. It's okay."

Ursula further characterized her husband as "good" because he did not restrict her spending too much. Indicating a pair of expensive shoes she had just bought, she told me she was excited to show them to him. She said that he would not have a problem with her having bought them. "He's very good that way. If I did five of these in a month, he'd be like, 'Get a grip.'" (She also underscored that she had gotten the shoes for 50 percent off.) Several other women also described their husbands as "very good" about not interfering with their spending. These characterizations as "good" indicate that their husbands could be "bad," which would mean controlling the wives' spending. Thus, however they use it, the husbands hold the power to define acceptable and unacceptable choices. Indeed, Ursula told me later in our interview that she would like to have her own income "so I don't have to justify my pair of shoes from yesterday." This statement contradicts her earlier assertion that her husband is "very good," suggesting that perhaps he is more demanding of "justification" than she wanted initially to admit.[12]

When husbands trusted their wives to spend money and time intelligently and recognized their "consumption work" as legitimate labor that contributed to the family, conflicts were minimal.[13] And when they did not try to control their wives' spending, they avoided implying that their own contributions were more important by virtue of the fact that they provided the money. But when they did try to control women's money and time, denying their status as contributors and hard workers, conflicts over how their wives spent both money and time were more frequent.

Relationships of Recognition

In relationships marked by minimal conflict over money, the partners seemed to have found complementarity in their provider/consumer status. One key was that the husbands trusted their wives to spend wisely and did not interfere in their choices. Frances told me, "I'm in charge of literally everything" having to do with the household and family. But, she said, "I'm so super lucky that I married someone who never makes me feel like I'm contributing less. And never questions what I'm spending money on, and we have a really good division of labor. . . . I have wonderful friends who are on a budget. Which, I mean, if [my husband] ever came to me with a question [about spending], like, game over. That wouldn't work. But like I said, I'm just lucky that I married somebody who doesn't ever—if anything, he'll complain that I don't spend enough on something." Frances and her husband do sometimes disagree over spending, as she says, because she wants to spend less. But this difference in spending style doesn't create major conflict because Frances doesn't feel as if her husband is trying to control her. Yet Frances is clearly aware of the possibility that her husband could try to control her spending, as it is an issue for other women she knows.

The second critical dimension of this complementarity is the husbands' recognition of the wives' unpaid labor as a legitimate contribution. Frances told me that her husband "will often say he couldn't do what he does and be as successful as he is if I weren't managing this part of our life. If he couldn't be totally secure that I had this down, in terms of raising our kids and managing our home, he wouldn't be able to do what he does. So I feel like I'm contributing economically in that way." Frances's husband explicitly recognizes and legitimates her labor, which allows her to see it as an "economic" contribution and highlight its "managerial" dimension. Perhaps not surprisingly, then, Frances said she did not miss having her own income.

Teresa's husband, as previously noted, worked long hours on Wall Street and traveled frequently. He saw his two children only briefly during the week, although the whole family spent weekends together. Teresa had not been reluctant to stop working for pay, but she had struggled to "come to terms with" the fact that she was fully responsible for the home, which included employing both a nanny and a housecleaner. But now, she said, "I am the CEO of this house, and I run the ship, and that's how I like it." She highlighted her husband's recognition of her work and her contribution:

> He's really cool and laid back. You know, I don't cook like I would like to, and he'd never, ever, complain about me not cooking or having a dirty house, or not getting the laundry done. It never ever would cross his mind to complain about that. And he gives me all the credit—I'm selling it so great—but he gives me all the credit in the world. A couple of months ago—my daughter can be a pain in the ass, and he spent a day with [the kids], and he's like, "I just don't know how you do this. You've got the hardest job in the world." And he's always said that, which makes all the difference.

Teresa's analogy of "the CEO" gives her labor legitimacy through the reference to paid work involving managerial authority, as does her husband's labeling her work a "job." Her job is firmly anchored in the home, again suggesting that this recognition further cements the traditional division of labor, typically imagined as complementary. (Notably, her interjection "I'm selling it so great" indicates some self-consciousness about presenting the situation so positively to me.)

Like Frances, Teresa said she did not feel conflicted about not having an independent income, although other women she knew did. But, although she managed the money in the household, she claimed, "I manage it poorly." She couldn't tell me the amount of their rent or her husband's precise income, claiming that "numbers are something my head does not enjoy." Yet she went on to say, "I think not really having a grasp of the total picture of income helps with not feeling bad about spending my husband's money." This kind of comment signals that at least some women, even in couples with less conflict, are ambivalent about their entitlement to spend money they see as belonging to their husbands.

Some women said they appreciated the discipline their husbands encouraged. Talia, for example, indicated that she and her husband shared a spending style, saying, "We're savers." It turned out, however, that her husband was actually the more natural "saver." She continued, "My husband, especially, drives the saving, which I'm so thankful for. . . . He, in life, he is very thoughtful about what he wants to do in the future. So he knows that in order to do those things we can't, like, just spend [a lot], which is good for me, because sometimes I need someone to rein me in." They had established specific measures to limit her spending, which suggests that it must have been interpreted as a significant problem (perhaps more than she admitted to me). She said, laughing:

> One thing we did institute was an incentive program, where if I spent below a certain amount of money it would [go] to a profit share. So the cap was like, two or three thousand dollars. And whatever I spent below that, you know, if I [only] spent a thousand I would get five hundred dollars. It was great. . . . But I really only succeeded at that for, like, two months, just because being [in their summer home] I ironically have been spending more money, at like Toys R Us, Target, you know what I mean? I don't even know what I've been spending money on.

Talia was quick to assert that she was never extravagant, saying, "Not like I would ever totally go overboard. I don't have, like, really expensive tastes." Yet she clearly has some conflict about what she *should* desire. Her husband helps anchor her in a morally more desirable place, as a saver, not a spender, thereby helping to constitute her as a morally worthy, prudent consumer.

Talia also felt that despite his financial discipline, he recognized *her* needs, such as child care, as legitimate. She said, "I'm very lucky, like, I have a babysitter. . . . I have a lot of freedom during the day, and that is one thing that we spend money on, because . . . my husband knows that for me to be happy I need to be able to walk away sometimes." Talia and her husband both see the babysitter as "her" need because it is her job to take care of the kids, but he recognizes this need as legitimate. This comment also shows that his is the final word on spending, which determines the conditions of her labor.

Although Talia and her husband have some conflict over her spending, they appear to be fundamentally aligned in terms of what they *imagine* legitimate needs and contributions to be.

Failures of Recognition

In some single-earner couples, however, the provider-consumer dynamic was conflictive rather than complementary. In these couples, the husbands felt that the wives were spending too much, but the wives did not agree with these assessments. These husbands tried to control their wives' spending, casting them as untrustworthy with money and as profligate rather than prudent. They did not see family and lifestyle labor as real work, thus failing to acknowledge their wives' contributions, triggering fears of dependency among the wives rather than reinforcing mutuality. These couples fought more about money, and they seemed more likely to be secretive about it with each other. The women with these difficulties reported both knowing less about the family finances and hiding expenditures from their husbands.

As we saw at the beginning of the chapter, Stephanie was a stay-at-home mother married to an architect who owned his own business. She appreciated that her husband was a "saver" and had put money away for college for their children, but her narrative made it clear that money was a great source of stress in their relationship. She was often confused about their financial situation. He would tell her, in her words, "'Things are tight, you've got to watch what you're doing.'" But then he would make big financial commitments to his parents or spend money on entertaining. She lamented, "It's always mixed messages all the time."

He also questioned Stephanie's expenditures, which bothered her because she felt that she was buying necessities. She said he didn't understand how much having kids cost, and because he hadn't taken care of their summer home in a long time he "conveniently forgets" what it costs to do landscaping, maintain a pool, and so on. He got upset with her for spending money, she said,

Even though it's, like, for the house. He goes, "I just don't understand where all the money's going." And it's like, I don't go shopping. I don't—you know, I painted my own nails this morning. Cut my own hair today. Like, thinking all these things I could do to, like, not spend. And I don't spend money on myself, other than—you know, maybe I'll splurge on a couple T-shirts at Target. But still, it's like, this is what groceries cost. This is what booze costs. That's a big expense in our house. You know, Costco, and—they just don't want to know. Camp! Swimming classes. And, like, I know he thinks in the back of his mind, like, "Oh, we never should've [renovated] the house. Because then I'd still have, like, you know, a hundred and fifty thousand dollars just sitting in the account."

Stephanie defends herself against real or imagined accusations of illegitimate spending (on herself) by talking about *legitimate* (family-related) expenses and suggesting that her "splurge" happens at Target. She also asserts that the problem is with prices, not with her choices. But her husband fails to recognize both her expertise as a consumer and the work she does to navigate markets (and to avoid them, in the case of her body labor).

She felt that her husband did not appreciate her family labor, either. As I showed earlier, Stephanie was proud of her work taking care of her child, baking cookies for his school, and making his Halloween costume. She was also proud that she did not have a nanny. But her husband did not appear to see this work as productive or valuable. She described a conflict with her husband in which he implied that she was privileged because she did not have to work for pay. She said, speaking of working moms,

And I'm like, "You know what? They're lucky. They go to work. They go to work, that's all they have to do all day." I feel like sometimes I'm paddling upstream. I have so many things. And I'm not complaining. But we have three homes. And I've gotta deal with the leak in this one, and the electrician that's come out to that one. It's like, I'm all over the place, all the time. It's stressful, having three homes. You know? There's always something going wrong. And then when there's something that goes wrong that costs money, I hate being the bearer of bad news. Because I'm the one that deals with all of it. . . . I manage. But it's stressful, and—and then my husband, yet, thinks that I'm, you know, eating bonbons all day. It's hard.

Stephanie's husband doesn't respect her consumption labor and doesn't share knowledge with her about their financial situation. Yet because she is doing the consuming, she has to be "the bearer of bad news"—as when she had to tell him about a missed payment to their contractor of several thousand dollars—leaving her with an image that highlights her subordination to him and her distance from the family's long-term money management.

Especially notable here is Stephanie's disclaimer "I'm not complaining" about managing their three homes. In saying this, she recognizes that she is privileged, but her privilege is subsumed into the conflictive dynamic she has with her husband, who thinks she is "eating bonbons all day"—the quintessential image of the pampered, self-indulgent, nonworking housewife. When I asked her what she would do if they had more money, she mentioned maybe buying a new winter coat. She then said, "I don't feel like I'm really missing anything. I'd just rather have less grief, you know, from him. About everything. You know, what the bills are each month, or whatever." His failure to recognize her contributions to the family looms larger than any material desire.

Conflicts over consumption work sometimes included an explicit struggle on the part of the woman *herself* to see the labor of lifestyle as legitimate. Helen, for example, had loved her job in banking and left it only when it became clear that she could not reconcile its demanding hours with her family life. She told me, referring to her husband, "There are power dynamics where he's the breadwinner now, and I'm really not. And yet, I do so many things for the family that you can't put a number on it." She continued, referring to herself,

"And yet, you're well-educated. I had a career. You know, where is all that now? And it's hard, I think, to negotiate all those things. I was always scared that, 'Oh my gosh, I'll stop working, and then I'll be working for him.' And I feel like, you know, on some level, that's how it feels sometimes. So I have to really work hard to claim my own stuff." Helen went on, "It took me a long time to bridge that gap, sort of. And to feel like, 'Well, listen. It's my job here as, you know, managing the household. Like, I'm supposed to be spending the money.' But I wasn't comfortable for a long, long time." Helen fears being her husband's subordinate and losing her identity. Her labor, because it is unquantifiable, is hard to recognize, and even she has trouble seeing it as "my job."

Like Stephanie, Helen resists the idea that she is spending money on herself, which would be illegitimate, emphasizing that she is being frugal or forgoing the little luxuries others might take for granted. Helen said her husband

> just sort of feels like I'm, like, spending all this money on things. And yet I feel like I don't spend money on things the way other women do. I do very little self-maintenance. . . . I know all these women who do all these beauty treatments. Like, I don't get my eyebrows done. I don't get waxed, I don't do that. . . . When I buy, I try to buy 70 percent off, with sales. That's just me. . . . But, so, he thinks I spend all this money. And yet I look at him, and he's, like, very into rare books. So we have all these books that he buys. . . . He's comfortable calling the shots, because [he's working], and sometimes I feel like, "That's not fair."

Her husband gives himself more latitude to spend because he earns the money, while implying that her spending is frivolous because she doesn't.

Although they do not use this language, Helen and Stephanie are describing the work of mediating between their husbands and consumer markets. They must convince their husbands that the amounts they spend are necessary—simply reflecting what products and services cost—rather than excessive. Although these husbands distrust their wives' ability to do consumption work well, they do not want to do this work themselves. When I asked if Helen's husband paid close attention to what she spent money on, she responded, "Not in any detailed way. He just says, 'We've got to bring the credit card bills down.' I'm like, 'Okay. Tell me where.' There's never been an answer to that question."

Some men wanted to control how their wives spent time rather than money. Alice's husband, for example, trusted her to spend prudently; she said, "He knows my personality, so he knows that I'm not going to just be excessive and sort of throw away money. . . . I go to the ATM machine a lot and take out a fair amount of money. And he's never, ever questioned me." Alice and her husband also had similar spending styles. However, he chided her for doing too much volunteer work and spending too much time working on the renovation of their second home. Alice described herself as obsessive in terms of trying to find exactly the right fixture or piece of furniture, or to do tasks perfectly, and said her husband "feels like I can't just let it go." He believed that she should pay people to do more of this work. "He's like, 'Just hire someone, let them do it. I don't care if you're going to pay 25 percent more than if you did it on your own.'"

Alice felt that her volunteer and renovation work were "totally" analogous to a job. These projects felt like something she was doing "for the greater good" that allowed her to "use [her] mind in different ways." But her husband saw these as illegitimate uses of her unpaid time, because her job as a mother was supposed to be primary (though her children were in school). When I asked her why it bothered him, she said, "Because, you know, the reason I'm home is to be with my kids, not sitting in front of the computer and going to meetings and doing all that stuff." He told her, in her words, "'I want you to enjoy yourself. Be with the kids, do whatever, not— you know, be doing that stuff.'" It seemed to me, however, that Alice did enjoy the projects she was doing and that it was her husband who saw her responsibilities differently.

It became clear that Alice's husband wanted her to prioritize caring for and spending time with him as well as their children. She said, "He works hard. He values his time and his family. So when he isn't working, he wants to be with his family. And, you know, doing something that he enjoys." She explained,

> He's like, "I leave the apartment at seven in the morning. I get home at seven at night, or six at night, whatever. You've got twelve hours. Like, the fact that you can't fit this stuff into these twelve hours, and you're staying up late, or you're on a computer, you know, after dinner, checking your e-mails," that's what bugs him. You know, weekends and stuff like that. So I think it's more that he feels like I can't just let it go. But I sort of say, you know, "We're just sitting in front of the TV hanging out. So what's the difference between [that and me] being in front of my computer?"

Unlike some husbands, who think wives should "do it themselves" when they're not working for pay, Alice's husband doesn't mind paying for someone else to do it. But his schedule is supposed to be the primary one, and she is supposed to be available when he is. He is, in a sense, telling her how to do her job.[14]

Ironically, at one point Alice suggested that part of her attentiveness to money in the renovation might be related to her lack of independent income. She said she didn't really care about earning her own money, both because her husband didn't hassle her about spending and because, after having a job for many years, "I feel like I sort of proved—you know, I did that."[15] But, she continued, "One of the reasons why I try to save money . . . or spend that time maybe [on the renovation]—you know, even subconsciously—maybe that's why. Because I feel like I'm spending someone else's money." Alice and her husband are, in a sense, at cross purposes: he wants her to spend money and contribute time, but she chooses to "spend" time, at least in part because she is not contributing money.

Some husbands were concerned about how their wives used *both* time and money. Alexis told me that she and her husband shared the same spending priorities: they were willing to pay a lot for quality and for experiences like vacations, but they were "moderate" in general. However, as I described earlier, they also fought about her spending on what she called the "little things." First, she said, "It's not like I'm buying— it's just, things add up. Diapers.com and the groceries. Stuff. Stuff just adds up. You know, he's very, like, organized, and he has a budget of all my expenses, and he wants me to, like—he has a goal for the monthly credit card bill, and keeping it at that." She casts her expenses in the language of legitimate family spending, contrasting them implicitly ("It's not like I'm buying—") to something more extravagant.

But ultimately, like Talia, Alexis described her husband as being reasonable in his desire to discipline her, saying, "He's right. I don't need anything. I don't need another shirt, another piece of jewelry, another pair of shoes. . . . But it's hard. Like, I go out, and I see something, and you know, I want it! But I'm getting better at that. And I try to be better. . . . I mean this very seriously. Like, I really want to try to be better all the time." Alexis wants to be "better"— meaning more controlled, which also connotes morally "good"—in her consumption. She attached this desire to a history of having been a spendthrift, never thinking about money when she was single and working in finance. Now in a different life stage, she found it important to conform to the norms her husband wanted to enforce. But, at the same time, she admitted that she didn't tell him about some expenses. When I asked if he noticed, she said, laughing, "Well, there's one credit card bill that he doesn't see the details of. So I use that one. You know. I've figured out ways. Like, 'Amazon.com' is so vague." Keeping these purchases secret not only helps her avoid conflict with her husband but also allows her to keep thinking of herself as "good."

As Alexis discussed these issues, it became clear that her husband wanted to control her time and her labor as well as her spending. Soon after their first child was born, she realized that she did not want to return to her job because she did not want someone else taking care of her child. But she "felt guilty" about the prospect of not making money. So when her husband admitted that he also wanted her to stay home, she said, "a weight was lifted." When I interviewed her a few years after this decision, however, Alexis's use of paid child care had become a bone of contention between them. He made fun of her for hiring babysitters because he thought she should be taking care of the kids herself. Although she initially described this as "only" good-natured teasing, she eventually remarked, when I asked about it, "Maybe he does make me feel a little guilty about it."

As a consequence, as I noted previously, Alexis sometimes lied to her husband about how much babysitting she used when she was at their summer house and he was working in the city. She said, speaking haltingly about the lie:

> Sometimes I lie about how much—because he doesn't really—like, I pay—like, he doesn't really know all the time how much help I'm having. It just makes me happier. Because I can get things done. I don't like [it] when my life backs up. You know? And if I have the two kids on my own, I have to be with them. Busy. So, I'm not doing, like, administrative things on the computer that I need to be doing, or emails, or planning [a child's] birthday party . . . or doing the dishes, or the laundry. You know, I like to keep moving. Getting all my stuff done, and multitasking. So it helps me do that. Makes my brain happier.

Like other women I discussed in chapter 2, Alexis frames her use of paid child care as facilitating other morally worthy work, which mitigates a sense of illegitimate entitlement. But her husband doesn't echo this interpretation, because he doesn't think she should need this "help." Lying to him about it allows her to avoid conflict with him, just as seeing him as "teasing" rather than "shaming" allows her to avoid confronting the real gap in their valuations of her labor. It also permits her to see herself as morally worthy, because she does not have to confront his critique of her consumption as unreasonable and therefore can avoid thinking of herself as a "snob," a fear we saw in chapter 2.

Marie, a stay-at-home mother married to an executive, also recounted ongoing conflict with her husband over money. They struggled both over money and over the legitimate use of Marie's unpaid time. She described herself as "a spender," while her husband "spends nothing, ever." Marie and her husband had been in counseling at least partly to address these issues. She felt that her husband was "watching" her spending. Marie also thought her husband took her (unpaid) time for granted, assuming she would always be available because she did not have a job. For him, time spent on paid work was symbolically (as well as economically) valuable and legitimated spending; unpaid work was not and did not count as a real contribution. Yet, at the same time, she thought he was conflicted, because at some level he was glad that she did not work. She said, "I think that he believes that at a certain point, it's good for you [the wife] to quit work because you [the couple] are at a certain level. None of his friends' wives work. None of them. And in general, I don't really have that many friends that work, either. But I do have some. But I always think that [husbands] think, 'But what are you doing? What are you doing all day?' . . . I think that he thinks I never have to do anything if I don't want to, because 'What are you doing, you're not working.'" Marie's husband seems to desire the status of having a nonworking wife (much as Veblen would have predicted) but not to believe that her unpaid labor is valuable.

Marie described the same struggle that Helen did, to feel that she had a right to the money her husband earned. She said, "It isn't a comfortable place to go—when I first quit, to now have to figure out how money would be spent. Because I'm still the same person that's been socialized to believe I would support myself. And now I'm looking to someone else to support me. And the truth is, in the marriage, it's both of our money. Legally. But it's a mindset that you have to get over." She went on, "But it's also hard for [her husband], as the person that's working, to have no control. I can see him feeling that way. And I remember having many arguments with him and saying, 'Whether you like it or not, whether you're comfortable with it or not, whether I am comfortable with it or not, if something should happen to this marriage, half of this money's mine. So, you can work a hundred hours a week. And for whatever you make, half of it's mine. So you've got to get used to that.'"

Though Marie knows that *legally* she is "entitled" to the money her husband earns, she has trouble *feeling* that entitlement, "getting over" the "mindset" that it is not her money. She continued, "And *I've* got to get used to that. So I started kind of unapologetically spending money. And so, then you're not a team. You're just spending to assert that you can. You almost have to be in your [husband's] face, to overcompensate for the fact that you feel uncomfortable about it. And you do. And so I am." Marie is responding to her own discomfort with her lack of earning, as well as her husband's; she uses aggressive spending as a way to assert her right to her husband's money and her power in the marriage.

Maya took a different tack. As we saw in chapter 3, her husband set strong limits on her spending overall (she said, "He doesn't give a shit if I have a nice handbag"). She claimed not to know how much his salary or assets were, and I believed her (again, this was not always the case among the women I interviewed). She told me she would propose certain expenditures, "and then he'll be, like, 'This is crazy' or not." But he appeared to give her autonomy within the amounts he allocated to her. I asked if she missed working and having her own income. She responded, "No, I don't, because he doesn't get into my business. Like [her friend], she works, and her husband looks at every credit card [bill]. If [her husband] was doing that, we'd have real problems. We'd have real problems. But he never questions—I don't tell him everything, but if I told him everything and he questioned, which he would if I told him, then we'd have a problem. There are no questions asked, it just kind of goes. Now I'm also not crazy. I'm not crazy at all. If I was, I think questions would get asked, but I'm not." Maya doesn't feel that she needs her own earnings because she can spend her husband's earnings freely—and she represents her own desires as "not crazy." But this is possible only because of a "don't ask, don't tell" policy of not discussing what she is spending money on. Avoiding overt conflict about money, Maya has accepted her husband's limits, and he has accepted her right to control what he gives her.

A shadow issue in these stories was the question of the women's dependency on their husbands and what would happen if they split up. Marie was sure her husband had money in accounts she didn't know about. She maintained a secret account herself, with "under a hundred thousand" dollars she had "saved" (from money he earned, it seemed). She explained, minimizing the amount, that this money was to "buy toothpaste" if she and her husband ever separated. Maya was also anxious about her own ignorance of the family's finances as it related to her dependency on her husband, although she spoke about this very vaguely. She told me, "I think I probably should understand more of the whole picture, and I don't." When I asked why, she said, "I just let it go. . . . He was kind of like, 'Let's not worry about it. You know, I'll take care of it, and blah, blah, blah.'" She haltingly explained that she felt that she *should* know the size of the "whole pie" as part of a "safety net." Instead, she said, she had made the "naïve" decision to trust her husband and, as a last resort, the legal system. She had saved some money from working, about $1 million, but she did not seem to feel that this would be sufficient. As in Marie's case, the law outlines what Maya should be entitled to in one sense, but it does not suffice to make her feel comfortable with the situation.

These conflictive dynamics clearly interfered with these women's self-conceptions as hard workers and prudent consumers. Men's refusal to recognize women's volunteer and philanthropic activities also delegitimated their attempts to "give back" more explicitly. Marie said, for example, "My husband would like to see all that volunteer work going to a paycheck." She also told me that her husband would prefer to reduce their giving to $50,000 per year from $75,000 (on an income of over $2.5 million).

Furthermore, such conflicts engender a sense of *scarcity* among these wives. The conflict locates the question of entitlement to and use of resources between the members of the couple rather than between the couple and the rest of the world. All of the women who mentioned these problems were "upward-oriented" in the sense that they did not tend to describe themselves as privileged. Alexis and Stephanie were among the very few in my sample who did not make charitable donations. Alexis said, "I don't feel like we have money to be giving away right now." Stephanie said, "I don't have any money to [give away]," although she described making some political contributions. They may feel that they do not have enough to give away for multiple reasons, but it seems likely that these constraints and conflicts with their husbands play a role in stifling a sense of self as privileged.

Stay-at-home mothers married to earners seemed less susceptible to these dynamics if they had significant resources of their own, accumulated through earning and/or through family wealth. These women did not talk about conflict with their spouses. Zoe, for example, had worked in corporate law and also had inherited wealth. She told me that she and her husband didn't disagree about spending: "One, because he's not petty at all about it. And two, because I bring just as much." She explained, "He's the only one working now, earning money. But I've got my own money. So, when I want to buy my own pair of shoes, or buy myself a bag, or whatever, I certainly don't feel like I have to ask permission. And I can do it myself, and never have to tell him how much they were, because he'll never see it. Like, it's my own account, and my money. We have everything together, as well. But he's certainly not looking through my credit card bill, thinking, 'What is this?' . . . And anything related to family, whether it's groceries or home, he's like, 'Spend as much as you need.'" When her husband says, "Spend as much as you need," he sounds like other husbands, who ultimately have power over the couple's money. But her financial independence means he can't control her spending (though she does echo the idea that spending on herself should come from "her" money).

Danielle had been a banker before leaving paid work. Like her husband, she had inherited wealth, from which she paid herself a "salary," as we have seen. She told me, specifically alluding to her primary role in household consumption, "I don't understand how you could be the one who spends the money and not know. That would make me real nervous. . . . I need to know the cash flow. I need to know what the [balance] sheet looks like and, you know, like how all that stuff affects the long term." Unlike most of the other stay-at-home mothers I talked with, she links her desire to understand money to the fact that she is spending it. That is, spending, not earning, justifies control. I believe it was easier for her to take this position because she brought her own money to the relationship, so she did not feel as if she was spending "someone else's" money.

INHERITANCE AND ENTITLEMENT

In heterosexual couples living primarily on inherited wealth from one inheritor, the household division of labor and the fact that one person was the source of the money played out somewhat differently. Like stay-at-home mothers, women in these families (including female inheritors) still did the majority of the daily household management, including food preparation, planning for the kids, and supervising domestic workers, even though they almost always worked at least part-time for pay. But men in these families tended to take a more active role in some aspects of this work (especially child care and renovation) than did high-earning men, in part because they worked shorter hours and in some cases because they had more progressive politics. Because they almost always worked for pay, the women had strong identities as paid workers. And because the bulk of the household assets did not come from paid work, the money did not confer quite the same legitimacy on the inheritor as earnings could, as we saw in chapter 2.

For all these reasons, I saw less discord in these couples over whether consumption and family work counted as real labor. They also felt less economic anxiety than earners because their significant assets shielded them from the risks of job loss. But questions of control over money did arise. Most prominent was whether it was "our money" or the money of the inheritor alone. Couples who could experience the money as "ours" (a status less enshrined in law than it is for couples who have earned wealth since marrying) seemed to experience less conflict. Both male and female inheritors talked about trying to equalize these relations, although the women seemed to be trying harder to create balance.[16] Here issues of legal transfer —of inheritors to their spouses and of inheritances to children— became central.

In these couples, money was usually managed by the inheritor, male or female. Scott, for example, was in charge of what Olivia called the "care and maintenance of money," dealing with their accounts and all the "emails and signings."[17] She preferred this arrangement, characterizing her attitude as "your family, your money," though she also recognized and lamented that this stance was conventionally gendered—that she as the woman didn't know much about what was going on with the money. Inheritors also often held significant assets apart from those of their spouses, sometimes because they were tied up in family arrangements for wealth management.

It seemed to me that the inheritors' control over the wealth was taken for granted in these families, for the most part. And I did not get the sense that inheritors were policing their partners' daily spending to the same extent as earners. But power struggles over consumption decisions still emerged. Grace, who worked part-time in nonprofit consulting, very explicitly illuminated the relationship between the source of the money and the power to decide where to spend it. She said that sometimes her husband, who had both inherited and earned wealth, "gives me a hard time about buying [something]. And I'm just like, well, how am I ever going to be able to have—I can't make enough money to impact our life. And how am I ever going to make enough money to deserve something, like, if I don't just say, 'I worked for this, and I made this money?' Even if it's not impacting our life. It's frustrating. It's hard." She ties "earning" to "deserving" specifically in the context of having the right to control how household money is spent, even though she provides very little of it. She continued, "Or, I can't be like, 'Well, I know you don't like it, but I'm buying it.' Do you know what I mean? Whereas [her husband] can. He can be like,

'I know you don't like it, but I'm going to buy that car.' Because he could. Whereas I don't have the background money to do that." Because her husband brings the money to the family, he has the ultimate power to define legitimate needs in the household.

Grace also missed the psychological boost of financial accomplishment and contribution. When she worked in a regular job, she said, "Like, if I got a raise, I'd buy myself something. I'd buy myself something small or go out to dinner or something to celebrate, and I don't have that now. It's just not the same. I can't be like, 'I put money into this renovation.' I think there is a pride there that is lost, and it's hard." She thus turned to her own work as an important source of autonomy. It was crucial to her to have her own money, which she earned, and to keep it separate from the household money. This was partly because, as she said, "It is all mine, and I can say it's mine." Also, she said, "There is a part of me that needs to have my own access [to money]. . . . If anything were to happen, like, I have access to my own—I don't have to worry. It's a little bit of a security blanket." She also told me she did not give away much money to charity, both because she didn't feel as if her husband's money was hers to give and because she felt as if she had to hold onto her earned income. As in the case of the stay-at-home mothers described earlier, these tensions over control create a sense of immediate scarcity that can overshadow the sense of privilege.

Struggles over control also played out between Kevin and his husband, Dan, who had inherited wealth. But unlike Grace, Kevin was *less* likely to want to spend. Kevin said, of the differences in their financial situations, "I mostly would say I don't think it matters at all." He told me, "In many ways, [Dan's] values are super close to mine. He's not at all identified with having this money. I mean, I think what's beautiful about it is, he sort of sees his money as allowing him to do things sort of with his own life, and sometimes in support of his friends, that he wouldn't be able to do otherwise." They also had an egalitarian division of labor, Kevin said. But Dan's definitions of need, which involved spending money more freely, were likely to prevail. Kevin described the tension between spending to change something and accepting it the way it is as "always in our lives." Dan would argue, Kevin said, "'If we can afford to do it and we kind of want this thing, whatever it is—this new sofa, or, you know, new shelves, or whatever—then let's just do it.' And I much more have this feeling of like, do we really need that new sofa? I mean, yeah, our sofa looks like crap, but it's still functioning, and is it so terrible to have a crappy-looking sofa? So that kind of justification question is often in my head." Dan also wanted to pay others more often to do things Kevin felt they should be doing for themselves, such as taking care of their children.

In the end, Dan's definitions won out more often. Kevin said, "I think the fact that some of the money isn't mine almost means that I am more willing to kind of say, like, 'OK, whatever.' And I'm willing to kind of defer to his 'Hey, we can afford this, we should do this.'" This imbalance had caused problems, especially in their renovation, which Kevin described as "contentious" and "fraught." He had been inclined to make fewer changes, while Dan had wanted to do more. "And I think," he said, "the renovation was a big wrestling with [money tensions] in some ways. In moments, it felt very significant to me. Like, 'Whose apartment is this? Am I just, like, a guest in, like, your apartment? Or your and your family's apartment?'" Now, he said, "I mostly feel like to the degree that we did have these tensions around [money differences], it's mostly resolved."

Miranda described struggling with her husband over hiring paid labor. Although they both worked for pay and had relatively flexible schedules, Miranda was also in charge of her young children's food, their classes, and their play dates. She was responsible for supervising and communicating with the nanny and the housecleaner, on his behalf as well as her own. Her husband had resisted hiring an interior designer for their renovation because he wanted their home to reflect their aesthetic vision rather than someone else's. But Miranda, who was responsible for executing this vision, wanted someone to help her find all the necessary fixtures and furnishings for their home. Her husband didn't see her desire for this assistance as necessary—but he wasn't willing to do the work himself.

Heterosexual male inheritors I interviewed sometimes acknowledged these issues, but they tended to frame themselves as *not* controlling their wives. Gary told me, "I have made a real point of not applying [to her] controls or judgment to the use of our money." In fact, he wanted her to take more of an interest in the management of their money, partly because he had watched his mother's "deep infantilization all through her life, around any financial affairs." Donovan told me, "I manage all the finances," but his wife was in charge of the family spending. When the credit card bill came, he said, "I look at the gross number, and if it's a big bill I look to see what was the money being spent on, but I never say anything about it." He said, "By and large, my wife and I have very few financial arguments. One that we had was about the budget for our bathroom. I'm not going to remember numbers, but she was interested in putting in marble tiling, I think it was. And that's where I drew the line. I just said, 'No.' It was quite expensive, and, more fundamentally, I just—it rang contrary to so many of my beliefs about the proper use of money." But he insisted it was the only decision he had ever vetoed in the course of their long marriage. The fact remained, of course, that, like the male earners I have described, he did have the *right* to prohibit the expenditure.

Not only the status of inheritor or spouse, but also the gender of the inheritor, mattered. Female inheritors married to men appeared less likely to try to control their husbands' spending, either directly or indirectly, and they talked more about their spouses' feelings than male inheritors did. They were not monitoring what their husbands spent. Instead they felt impelled to compensate for a feeling of powerlessness that their husbands might have related to their contributing less. Ellen, the progressive financial advisor mentioned in chapter 2, told me:

> I work with a number of women with inherited wealth. And the pressure that it puts on heterosexual relationships is troubling. . . . When men have inherited wealth, and marry a woman, there is no swimming upstream for our culture because of the sense

that the man is still taking care of the woman. And so he got it from inheritance? Who cares? Or he got it because he goes to work every day, or he got it—you know, no one cares. When the woman has the money, then it is swimming upstream. Because it's against the messages that we've all had from birth of "He should support his family."

Ellen said husbands in these situations sometimes felt that "they have to go work really hard to make some money that's equal to that, or they have to gain it, in the sense of, they have to use it to invest." Even when the family had enough money, she says, "often I'll see that men make short-term bad decisions around money. . . . And they end up risking and losing it, because they were so eager to have their footprint on the money."

Sara reported a similar dynamic with her husband. She had inherited over $10 million. Her husband worked in finance, earning about $250,000 annually; he had some family wealth, but his assets paled in comparison with hers. They lived in a rental apartment costing nearly $6,000 per month. As we saw in chapter 3, they were trying to work out what their spending limits should be. Having recently had their first child, they were beginning to consider buying and furnishing a more permanent home. Sara wanted to buy a place, but her husband was thinking about quitting his job, in which case they might leave the city. She wanted to upgrade her furniture and maybe buy some art, but starting this project proved difficult without knowing where they were going to live.

Also crucial, however, were her husband's reluctance to spend "her" money and a lack of clarity around who was the ultimate decision maker about spending. Sara told me, "We've fallen into a dynamic that we're trying to get out of. Which is, like, I want to spend money. He's in the awkward position of being, like, 'No, I don't think we should buy that art or go on that vacation.' And I'm like, 'But we can afford it.' And he's like, 'Well, it depends on how you define "afford."'" And then, at the end of the day, it's my money. And so it puts him in this really awkward position. So we're trying to get through that. And we both agreed that having a budget that we agree to will be a good proactive way to say, like, 'We agreed that we can spend X amount on trying to finish our apartment this year.' And, like, work within that." In part, her husband had a "Puritan ethic" about spending in general; but also, she said, "for him, I think a lot of it is like, 'I shouldn't be spending your money.'" She told me that her personal giving had declined to 5 percent of her income from 10 percent since she had started making decisions jointly with her husband, which seemed related to their general lack of clarity about how to spend.

Rebecca thought recent money problems she and her husband had had might actually have helped their marriage. Her husband had felt left out of their renovation process, she said, because the money they had used to buy and renovate their house came from her inheritance. She recounted, "I think that [he] felt like I was just throwing money at a lot of stuff to solve problems. And I think that he didn't feel, maybe, like he was part of the game." But, when they ran into economic challenges, she said, it became "less of a problem. . . . Like, we've had to actually come together to figure some of this stuff out. . . . I think that it might have actually been a good thing for our marriage, to have had a financial stumbling block." Having more limits created a greater sense of equality between them—and having less money perhaps gave them a sense that it belonged to both of them.

A central way that both male and female inheritors compensated for this asymmetry was to transfer assets to their partners legally. Rebecca, for example, spoke of doing some "legal rearrangement" to make sure her husband felt that their home was "his house." Although Sara said of her money, "I'm not entirely ready to *not* treat it as mine," after a lot of discussion she was planning to transfer some assets to her husband and see how that felt to both of them. Donovan told me, "When I was working—and I made a lot of money on my own—what I did was, I paid our expenses. And anything that was left over—and there was a lot left over—I split evenly. Half went into her account, half went into my account. So she actually has a substantial amount of money of her own, and I've emphasized repeatedly to her, 'It's your money!'"

Olivia's husband had given her significant assets as well. Yet Olivia, like several others I interviewed, had signed a prenuptial agreement that protected the bulk of her husband's family's substantial wealth. The prenup is, of course, a form of *preventing* transfer of assets. One stay-at-home wife of an earner told me that her husband had asked her to sign a prenup, and she had refused. But other earner families did not mention this to me. In part, perhaps, they simply did not want to tell me about it, and I did not usually ask. But if inheriting families are more likely to have such agreements, it might be because legal issues are different for inheritors, who tend to own the bulk of their assets *before* coming into the marriage, whereas earners typically accumulate them during the course of the marriage.

Legal transfer of assets became an issue, again, intergenerationally, particularly in terms of children's inheritance. Several partners of inheritors felt their partners' families played an outsized role in their own and their children's lives. It did not usually bother them that grandparents often paid for kids' private schools (a way of avoiding taxes on gifts above a certain amount). But grandparents also concerned themselves with establishing trust funds and other mechanisms of passing money down through the generations, which noninheriting parents often had no control over. One wife of an inheritor was frustrated at the way her in-laws treated their children on a quotidian basis in terms of values around spending. She said, of their preference to spend money freely and enjoy luxury, "I find it very hard to counter those arguments in a way that people who believe those arguments care about and will listen to." She said, "The times I've raised this [issue], it's sort of like, 'You know what? Your kids are going to grow up with luxury whether you want them to or not. Fuck you.'"

In a few families, the women had inherited wealth but they lived mostly—or talked about living mostly—on their husbands' significant earnings, thus framing themselves and their husbands as more like earning families. Nicole, as we have seen, tended to think of herself and her family as living on her husband's earnings, and she talked about her inheritance as something she tried not to touch.

Although her family members paid for her children's school, she said that if she had to, "I think I could swing that" (using earned income). Nicole told me that she had no idea how much she and her husband spent every month but that her husband "absolutely" did know, because he was in charge of the family's finances. She also said he trusted her to spend reasonably. "He knows everything I spend money on. Everything. . . . And I have absolutely no issue with it at all. I just don't care. . . . He doesn't give me grief about anything."

But it became clear that Nicole's husband had, in fact, been monitoring her spending and that she felt disempowered in the relationship in terms of entitlement to spend his earnings. She told me she had recently inherited a chunk of additional assets: "Actually, that's been great. Because for a long time, I was like, 'Brian, I need more money in my checking account.' You know. And now I don't have to do that anymore. Which is great. And I don't have to have a huge discussion about, like, whether [her daughter] Felicity is going to take, you know, science camp for a week. And in the old days, I'd be like, 'But Brian, she's really good at science. I know it seems expensive, but, you know.' And now I'm like, 'She's doing science camp.'" She laughed. "You know? Because I feel strongly about it, and I'm not going to, like—I don't know. I mean, obviously, we still have conversations about things. But it's nice to not always be the one who's asking for a check." Like Ursula, who said her husband was "very good" about not interfering with her spending and then said she wished she had her own income so she could spend without "having to justify" her new shoes, Nicole seems torn. She wants to feel that her husband doesn't control her spending, but in fact he does, at least sometimes. Perhaps ironically, Nicole does have her own money, which she could have spent on camp or anything else. But her desire not to rely on this money for daily living prevents her from tapping into it, even in order to avoid the feeling of supplication (and apparent subordination) she describes when she has to convince Brian to agree to spend the money.

The flip side of this question of control is the question of contribution. I asked Nicole if her husband ever felt conflicted about her inherited wealth, a possibility that Ellen and others had suggested to me. She was surprised by this question, saying, "It never even crossed my mind that he would feel weird about me having family money.... Isn't it nice to have a nest egg? Like, [I'd imagine] that he would feel a comfort." But she also told me about a moment when his income had dropped unexpectedly and her work as a photographer, which varied seasonally, had brought in a little bit of income: "I said, 'Well, isn't it good, then, that I'm bringing in all this extra money that we're not used to? 'Cause, you know, it can, like, fill the gap a little bit.' And he said, 'What you bring in would barely scratch the surface of what we need to come up with every month.' And I was like, 'What an obnoxious thing to say! I was not suggesting that I could cover all of our expenses. I'm just saying, it doesn't hurt. I mean, that's four thousand dollars you didn't have. Like, come on. Throw me a bone.' Obviously, I'm taking some pride in being able to, like, provide a little bit more than I have been, because it was a job that paid more than most. He didn't throw me the bone." It seemed to me that perhaps Nicole's husband's sense of recognition was zero-sum—that is, he could not recognize her earned contribution without somehow diminishing his own—and that this might have been related to the "nest egg" her inheritance provided.

Although these control issues mirror those of single-earner couples, inheritors seem to communicate more about them with their partners than did the stay-at-home mothers I interviewed. They did not mention being secretive about spending. Although the pool is small, it also seems likely that heterosexual female inheritors are more concerned about ameliorating their husbands' discomfort than vice versa, given the great threat to masculinity that can come from not being the breadwinner.

Not every couple, however, talked about these concerns. Eliana said, "I did nothing" to get the money she inherited. "I feel like that gives me the right attitude toward it. Which is, it's not mine. You know. It flows through. It flows to my children, it flows to the things I give it to. I'm a member of the economy. I employ people, I spend things. I just feel like a conduit; it doesn't feel like mine. So, sharing with my girlfriend, for example. No problem. Why would it be my money any more than hers? It's so arbitrary." This idea of "flow" explicitly denies attachment or ownership.

Kate told me that she did not feel "dependent" in her relationship with Nadine, first of all because she had earned her living for many years and could do so again. She also felt strongly that Nadine did not try to control the money, saying, "I don't think she sees that money as hers, either. She never has." Also referring to "flow," Kate said, "It kind of flows through us, but it's not really ours. And [Nadine's] really remarkable in that way. She's never made me feel like somehow she brings the money to the relationship, so that gives her a different sort of footing or standing or anything like that." Unlike most inheritor couples, they shared all the money jointly.

The lack of conflict may have to do with being in a lesbian relationship, in two ways. First, until very recently same-sex partners had to make extensive (and expensive) legal arrangements in order to gain the benefits of marriage in terms of taxes and inheritance, as well as many other issues. Thus these couples may have had to address these questions more explicitly. Second, in same-sex relationships questions of money do not map onto larger issues of male privilege that mark heterosexual relationships. Kate reflected on the gender issues associated with this situation: "I have to say, I think if Nadine were a man, I would feel differently. I know I would." She mentioned that her childhood had been "very gendered," saying, "And so if I was married to a man and I was totally dependent on the money that he had, it would bum me out." But as Kevin and Dan's story indicates, issues of control of money do not disappear in these same-sex relationships.

TIME OVER MONEY: DUAL EARNERS

Unlike most stay-at-home mothers and wives of male inheritors, women in dual-earner couples typically had a grasp of the family finances equal to or occasionally better than that of their husbands. Willa had inherited wealth and a significant income of her own, although it was only about a fourth of her husband's (with a household income of around $2 million, they were wealthier than most in this dual-earner category). She told me, of her husband, "I mean, almost from the first day we dated, he has not had any idea what's in our checking account. He has no idea how much money we have. I pay all of our bills. I manage all of our accounts."

These couples included the least affluent in my sample, and thus we might expect that they would struggle more over money. But I did not find that to be the case, especially in any gendered way. Margaret, for example, was a nonprofit fundraiser whose husband worked in entertainment. She earned a small proportion of their total household income of just over $250,000, but she was the one watching the family's expenditures, including setting limits on what her husband could spend on his lunch.

Instead of money issues, these couples clashed over the household division of labor. Unlike families with one earner (always male) and most of the inheritor families, in which it was taken for granted that the women were responsible for the home front, men and women in straight couples who both worked at least half-time struggled over who would do this work. Like inheritors, the men in these families seemed to spend more time with and take more responsibility for the children. But they were less active in other areas. Keith and Karen agreed, for example, that Keith was "a very involved dad." Keith said, "It pains me to be at work and not be in my kids' lives." However, he said that he and his wife had "hired a cleaning lady instead of a couples therapist." This claim suggests, of course, that the conflict they had about cleaning had been significant; like many other couples before them, they chose to spend money on the labor of another woman to resolve it.[18]

In almost every case, the women took greater responsibility for their homes in general, as women in all social classes typically do.[19] In this sense these women resembled those in the other types of families I have described, with the significant difference that they also worked full-time.[20] Margaret, for example, was responsible for the mental labor of taking care of the household. She said that her husband's work travel "puts me in that gender role again, where I'm the one responsible for the children, the schedule. I mean, he doesn't know what they have for homework, and all that. So yeah, absolutely, I'm definitely performing that gender role where I take care of the home and I take care of the kids, and I have my job as well, and so on."

Monica, the real estate broker, and her self-employed husband both worked full-time, but her account illuminates her much greater household responsibility, even as it shows the effort she makes to interpret her husband's behavior as a contribution. She sometimes hired after-school babysitters for her children, but, she said, framing these tasks as her responsibility alone, "I do all my shopping, I do all my cooking." When I asked about her husband's household involvement, she said: "Actually, he does a lot. I shouldn't complain. He does laundry. He'll do grocery shopping if I give him a list. I mean, he doesn't think of things that we need, but—you know, he'll go do whatever. Since [his time is] flexible, he gets [our son] from the bus and takes him to soccer or picks him up from wherever. It's easier, because he's uptown, and I'm all the way down here. So he does so much in that way." Though she said, "I shouldn't complain," she had not been complaining to me, so it seemed as if what she was saying was one side of a dialogue ongoing in her head. But although she might have felt like complaining, like some of the stay-at-home mothers described earlier, she also gave a lot of credit to her husband for doing even minimal tasks.

Even in couples in which the women earned significantly more than the men, the women were more responsible for their households.[21] When I asked Lisa, who brought in about two-thirds of her $600,000 household income, if it was an issue that she earned more than her husband, she said, "I think so. Not that he would admit. I don't think he would." She continued, "But earlier on, it came out in indirect ways, I think. Because maybe I was giving off a sense of my work was more important. Because it was!" She laughed and pointed out that without her income they could not afford their lifestyle. "So it can't be equal. If there's a choice, and the child is sick, and I have a meeting, guess who's not staying home? I'm not staying home. So it kind of came out in those ways. In, like, the division of labor. It was surprising how much I had to push to get what I needed. To support me in my work." Ultimately they hired a housekeeper, Lisa said, "of course." And they paid to have full-time child care even when the kids were in school, "because," Lisa said, "I wasn't going to have the stress of having to think about, 'Now I have to put something in place.' Like, it just needed to be there." Even this formulation ("I have to") shows that it was Lisa's job to make sure the kids were taken care of.

Miriam's case was especially striking. She worked long hours in banking and her $1.2 million annual income was about ten times that of her husband. Yet she told me that her husband had "the priority job in the family." This meant that she was the one who dealt with emergencies, such as staying home with the kids when the nanny was sick. She initially attributed this arrangement to her greater job security and to being more able to deal with chaos; she also felt that her husband's ego was more wrapped up in his job than hers was. She went on to say, "I think there's a gendered thing that happens, where women who work also are the CEO of the house and the men just work. And even in the most progressive-minded man, that's just what happens. It's very rare in my experience to find couples who have a better balance."

Echoing Margaret, Miriam also said that in "most couples," "the woman carries the whole mental burden." Examples of things her husband did not think about included school tests and applications, classes for kids, life insurance, and homeowners' insurance. She said, "He doesn't take that on. Having said that, he does way more cooking than I ever do. He does the laundry. He tidies. He does all these things. . . . But I carry a much bigger burden." Initially she seemed to me to be justifying her husband's lack of participation, both by legitimating his job insecurity and by asserting that few other couples did it better. But by the end of our conversation it was clear that her household responsibilities (which she called "running the details") made her exhausted and angry and that they had numerous conflicts in which her husband failed to see the sacrifices she made. He asserted, for example, that his job "always came second" or quickly vetoed renovation possibilities she had spent hours coming up with. And she had almost no time for herself.

Although Miriam was the primary earner, she did not seem to try to control her husband's spending, as a high-earning man might try to control his wife's. In fact, she went out of her way to recognize his contribution.[22] For example, her husband invested her income as well as his own. She recounted, "He feels like that's a way that he can contribute. That he can make my money into more money, you know? And it's not really—I don't think of it as my money, either; I think of it as our money. But he can grow it for us, and that's a way he can add value." This is exactly the process Ellen described previously, in which men want to invest the money so they can "have their footprint" on it.

Unlike some of the high-earner husbands, Miriam also made an effort to maintain her husband's feeling of financial autonomy. She said, explaining why their accounts were not entirely joint, "He likes having a nest egg of money so that he doesn't have to be in the position of asking me for money." He had not wanted to use "his" money to solve a temporary cash flow problem with the renovation, even though she had explained that she would repay him with her end-of-year bonus. He seems to feel—like the stay-at-home or low-earning women discussed earlier—that he needs his own money to be protected. And she is willing to legitimate this need and preserve the "family myth" that he is financially independent.[23]

GENDER, CLASS, AND CONTRIBUTION

As Viviana Zelizer has written, "In organizing their economic activities, household members are actually negotiating the significance of relations among themselves."[24] As they negotiated household consumption and labor with their partners, the people I interviewed were also working out the value of their own contributions to family life. These negotiations are common across classes, of course. As previous research has shown, couples in all economic strata have to navigate these same questions of money, power, and paid and unpaid labor. This research has established that both the person who earns more money and that person's gender matter for power and labor relations in the family. Female breadwinners, for example, may actually do *more* household work once they become the primary earners, while their husbands do less, and such women do not gain greater power over financial and other kinds of decision making.[25] The idea of the female breadwinner goes counter to ideas about appropriate gender identity held by individuals and enshrined in institutions.[26] The same is true among my interviewees. The dual-earner households I studied also appear to be similar to those studied by others in that unpaid labor becomes a contentious issue.

The kinds of conflicts my interviewees describe are specifically inflected by class, however, in multiple ways. One class issue is the context of abundance in which these families operate. In the case of single-earner families, the stay-at-home mothers are doing the "labor of lifestyle" rather than (or in addition to) more basic reproductive labor such as cleaning, child care, and cooking, much of which is performed by household workers. As we saw in chapter 2, such labor is harder to construe as a contribution, especially because it largely consists of consumption, which is associated with the imagined excesses of women in general and wealthy women in particular. Some earner husbands—probably the majority in my sample—see this labor of lifestyle as a legitimate contribution to family life. But others seem to see it simply as a drain on their hard-earned assets. Furthermore, some of these highly educated women are themselves ambivalent about the contribution they are making and their own entitlement to spend money they did not earn—even when they are legally entitled to do so.

Second, the structure of and compensation associated with careers in finance and related sectors also contribute to these dynamics in a single-earner household. The extremely high incomes in these fields mean that the earner—nearly always the man—brings in enough money that it doesn't "make sense" for his wife to continue to work, which means they both spend more money on behalf of the family and accumulate less wealth for themselves.[27] The time demands of these careers further create incentives for women not to work for pay, or not to work very much, because their husbands work such long hours and often travel frequently. But the risk associated with these often unstable jobs may also make men more fearful about the future and therefore more inclined to police their wives' spending.

Third, these questions of power in relationships have mostly been addressed in terms of who *earns* the money. This chapter shows that similar gendered dynamics of control play out in relation to *inherited* wealth. Inheritors control their wealth, no matter what their gender, but female inheritors appear to be more attuned to the ways in which contributing less financially challenges their husbands' gendered desire to be providers. Legal transfer of assets to the noninheritor is the preferred method of attempting to equalize these relationships.[28]

Fourth, entitlements to recognition in the family are tied to broader questions of class entitlements. Joan Acker wrote in 1988: "The twentieth-century American emphasis on love as the basis of marriage tends to obscure the character of marriage as an integral part of the society's system of distribution." Acker was pointing out that marriage appears to be only an emotional relationship between two people, but it is in fact an economic relationship that, in many ways, regulates the distribution of resources, especially from men who work for pay to women who do not. Because money appears as "a personal issue" within marriage, "the question of how the society should provide for distribution is obscured as it is transformed into a problem of interpersonal conflict."[29]

Acker was talking about gendered access to resources, not broader class distributions. But the point applies in a new way in these families as well. Struggles over entitlements in intimate relationships take up an enormous amount of space in participants' psychic lives and daily routines, displacing awareness of their social advantages. It is hard for someone who feels as if she is fighting for equality and recognition with a partner to feel privileged relative to others in the world. These struggles also engender a sense of material scarcity—when expenditures and entitlements are contested, it is difficult to recognize abundance. As I noted at the beginning of the chapter, it was hard even for me to hold onto an awareness of the privilege of Stephanie and Alexis as I saw them grappling with these issues.

Finally, struggles over spending, which are also struggles over labor and power, are tied to questions of worth—the worth of the person as well as the object. These affluent New Yorkers look to their partners to confirm their self-conceptions as legitimately privileged hard workers and reasonable consumers. Feeling legitimately entitled is most difficult for the stay-at-home mothers without independent wealth, not only because they have no income but also because—due to their class position—their labor consists largely of consumption rather than traditional mothering work, such as cleaning, child care, and cooking. When their husbands reflect images of their labor and consumption as reasonable, they confirm their wives' entitlement. When they don't, conflict ensues. Similar dynamics obtain in other types of couples as well, though when both partners work for pay they can draw more easily on earning as a source of merit.

Overall, regardless of the type of couple, because men's labor is paid more often and more highly and women are more likely to do the less-valued household labor, it is harder for women to be legitimately entitled. Chapter 6 explores questions of legitimate entitlement in another family realm: the raising of children.

6

PARENTING
PRIVILEGE

CONSTRAINT, EXPOSURE,
AND ENTITLEMENT

Lucy was the stay-at-home wife of a global business entrepreneur, with assets in the tens of millions. She and I talked sitting at the dining table in the large, open kitchen/dining room/living room area of her apartment, the renovation of which had combined three smaller apartments. For the first hour of the interview, until her nanny came to entertain them, her three small children played nearby. Every once in a while the youngest, a 2-year-old boy, toddled in for a snack or to climb onto Lucy's lap for a cuddle. The children also showed up frequently in our conversation, especially as Lucy described her fears about how to raise them. She said, "I just don't want them growing up with a sense of entitlement. You know, everybody's got entitlement concerns. And I still really struggle with that. Creating a sense of, kind of, hunger and drive. . . . When you get everything you want, you don't have to work for it, you don't appreciate it." There was a "level of affluence" at her children's private school that, she said, "really troubles me." She had considered moving them into public school. And she regretted having set up a trust fund for them because, she explained, "I don't think that anything good ever comes out of a trust. It can only be incendiary in somebody's life." She was relieved that the trust would mature only when her children were much older, so they would have to earn money before they inherited it.

Actually meeting interviewees' children was unusual for me during this project. I usually just saw traces of them, such as drawings on the fridge or toys in a corner. But, like Lucy's, many parents' narratives were brightly threaded with anxieties about the kind of people their children would turn out to be. Also like Lucy's, their anxieties turned particularly on the threat of "entitlement," a concept they brought up frequently, usually unprompted. In general, as we have seen, to be "entitled" is to believe (or behave as if one believes) that one should receive certain benefits simply by virtue of who one is.[1] Implicitly, these parents grouped a number of different fears under the umbrella of entitlement. They worried that their children would lack a work ethic and would expect others to do everything for them, that they would think they could have everything they wanted, that they would be covetous and materialistic, that they would not be aware of their advantages relative to others, and that they would treat other people disrespectfully. Instead, these parents wanted their kids to grow up to be "good people": hard workers, with prudent consumption desires and practices who respected others, were aware and appreciative of their advantages, and gave back. Although such ideals are common to parents across social classes, these privileged parents are specifically concerned with how their children can be best prepared to occupy their social position, as we will see.

In order to cultivate these characteristics, these parents used two strategies: *constraint* and *exposure*. First, they talked about limiting children's behavior and their consumption of material goods, experiences, and labor. Placing boundaries on kids' entitlement to consume would, parents hoped, also constrain their sense of entitlement more broadly. And requiring labor of them would instill a strong work ethic and a sense of self-sufficiency. Second, these parents tried to *expose* their children to class difference, in both imaginary and concrete ways, in order to help them understand their advantaged social location and get a sense of what a "normal" life is. These ideals had instrumental aspects—that is, parents imagined that having a solid work ethic and being comfortable with people different from themselves would help their children succeed in a risky world.[2] But they also cared about the moral integrity of their children, both for its own sake and because it reflected on the parents themselves as moral actors.[3] As Eliana put it, "Another moral warrant" for her was that "I'm raising people with good values."

However, creating limits stood in tension with a more conventional form of cultivation: giving children more. As previous research would predict, elite parents wanted their kids to have access to a vast array of experiences and opportunities, receive all the attention they might need, and be able to develop any interests and skills they might desire. So they struggled with the idea of limiting these and thus the children's "boundless potential."[4] Furthermore, as we have seen, the parents themselves were conflicted about how much is enough—for their children as well as for themselves. It was also a challenge to define exactly what was "normal," and for whom. They wanted their kids to *be* "normal," meaning similar to others with less; but they also wanted them to be aware that they were *not* normal and appreciate their advantages.

I came to see that the kind of entitlement parents wanted to avoid was behavioral and emotional, not material. As long as they don't *act* or *feel* entitled, children remain legitimately entitled to resources. Their advantages remain essentially the same. Ultimately, the parents are not challenging their children's advantage but, instead, teaching them how to occupy their advantaged position appropriately. They inculcate an identity, or a *habitus*, as Pierre Bourdieu called it, of legitimate privilege. This legitimately entitled self faces the contradiction we have seen before: between *erasing* class difference through treating everyone the same and *recognizing* this difference through "awareness" of privilege.

DISCIPLINING THE SELF: BEHAVIOR AND CONSUMPTION

One central parental concern had to do with how their children acted vis-à-vis others. They wanted to teach their kids to take other people into account and to be generous in the world more broadly.[5]

Paul told me, "I think one thing [his wife] and I are, very, very, very—it's very important for us, is that our kids are, at a minimum, respectful to people. They're nice. That's number one." Nadine said, "I don't want my kids to be entitled or snobby or spoiled in any way. I come down pretty hard on them about—I mean, the main thing is, like, 'You're going to be, like, a good fucking person, you know? Like, you're going to say please and thank you, and you're going to be, like, kind towards other people. And you're going to be responsible for yourself and make good choices.'" Sara planned to be "intentional" about "making sure that my kids understand that there's an obligation to give back."

Although these parents often expressed their concerns as *behavioral* imperatives such as saying please and thank you, they conceptualized such behaviors as signs of a deeply rooted nonentitled *disposition*, a fundamental understanding of self and other. Eliana described this disposition succinctly. When she said she did not want her children to be "entitled," I asked what that meant. She responded, "To take privilege for granted. To think it has something to do with you." She laughed. "Instead of just luck. I think one of the things that really concerns me is the many different faces of supremacy. And so, anything like that. If you think you've got anything on anybody else. Like, lack of respect. And not just respect, but full consideration. That all humans are as valuable as each other."

Asked what she wanted for her kids, Monica talked about the kind of people she wanted them to become rather than about their professional paths or other achievements, and she linked behavior to a generous disposition. She said, "To think about other people when they make their decisions. Even now, with their friends. Their tone of voice when they speak to people. Just be conscious of it. It's not that you're always going to do the right thing. But, just catch yourself. And thank people, or—you know, that kind of thing." She continued, "You can't just exist. You have to give. However that is. Emotionally, your time. It's not a financial gift. It's more of yourself."

One very significant aspect of shaping children's dispositions, of course, is shaping their consumer desires and entitlements.[6] Helen said, "I think we all worry. My husband and I worry about our kids, like, falling into this kind of thought that, like, you can just order everything online, and it all comes. And, you know, money feels a little bit like it grows on trees kind of thing." Ursula said, "You have kids that talk about they never fly, you know, commercial planes or they've never flown coach. I think it's crazy. . . . We [she and her husband] really know the value of what we have and understand how fleeting some of this can be and how important it is to not, you know, feel like you have to keep up with the Joneses, because you just—there's no stopping. But for young people whose minds are not fully mature, it's work."

Nearly all my interviewees portrayed themselves as setting limits on their children's consumption as a way of forestalling an excessive sense of entitlement.[7] Olivia, for example, did not want her children to become "trustafarians." Asked how to prevent that, she said, "I mean, I think the biggest thing is, they just don't get everything that they want." Chaz said, "I think by just living in New York, it's easy to be overcome with too many luxuries. And you've got to make sure that they don't get everything they want at this particular moment. Make sure that kids understand that they have to have fun, but nothing is to be given. You've got to earn things." Some parents with older children used an allowance to help them learn limits. Eliana not only gave her children an allowance but required them to "spend some, save some, give some."

Not surprisingly, these parents also used consumption in order to enforce appropriate behavior. Zoe described herself as having strict limits. She said, of her children, "I don't buy them random things for no reason. We definitely wait for birthdays. Or, even an ice cream. Like, [her daughter] has to earn it. Yesterday we promised her an ice cream, but then she behaved horribly. And I said, 'Then I'm sorry, ice cream is for girls that behave. And that's not you today. Maybe tomorrow.'" As Zoe's comment indicates, consumption not only depends on appropriate behavior but also is framed as a birthday "treat."

Like Lucy, many parents were concerned with the possibility that their children would not want to work. Scott said, "That's one of the things I think about and talk about a lot. Is, like, how do you instill in your kid, in your wealthy kid, the desire to work? You know, just the satisfaction that comes from, like, 'Paycheck. Yes. I did it again.' It's a very deep-seated feeling. I don't know where it comes from. And I'm terrified that my kids aren't going to have it."

These concerns with consumption, reciprocity, and the work ethic came together in the question of how much of other people's labor children had the right to consume. Olivia said, referring to both politeness and labor, "The manners thing, I think is really important. And entitlement. Like, you shouldn't feel entitled to leave your stuff at the table, or not clean up after yourself. And you know, the worst thing is when you say [of the family's assistant], 'Look, Nancy's going to [do it].' No, no, no. I will make it so that Nancy doesn't come. You know, you will take care of this." Danielle told me, of her two young children, "I mean, they live in an incredibly entitled environment. So yeah. Squash it down, every time I see any, I go squash." She laughed. I asked, "When do you see it? How do you do that?" She responded, "They say, 'Get me a —.' I say, 'You have legs. Your legs ain't broke, you get that. You put that away. You pick it up.'"

This emphasis on self-sufficiency and work also meant *requiring* labor of children in the form of chores. Asking me if I had read a recent *New Yorker* article that described a 6-year-old child in the Peruvian Amazon who cleaned, fished, and cooked,[8] Lucy said, "That article changed my life. I'm not kidding you. I was like, 'My six-year-old doesn't know how to do anything.' So the next day, I was like, 'You are doing your own laundry. Here's the liquid detergent. Have at it.'" She laughed. "And now he does. He does his own laundry." She and her husband had also instituted a system of points their son had to earn for making an effort in areas where "he feels he needs to improve" (e.g., participating more in school), which he could redeem for activities of his choosing, such as art classes—activities he had gotten for "free" when he was younger.[9]

Frances had been raised upper-middle-class and attended private school and an Ivy League college, but her family's current lifestyle was far beyond what she had grown up with. (She told me, "We were well off, but not to the extent that my nuclear family is now. It's pretty different.") As her own father had, Frances enforced expectations for her kids through their allowance. She said,

> Yes, my kids definitely have an allowance. And it's tied to their chores. Which is something that I carry over from my own child-hood, which I really value. It's a huge pain in the ass for me. But I fine them when they don't do their chores. . . . Everything has a value. It's like, "If you don't turn off your lights, if you don't make your bed, if your clothes aren't in the hamper," those are fines. "If you don't set the table, if you don't clear the table, if you don't put your sports bag away," those are all fines. . . . And every time I describe to friends what I do, they think I'm a nut job. That I'm crazy to spend the time I'm spending. But that's how I grew up, and it is a huge pain, but I'm hoping that it pays off, and that they appreciate—that they get something from it later in life (laughs). I don't know.

Like Lucy's points scheme, the system Frances has created consti-tutes constraints on her children's entitlements. Though the system creates work for her, she hopes it will "pay off" for them, although she cannot exactly articulate how.

As this example indicates, respondents who were raised with less money than they have now often referred to their own upbringings in talking about their children. Many who had grown up facing ma-terial limits now imposed symbolic ones on their kids. Miriam in-sisted that her two daughters share a room, a decision she attributed explicitly to her own upbringing and her discomfort with her own privileged financial position, as well as to her desire for her daughters to have "normal values":

> I just wanted them to share a room. I always shared a room grow-ing up, and I have weird feelings in general about—like, I didn't grow up with any money, and I didn't set out to make money, but I do make a lot of money. And it's a weird thing. And I'm

like, what does it mean for my girls to grow up with money? What does it mean for them and their values, and how do I instill normal values in them? So I was like, they need to share a room. . . . I think I just feel like [sharing a room] will show them that they're not the only person in the world. That, you know, they can't have everything they want. Maybe they feel like they should have their own room 'cause their friends have their own room. Well, too bad.

Miriam also criticized parents who said they "had to" give their kids separate rooms because they would fight otherwise. "I'm like, you don't *have to* do anything. You know? We didn't have the option when I was growing up, and so we fought and we had to share a room."

Like Miriam, other respondents drew boundaries between themselves and other parents who seemed to indulge their kids. Willa said she had known other kids growing up whose rooms had been built to be the maid's room (as is the case in many prewar buildings in New York). But now, she said, "people don't want to put their child in a maid's room. Talk about entitled. Because it's small, it's in the back, it's next to the kitchen." Zoe deprecated "mothers cooking three different meals, depending on what their kids want." She said that she, in contrast, would send her daughter to bed hungry "if she doesn't want what I cooked for dinner. . . . I've put her to sleep many times without eating dinner. I'm not afraid to do that."

Yet, as we saw in chapter 3, parents also framed children's needs as especially legitimate. Therefore, despite their commitment to limits *in general*, these parents were torn about what *specific* limits were appropriate, especially when these constraints stood in tension with the children's happiness, comfort, or sense of belonging, as well as their enrichment. As Olivia said, using the example of refusing to buy an iPhone for her children, "I think that's actually one of the biggest challenges, you know, in terms of spending money and making decisions, like, when do you say, 'All right. No. We can, but we won't. And here's why.'"

Frances had had no problem refusing to buy her teenage daughter a $400 ski jacket, which seemed too extreme. But she struggled to set limits when they might affect her daughter's social life. She told me, of her daughter's obsession with brand names:

> I definitely entered that [phase] with her, where—you know, if it doesn't say Ugg on the boot, it's not actually a boot. [She laughs.] If it doesn't say Hunter, it's not really a rain boot. And that drives me crazy. Because my parents never bought me any brand-name anything. I'm weak on that score, though. Because she's a good girl. She's a nice girl. She works hard. And I cave. Because it's easier to buy the Hunter boots than it is to say, just on principle, "You're gonna be the one girl in [her school] who wears the rubber boots from K-Mart, because that's how I grew up." And I'm sure I'm doing her a disservice by letting her have all the brand names. But again, it's one of those things where you pick your battles. . . . I tried very briefly, when she was in fifth grade or so, to buy the non-brand-name stuff. And then she didn't have a lot of friends, and she got all these pimples, and I just [felt] like, "You know what? Okay. You can have the Ugg boots, as long as you appreciate that you got them for your birthday!"

Frances is trying to establish a sense of constraint that echoes the limits she grew up with, but she does not want to make her daughter suffer in her social milieu by not fitting in.[10] She thus resigns herself to buying the boots, though she wants her daughter to "appreciate" that they are *special*, a birthday treat. This kind of consumption, she hopes, will not be taken for granted. It is also notable that she describes her daughter as a "good girl," "a nice girl," who "works hard." Because her daughter does not act *behaviorally* "entitled," she becomes *materially* entitled to the boots.

In this conversation, both because I remembered my own anxiety about not having the "right" clothes at that age and because I wanted to be sympathetic, I said I could see her daughter's point of view. Realizing that we were the same age, Frances and I ended up reminiscing about what it was like to be teenagers and be denied the brand-name items that were fashionable (for us, Tretorn sneakers, all the rage in the mid-1980s). In a telephone conversation a few days after the interview, in which I was following up on a couple of questions, Frances mentioned without prompting that that part of our conversation had "crossed my mind a dozen times." Saying, "This is so messed up," she admitted feeling that since a "well-educated, hard-working" person (i.e., me) had sympathized with her daughter's position, she felt better about buying the name-brand clothing rather than getting it at Target. I had not expected that my opinion would loom so large in Frances's mind. Her comment signaled to me that she was genuinely worried about the situation and looking for reassurance—from a particular kind of source. Because I was coming from a position opposite to the one her daughter was in—that is, I had been denied these items—she could have read me as evidence that if she wanted her daughter to become "well-educated and hard-working" she would refuse her child's requests. In fact, she had said that maybe she herself was a better person for not having been given these goods. But instead somehow she was able to read my *sympathy* for her daughter as the green light to stop worrying about these purchases because it legitimated the daughter's psychological need.

Protecting kids from thinking or worrying about money—itself another form of privilege—was a priority among these parents and demonstrated another dimension of their concern for their kids' psychological well-being. Several told me they did not want to talk about money with their young children. Donovan, an inheritor and earner of wealth of over $10 million, said of money that he had tried to give his kids "the gift of allowing them to ignore it." But again, this approach sometimes conflicted with the notion of setting limits. Karen had been "raised with a money problem" and struggled to decide how to restrict her daughter's spending after school at Starbucks. She said, "I mean, I definitely don't want her to feel worried about money. But I also want her to feel like there's some real limits to what she can spend." How to impose the "limits" without also imposing the "worry" was the dilemma.[11]

STRATEGIES OF EXPOSURE: LOCATING THE SELF

Many parents I interviewed also used strategies of exposure as a way of mitigating entitlement. They wanted their children to be "aware" of and "appreciate" their privileged stance relative to others and to inculcate a sense of what kind of consumption was "normal" in the world. Ursula, for example, said, "I do sometimes worry the kids feel everybody has a house in the Hamptons [as she did]. That this is normal. And it's not. So we try to teach them that. But I don't know if it's getting through." Questions about exposure emerged in relation to consumption decisions and the social environments kids were in, especially schools, as well as the possibility of working for pay.

Consumption and What Is "Normal"

My respondents saw consumption decisions and the constraints discussed earlier as important for how kids would locate themselves in relation to the rest of the world. They tried to model appropriate consumption for their children, often using the word "normal." Gary and his family were invited to a wedding in India that he and his wife "would have loved to go to." But they did not attend, in part because the wedding fell just a few weeks after another international family trip but also because it felt "over the top." Gary said, "it was this feeling that, what's the message we're imparting to our kids?" Parents struggled frequently over these decisions, which, like Gary's dilemma, often clustered around leisure travel.

One very wealthy mother said her biggest disagreements with her husband were about spending money. When I asked for an example, she first reiterated how confidential our conversation was. She then recounted:

Like, he would fly privately all the time. And I want our kids to not get too used to that. Every once in a while. But, I don't know. I value that I went to public school, and I slept in many motels, and I drove long distances in cars. And the way I grew up is still much more affluent than the way most—but I feel like I have somewhat of an understanding. I think it's important to understand the way everyone else lives. That doesn't sound right, but . . . but . . . so, I just don't want our kids to go to college and never have cleaned a toilet. And never have slept in a motel instead of a hotel. And then to appreciate that there are some kids that don't even ever sleep in a motel. I mean, so I just want our kids to have—you know, a reality check every once in a while.

This mother resists her husband's desire to live lavishly in order to instill an understanding of how "everyone else lives" in her kids. In talking about his clients' conflicts around money, Robert, a real estate broker, spoke approvingly of this kind of modeling. He said, "I have some healthy clients. I have one client—very rich people. She said, like, when they fly with the kids . . . they fly coach. When the husband flies by himself, he flies first class. They're constantly struggling to set an example for their children that, 'just because we have, not everybody else has.' They're trying not to turn their kids into assholes."

Many parents encouraged their children to interpret such experiences as "special." Olivia said her family flew business class "a lot." She told her kids, "'It's a privilege that you get to do this. And it's great that we can do this as a family. But I expect behavior and good manners.' And they [behave]. There's no wild acting out. And it's a big treat." Olivia asks her children to experience this travel as both a "privilege" and a "treat"—typically defined by being exceptional—even though it is something they do often. Furthermore, she is teaching them that high-end consumption is acceptable as long as it is inhabited appropriately in a behavioral sense.

Similarly, Danielle emphasized to her kids that they had experiences many people could not afford. She said, "I've told them, the kind of [private] education they're getting, I'm saying, you know, 'That's a valuable thing. Not everybody gets to do that. Appreciate it. Appreciate it, because it's kind of a special thing.' Or, you know, 'Not everybody gets to have a fun summer away, like, enjoy that. Like, understand that's a special thing.'" To be *aware* of the specialness of these experiences and to *appreciate* them is to avoid entitlement, as we also saw in the case of Frances's daughter and the name-brand boots.

These practices and discourses illuminate two meanings of *normal*. The explicit meaning, which parents invoked to try to help their kids situate themselves in relation to others, is what most people have—that is, people who are less advantaged than they are. But the normal that kids actually experience, in the reality of their daily lives, is the more advantaged form. Rather than acknowledge this tension, parents represented certain goods or experiences that were actually normal for their children as a "treat" and hoped the children would experience them as such. This kind of consumption is *not* special for their children. But these parents want them to see that it *is* special relative to the rest of the world.

Not surprisingly, then, these parents sometimes got tangled up in discourse around this question of "normal" consumption. For example, Allison, the stay-at-home mother with a household income of $3 million, gave a somewhat disjointed account of how she wanted her middle-school-aged kids to understand the two vacations her family takes each year. She said, "Some way or another, we have to instill in the kids that we're doing this, but it's not extravagant. So you try to not make it too extravagant." I asked, "And why do you want to instill that in the kids?" She replied,

> Because, you know, I think it's just a value system. Like, it's not—
> you know, they've done nothing to—you know, deserve to have
> these, like, two vacations. You know. Although they work really
> hard. Not—I wouldn't say—nobody deserves two vacations. It's
> extravagant. It's extravagant. It's not about deserving it. I don't
> deserve it. It's extravagant. I just want them to know, this isn't the
> norm. You don't want your kids to think that—take these kinds
> of things for granted. You know . . . [to know that] most people
> don't live this way. And that this is not the norm, and that you
> should feel this is—this is special, and this is a treat.

Allison's reasoning illuminates her ambivalence about her own privilege as well as that of her children. She jumbles multiple discourses, first suggesting that the legitimacy of entitlement rests on hard work, then indicating that legitimate entitlement is impossible ("nobody deserves it"), and then alluding to appreciation as the legitimate mode of experience. Allison and her husband addressed this problem *practically* by flying in first class while the children sat in coach as a way of controlling the kids' access to privileges they had not yet "earned."[12] But they *were* entitled to the vacation itself.

Environments and Social Others

In thinking about their children's self-location, parents were also concerned about the social others to whom their kids were exposed. They therefore thought carefully about the environments their children spent time in. Many parents worried about their children's exposure to those with *more*, fearing a kind of contamination from other kids and families about what constitutes reasonable consumption. As we have seen, Sara was at a transitional moment with her husband, trying to decide whether they would stay in the city. In speaking of the challenges of raising wealthy children, she said:

> I mean, that is a huge reason why we're like, "Maybe we want to leave New York." Because we're still kind of like, even if we could afford the fancy apartment, we don't want our kid to think that that's—you know, to be surrounded by everyone else with fancy apartments. I don't know. A colleague of [her husband's] went on vacation with his family. You know, like, a nice vacation. They went skiing for a week, stayed somewhere super nice. He asked the son, who was, like, eight at the time, "What'd you think?" And the son was like, "It was great, but next time we fly private like everyone else." . . . He spent, like, you know, ten grand on this vacation, with, like, ski lodge—you know, a ton of money. What do you do? He's like, how do you insulate kids, you know? I don't know what you do.

Speaking of her children's summer camp, one stay-at-home mother said,

> I worry because my kids are at camp, sleep-away camp in Maine. And the whole idea to send them is for them to learn independence and a little bit of social acceptance and, you know, how to fend for themselves and the whole thing. And my daughter's going to a place where there's no electricity, and we're sitting here in the air conditioning, and she has really hot days and really cold days and learns to live with it. Which I think is all a good thing. But then you have the kids that show up in their private plane . . . It's just warped.

This mother is trying to engineer a sense of deprivation for her daughter to promote her learning how to be independent, but because she is doing this in an environment of wealthy people, the child is still exposed to people with more. As I discuss later, this concern permeated decisions about schooling as well.

Although parents did *not* usually want their children to be exposed to those with more, they *did* want them to be exposed to those with less. Using an especially compelling phrase, progressive inheritor Eliana said she wanted her children to have "fluency outside the bubble," by which she meant an exposure to and understanding of the lives of people with less. Yet it was not always clear to me which social others Eliana and my other respondents were invoking and what kind of contact they desired. Some parents wanted to instill a sense of awareness of and obligation to *poor* people, often in a relatively abstract sense, in a way that was reminiscent of noblesse oblige. Others seemed more interested in their kids' having ongoing relationships with people who were "normal"—that is, not poor, but not as privileged as they were.

Some parents recounted trying to have conversations with their kids about poor people, such as impoverished kids in Haiti or the residents of the homeless shelter around the corner. A few parents told me they required their kids to give away one or two birthday gifts or to participate in charitable enterprises such as a swim-a-thon. Paul said, of his kids, "Always for their birthday we ask them to pick one present and donate it to kids who are less fortunate, because they understand not everyone gets what they get."

As Paul's comment shows, these practices also served to remind children of those with less (though such people were not actually visible to the children), thus cultivating awareness and appreciation, as well as a feeling of obligation to give back. Paul said, "I don't think I feel entitled, but our generation as a whole is, relative to our parents and grandparents. And I try to continuously—even though my kids are spoiled fucking brats—they are. I mean, they get everything they want. But I try from an educational perspective to continue to just make sure it's ingrained in their minds over and over again—whether they hear it or not, at some point they'll get it—[this lesson about] what they have versus what other kids have." What is fascinating here is the distinction Paul makes between actually receiving "everything they want" and having it "ingrained in their minds" that they have more than others. Here again we see the tension between the child's lived experience of what is "normal" and the parent's desire that he understand it as "not normal."

A few parents saw community service or volunteer work as a way to cultivate understanding of others in their children. Alice, for example, lamented that her pre-teen son had not yet done volunteer work. When I asked her why that mattered, she said, "I think it's a big element of being a good person, you know. Being a good person. And when you, you know, have all these things, if you don't, you know, understand the value of volunteerism, and empathy, and all of those things—I think it's a key element." Susannah, another stay-at-home mother, struggled with how best to expose her children to the lives of others through charity work. She said, of her three kids (all under seven):

> They need to know about diversity in the world and have experiences outside of their school and outside of their home, and know that not everybody—you know, we—we—[she sighs]. I

don't think this has set in with my kids yet. But, you know, I do a lot of charity work. I take them to food pantries. We make bags to give to kids less fortunate. But it's been very hard for me to show them in person what it means to be a kid who's less fortunate. You can't go to the hospitals. I can't really take them to a homeless shelter. There's not a lot of children [there]. The only place that I think that I can take them is an elderly home.

Monica said she felt a responsibility to those with less: "We help out. We go to public schools around the city that are—you know, there's this thing where you go and you help them paint it, so it looks better and it doesn't look like a dungeon. My kids should know what the other places look like, down in the outer boroughs, where other kids have to go to school. Be thankful for what they have. Sure. We do that kind of stuff. Not to prove that we're better, but just to take part in a community. And my son does community service."

Monica's remarks highlight a tension present throughout these parents' accounts: that between "being part of a community" and making clear that these poorer children are completely other ("my kids should know what the other places look like") and exist primarily to help her kids in order to "be thankful for what they have." Indeed, these accounts demonstrate that, as Rubén Gaztambide-Fernández and Adam Howard put it, a "conception of the wealthy as moral and deserving . . . requires suffering others (i.e., 'the people') as a way to enact 'good citizenship.'"[13] Furthermore, there is a class assumption here that these parents' children should have access to the lives of others even when they would not want those others to have access to their own lives.[14]

Some parents were concerned about a different kind of exposure: creating meaningful everyday networks for their children that included socioeconomic diversity. As Danielle put it, "I think there's something instructional about growing up in a community that is economically mixed." A few mentioned class diversity in their own families as one avenue of exposure to difference. But many had to engineer this kind of immersion. Kate told me, "Just the other day,

Nadine and I were thinking we have got to figure out a way, once the kids are a little older, to really expose them to the way most people live. The way most people live. And not in a, you know—in a concrete way." Kate's allusion to a "concrete way" implies a critique of an artificial or superficial approach. Scott and Olivia had chosen a church that was diverse in terms of race, ethnicity, income, and sexual orientation as a way to include their kids in a different kind of "community" because they had "a fairly homogenous day-to-day experience," as Olivia put it.

One stay-at-home mother had lived with her family in a mixed-income rental building while their home was being renovated. She encouraged her son to keep in touch with the friends he had made there, who went to public school. She said:

> I just feel like it's a community that's grounded. . . . It's not this new world of, you know, private school in Manhattan. Almost all the kids that live there go to [the local public school]. My son has a lot of friends who go [there]. And you know, private school education in Manhattan is kind of a crazy thing. . . . And I feel like I want to keep our feet in something that's a little more normal. . . . I like the idea that [her kids] have this community, where, you know, you have three kids living in a one-bedroom apartment. There's a lot of that. You know? You know, two of my son's best friends, they live in a one-bedroom apartment with their parents.

This mother tried to keep her son "normal" by virtue of his inter-action with people who have fewer resources. At the same time, having chosen to place him in private school (primarily because of smaller class sizes, she said), she preserved his class advantages over those same people. These attempts to construct meaningful community with people who have less again highlight the tension mentioned earlier in the concept of "normal": between a desire that a child *be* more normal and a desire that the child know what normal is (and know that he is advantaged relative to it).

This pattern of exposure was less clear among African American and mixed-race parents. My interviewees, like many wealthier African Americans, had more class diversity in their families than many of the white respondents.[15] But their children spent time primarily in majority-white environments (mainly private schools). Rather than class exposure, then, they talked more about wanting to create ties to other African American children and families in the middle class and above. A couple of these parents had also left Harlem after living there for years. One mother told me, after recounting an incident between her daughter and a mentally ill man, "You don't want them to be afraid of other people of color." She had moved to a largely white suburb; now, she said, "What's important for us is to figure out a way that we can expose our children to other people of color." One way to resolve this challenge was to join Jack and Jill, a cultural and social organization composed of relatively affluent black families, to which several people I interviewed belonged.[16]

Talking about those with less or interacting with them sometimes meant talking explicitly about money, which some of these parents were loath to do. In fact, many parents clearly tried to inculcate the norm of *not* talking about money. Danielle told me, "If [her daughter] says, 'So, what did our house cost?' I'm like, 'That's my business, not yours. And you know, we don't talk about that. And there's a time in your life where you can have that information, but now is not that time.' And she says, 'Why not?' It's like, 'Because people talk about that, and it's tacky.' And I don't know if that's the right thing to do. And when she says, 'How much money do we have?' I say, 'We have sufficient money for what we need.'" Speaking of flying privately, Olivia said, "We've had to have conversations with the kids about it. And just basically say, 'This was really great. This is not something that you talk about. Because this is not an experience that most people you know will have.' And it's something that you kind of enjoy privately." In this sense they reproduce for their children the common prohibition against talking about money and class; the "awareness" they cultivate is silent.

A final kind of exposure, which overlaps but is not congruent with exposures to class and racial-ethnic others, is experience of cultural difference more broadly. My interviewees often talked about travel, especially outside the United States, as providing this type of exposure. Julia, a stay-at-home mother, said of her children:

> I want them to see the world as a big place that everybody, we all share in. [As opposed to] being kind of small-minded and just seeing your thing as the only important thing that's going on, whatever that may be. I want to travel with them a lot so that they see that people live in different ways. That you don't have to have a big house and have TVs and all that stuff to be happy. You can be just as happy living in a little grass hut in the Serengeti or whatever. You know? I don't know. I just feel like we're just surrounded by so much stuff. Which I love. I love all this stuff that we have. But sometimes that's not what's important.

Julia's statement represents exposure to class difference as a *subset* of exposure to cultural difference more broadly. It fits into the project of self-location, an awareness that "your thing" is not the only thing that matters. But travel also provides the lesson that material goods are not always "what's important." Julia expresses a dilemma common to most parents I interviewed: the desire to keep the "stuff" but without kids' thinking it is "what's important." Again, the fantasy here is that kids can have material and experiential comforts and at the same time understand that it is possible (for other people, at least) to live without them.

These parents hope exposure to those with less will discipline the affective selves of their children into appreciation and awareness. At the same time, exposure connotes an expansion of a child's experience in ways that might be valuable in reproducing advantage later. Both parents of color and white parents thought this kind of exposure not only instilled good values but also could cultivate certain skills necessary in an increasingly diverse world. Lisa, for example, thought exposure to diversity for her kids was important "because most of the world is diverse. And you have to be able to relate to people." Zoe similarly cared about traveling internationally with her children because she wanted them "to be worldly. And to see how other people live." She later mentioned what seemed to be a more instrumental motive: "The world's becoming increasingly diverse, and I think it's important for the kids to be exposed to that." Thus, as Diane Reay and her colleagues have pointed out, exposure to otherness serves *both* moral and instrumental purposes.[17] The idea of instilling particular values in kids goes hand in hand with fostering capacities for dealing with difference. These become a form of cultural capital, as Eliana's notion of "fluency outside the bubble" suggests.[18]

School Choice

These questions of exposure and advantage came to the forefront in talking about children's central social environment: school. In New York, as in many other cities, public schools are much more likely than private ones to provide the exposure to difference that many parents said they wanted. But, as noted earlier, most parents I talked with ultimately enrolled their children in private schools. Yet they struggled over these decisions, in two ways: choosing public versus private, and, once they had chosen private, deciding which private school was the best fit for their children.

Parents who chose or seriously considered public school expressed concern that private school would, in Betsy's words, "warp their sense of what's normal." They worried that their children would be exposed to too much "entitlement" in private school, and they liked the idea of the diverse groups of people that their kids would be exposed to in public school. Some of them had political commitments to public school. Yet they were drawn to the private schools because of smaller class sizes and more individualized attention, the possibility of a better education, including classes in the arts, and the perceived link to college admission.

When I interviewed Justin, the finance entrepreneur, whose parents had been social workers, he and his wife were trying to decide whether to send their children to private school. On the one hand, he was concerned that they get into good colleges, which he thought was more likely if they attended private school. He also wanted strong sports and arts programs. On the other hand, coming from a middle-class background (though lacking a political commitment to public school), he was afraid of the effects that a private-school environment would have on his kids. He said, "I want the kids to be normal. I don't want them to just be coddled, and be at a country club. . . . I think they come out [of private school] being really sheltered. Not really exposed to—I don't know. Economic hardship, or you think everyone lives in these huge houses, and just thinking that's the world." He explicitly associates private school with an environment of "coddling," contrasting it to a public-school environment that will produce "normal" kids. His fear that in private school his children will end up "thinking that's the world" implies that private school will lead to a failure of self-location (like that of the child Sara described earlier, who wanted to travel in a private plane "like everybody else").[19]

Similarly, Kevin told me that he liked the idea of keeping his son in public school. He wanted the son not to live in an "elitist" "narrow world," by which he meant one in which "you only know a certain kind of people. Who are all complaining about their designers and their nannies." Donovan's children had attended a suburban magnet school. He told me, "I love the fact that not only have my kids gone to public school, but they've gone to a public school that's not, in fact, in an affluent community. So they've been exposed to a much broader spectrum of kids than they would've even within our own public school system [in the suburb where they lived], and certainly compared to private schools." Miranda said of one private school she was thinking about, "My fear is that the kids might seem a little more entitled . . . and there's no, like, community service part of the school at all."

Despite their conflicts,[20] most of these parents still sent their children to private school, especially after elementary school, choosing expansion of opportunities and individual selfhood over exposure to a diversity of social others. Nicholas told me, "I never would have thought that I was going to send my kids to private school when I was [younger]. Just like, 'No way.'" But, he continued, "It's so much easier when you're 20 years old and indignant to take a stance than [later], when you're like, 'Oh, sure, it's my child. Let's make him a guinea pig.' Like, 'Let's not give him what we can afford to give him,' I guess." One African American mother had been involved in founding a charter school in her neighborhood, but after one year she had placed her own children in private school because her husband did not want them to be an "experiment." Even Kevin told me at the end of our interview that he was thinking about moving his son to private school, despite his concerns about the "narrow world" there, because the child seemed less happy in his public-school classroom than he had been previously. Kevin said, "I think I've allowed to enter my imagination more than I ever would have before the possibility of, well, maybe there is a school that he would be happier at."

Many of these parents identify something specific in their children that seems to *require* choosing private education. Most often this is a fear that the children will be bored in public school. Linda told me, of her decision to send her son to private school, that it "seemed really like the right place for him." When I asked why, she responded, "Just because he's like this kind of weird dude. I mean, he taught himself how to read when he was really young, and he loves learning and he wanted to learn. . . . [In the public school] he would just be in the corner bored out of his mind, I think." Beatrice described her son as "a super-duper high-energy kid who teaches himself a lot of stuff. He doesn't actually need a teacher to teach him very much. And when he's not learning stuff he's running all over the place and jumping on things, and I can just see the situation where he's bored and he's, like, crawling the walls. It's that combination of being very smart and very active that I think is going to be real trouble in a situation of 28 to 1 [the student-teacher ratio in the local public school]."

It is not private school for its own sake but rather the brilliance or restlessness or some other personality trait of a child that *forces* these parents to choose private school. This process, which Allison Pugh calls "the luxury of difference," "perform[s] a certain magic for upper-income parents by producing urgent needs."[21] The close-to-home need of the child takes priority over the more abstract goal of supporting the public school system, though many of these parents still struggled over the decision—and sometimes, as I have argued, saw struggle itself as morally worthy. Eliana called herself "a public-school believer" and thought it was "selfish" that "my child should have all the advantages. . . . What's special about my kid?" She felt bad about "using all my privilege to the advantage of my one [child]." But her daughter was not being challenged in her public school. Though Eliana spent a year soul-searching about it, she ultimately placed her daughter in a private school.

Typically, though not exclusively, those most concerned about these issues had liberal politics and were downward-oriented. Their position was summed up by Robert, the real estate broker mentioned earlier, who worked with wealthy progressives. He said, "My niche would rather buy [a home] in a bad neighborhood, because they want to show their kids a good example. And they want their kids to have everyday good examples of people, and people's lifestyles, and [to know] that 'not everybody has as much as we do.' But their kids will go to the private schools." As Robert's comment suggests, although these parents want to set a "good example" for their kids by exposing them to those with less, they are not willing to give up the advantages of private education.

Some parents—mainly those with less liberal politics and/ or less upward mobility, who tended to be upward-oriented— were not morally conflicted about putting their children in private school. These parents tended to see the advantages of private school as outweighing those of public school so obviously that public school would never be an option. Some of them had even chosen to enroll their kids in private or boarding schools despite ostensibly having moved to the suburbs because the schools were better there.[22] Yet some lamented that they felt they had to choose private schools, precisely because of issues of exposure to diversity.

One African American mother said of her daughter, who attended private school:

> Sometimes I worry that—it's just such a bubble. I mean, for a time in my life, I was going from [her upscale midtown office building] to [the private school]. And it was just like, "This is not real." Even for New York City. This is not real. And I think it's a disadvantage for her, in a sense. Not to have true diversity in her life. And it's kind of a bummer, that the trade-off had to be made, between wanting a certain approach to academics and learning and curriculum and all that, and feeling so strongly that, like, they have to run around. I don't want gym [only] once or twice a week. And they need to have art. And they need to have music. Like, it's fundamental. But it's a compromise.

Parents choosing private-school education did care very much about *which* private school the child went to. Partly they wanted to make sure the institution was a good fit with the child's interests and aptitudes and with the parents' educational philosophy. But they also cared about the diversity and "culture" of the school, nearly always stating a preference for a less "entitled" environment. Nicole, for example, had rejected one private school she called "elite." She told me the community at the school her daughter had ended up at would "look down on" wealthy people "who have a sense of entitlement." Grace planned on private school for her kids, but, she said, "I want to be really careful. You know, that the school doesn't have this type of [entitled] feel." Helen said approvingly of her kids' private school: "It feels like a public school. Because it's got a lot of diversity."

These parents also cared about avoiding materialism. As we have seen, Maya told me that this issue was paramount in her choice of private school. She said: "Most importantly, we don't want our children to grow up in an environment where that's what their friends think is important, having Ferragamo shoes and Juicy Couture clothes. And that's a really big piece." Rebecca hoped to send her daughter to private school if she could afford it. "But it has to be some kind of alternative situation, where I'm not, like, contending with [her daughter] needing to get a Birkin bag for her sixteenth birthday."

Parents of color were more concerned than white parents about having other children of color in their children's lives, as I have noted, but they expressed fewer conflicts about sending kids to private school. As one progressive African American parent with kids in private school said, "I could manufacture a conflict about it . . . but at this moment I don't feel conflicted about their education." The one exception in all my interviews to the negative usage of the word "entitlement" I heard came from an African American woman. She said, of white students at her Ivy League college, in contrast to herself (a product of urban public schools): "They were just so much more confident. They were able to talk to professors, and demand more, kind of. They had this greater sense of entitlement. And in—not in a bad way." This was a feeling she hoped her children *would* have.[23]

These parents were especially attuned to class as well as race dynamics in the schools, saying that socioeconomic status was sometimes more salient than race. Another African American mother told me, "The difference between black and white isn't as big as the socioeconomic difference between the kids who don't have money and the kids who do." She distinguished between kids whose families vacationed often, had summer homes, and "have money on the weekends to go have sushi and go see a movie" and those who did not. Her child was in the first category. Yet this mother and others also said that people in these private-school environments sometimes assumed that their kids were poor or on financial aid simply because they were African American.

Paid and Unpaid Work for Children

A final site of contention related to exposure and environment, which also manifested tensions around labor and consumption, was the issue of paid work for older children. As we have seen, some parents insisted that their kids do chores at home, and nearly all frowned on the idea of idleness. They said they wanted their kids to "do something" over vacation periods; Talia, for example, told me she would not want her kids to "waste time" in the summers when they were older, as she had. This stance supported respondents' allusions to hard work in general as a form of legitimation.

Parents varied, however, on whether they would require children to work *for money* when they were in high school or college. Asked whether her kids would work for pay when they were older, Lucy said, "Oh yeah, absolutely. That's pretty critical. That's pretty core, I would say, to us." As we have seen, Grace described feeling a "pride" in having worked for money and supported herself prior to her marriage to a wealthy inheritor. She said of that pride, "It's something that I think about for my children, that I want to instill. I'm like [intoning robotically], 'My children will work in the summer. My children will work in the summer.'"

Justin unequivocally saw paid work as a necessary experience. He said: "I had all sorts of odd jobs when I was a kid. Everything. Because I didn't have any money. If I wanted a toy, or a football or something, I would buy it. My parents wouldn't buy it for me. They couldn't. So I had every single job. Ditch-digging, trees. Worked in the florist, worked in a restaurant. Painting, golf caddy. Every type of job. I'm gonna tell my kids, 'You have to have a job. You have to have a shit job, like at a restaurant, or something—you know, where it's not fun.'" Justin saw the "shit job" as character-building; he similarly wanted his kids to play sports in school so they would get "yelled at" and "humiliated." He said, "It doesn't feel good when you're hearing it. But if you don't hear that until you're, like, 25, then you're shattered." Justin thus sees paid work, like sports, as crucial in terms of creating self-sufficient, not-entitled young adults.

More often, my respondents were conflicted about whether the constraint that kids would experience if they had to work was a more important form of cultivation than the expansion of opportunities and selfhood that might come from other activities. (This dilemma is analogous in some ways to their ambivalence over limiting kids' consumption.) Nadine and Kate had a running debate about precisely this issue, partly due to their different class backgrounds. Nadine, who came from a family with wealth, said:

> Do I want my kid to spend the summer, like, researching harbor seals in Alaska and, you know, getting her groove off, or do I want her to work in a greasy spoon? You know? I think they're tough questions. Yes, you want them to learn, like, the value of work, and getting paid for it, and all that stuff. And I don't want my kids to be entitled. I don't want them to be, like, silver spoon. But I also feel like life affords a lot of really exciting opportunities. And if you have money for any reason, it's for enriching your life and your kid's life, and making things happier. And giving back to the world.

Kate, who had grown up middle-class, was more inclined toward the position that her children should work. Referring to the "crappy jobs" she herself had held, she said, "But nevertheless, there was some value to it, there was some value to recognizing this is what you have to do and you get a paycheck and that's the money you have and then you budget it." She was "ambivalent" about paying her kids' college expenses. She said, "I'm like, maybe we shouldn't even plan that way. Maybe we should factor in that they're going to need to take some loans and work because there's no reason for that. There's no reason they can't. Then again, I worked in the library in college, and I remember I spent time doing that, and maybe I could have been doing something else. I could have been, I don't know, saving the world, and, I don't know. I could have been doing something more enriching overall than filing books. You know?"

Nicole had worked when she was in high school, primarily in retail and food service, despite her parents' affluence. Her response to my asking whether her kids would work shows explicitly that paid work is valuable primarily because it cultivates the self of the child. She said, "I'm very grateful that I had all of that kind of experience. . . . If you haven't served the people, in some capacity, whether it be retail or food, I think you've missed out. I think people should go through that experience." I asked, "Missed out on what?" She responded, "Just, like, a basic work ethic. You're not above scrubbing the floor. Like, nobody is. I think it's very, very valuable to have an entry-level job. To do the things that I assume someday you're going to be expecting other people to do." For Nicole, working teaches a child that she is not "above" doing certain kinds of work—even though she will never actually need to do this work later in life. The lesson is about humility and empathy for others who will ultimately be serving her.

Nicole continued, "So, in answer to your question, I would be a fan of it, if we could fit it into the schedule, and if they weren't giving up something important." While the lesson work teaches is desirable, she indicated, it is not critical. More "important" than paid work, of course, was likely to be schoolwork. Asked whether her kids would work, Alexis said, "Well, that's the thing. I think education's important, so I don't want education to be sacrificed. I want them to have time to do their [school]work, and study." But, she continued, "I think having a job is good," and she described having been a camp counselor herself. Ultimately she would want her kids to have "some sort of job. Something that makes sense. Something that teaches a lesson, without kind of being over the top [in terms of the] amount of time and energy they're putting into it." Like Nicole, Alexis wants her children to get the lesson about paid work without giving up the more significant work of studying.

Several parents of older children similarly said they saw homework as their children's "job." This is not surprising because, as children get older, these issues become less hypothetical and parents become more concerned with conventional forms of advancement, such as college admission, in a competitive environment. Indeed, only parents with children under 10 said their kids would work for money, and to my knowledge none of the children in the six households with high-school-age children actually had jobs. Miriam, whose children were quite young, said, "I would like for them to have to have summer jobs starting at a certain age, but I don't even know if that's realistic anymore. It seems crazy to say, but, you know what I mean, everyone's like spending all summer enriching their kids. And I'm like, 'Well, I think you should go scoop ice cream and earn some money, because if you want to buy some clothes for the fall . . . ,' you know what I'm saying? But, like, am I really going to do that? I don't know."

In articulating these concerns, parents sometimes invoked future risk, arguing that their children needed to know how to work hard because they could not necessarily depend on family money. For example, Marie said, speaking of herself and her husband,

> We had this conversation with our older daughter, who seems to think we're millionaires—billionaires. And so [her husband] said, you know, "The reality of it is, we could probably give you everything you want. We're not going to." . . . So we can give you everything you want now. But when you become an adult, we can't afford for you to be a screw-up. We don't have the kind of generational wealth that can support that. So at some point, you've got to stand on your own and figure it out. So why you don't get everything is because we can't support that, later down the road. You've got to be able to figure out strategies and ways to deal with it.

(Notably, Marie changes the word "millionaires" to "billionaires," perhaps because she realizes that she and her husband are millionaires.) Other parents also emphasized that it is especially important for their kids to have skills in order to navigate the unpredictable future.

Often, however, this risk was almost entirely hypothetical. Olivia told me, "I don't want my kids, actually, to be in a position where their whole self-worth, and their whole identity, and their capacity to function, is connected to what they have. 'Cause it can go away. You know? I mean, it can—things happen. And you want capacities that aren't attached to that." She described an imaginary scenario in which the family lost all its money, saying "I could go out there and work hard." She said she could work again as a social worker, or "go work at Starbucks. I have worked at Starbucks before. I can do it again." For this reason, she said she would be "much more comfortable with" her children's having real marketable skills rather than being, for example, conceptual artists. Yet in the end she said that this possibility was remote. I asked if she cared about these skills "because of this issue of risk? I mean, if it all went away? Or because there's something you think is morally better about that?" She responded, "I think it's a moral issue. Yeah, I do think it is a moral—because I think the risk is fairly minor."

So having a strong work ethic and marketable abilities is not only a hedge against risk; it also helps make children better people. Indeed, passing down this discourse of risk helps constitute children's legitimate dispositions in three ways. First, as Olivia's account shows, it teaches children that having a work ethic is part of being a morally worthy person. Second, it teaches children to *feel* at risk, which is another way not to feel entitled (as I argued in chapter 2 about adults). And third, it helps parents and children feel that they don't really *need* their privilege, that they could survive without it, which also distances them from being "entitled."

THE NOT-ENTITLED ENTITLED SELF

As I've shown, in their efforts to raise "good people" who are not "entitled," affluent parents employ strategies of constraint (on behavior and consumption) and exposure (to social others of various kinds). Presumably, of course, most parents want their kids to be moral actors, and, at least in the United States, entitlement is broadly seen as negative and undesirable in both children and adults. Parents across the socioeconomic spectrum also try to constrain their children's sense of entitlement and think about what kinds of influences their kids are exposed to. But some of these strategies are specific to affluent and wealthy parents. Such parents, as Pugh has shown, are especially prone to using "'symbolic deprivation'" in the context of having significant resources.[24] These parents, unlike those with more limited means, must also offer their children narratives about the high levels of consumption they ultimately do enjoy. Practices of intentional exposure to those with less are presumably more confined to these parents as well.

In these families, constraint and exposure also stand in tension with *expansion*, or, to pick up Kate and Nadine's word, "enrichment": the imperative to amplify children's experience and develop their potential. In the end, of course, expansion mostly wins. In terms of consumption, what is taken away from these children is at the margins, and what is required of them is relatively minimal. They live in spacious homes, usually with their own rooms (and often bathrooms). They play music and sports and travel internationally. They receive significant customized attention from paid workers including tutors, teachers, and therapists of many varieties. And their parents spend significantly on the "pathway consumption" that ensures their advantaged futures.[25] In terms of exposure, parents try to help their children situate themselves in relation to others with less, but only inasmuch as such exposure does not interfere with their getting a wide range of life experiences and the best schooling for their individual needs. They are *told* how "normal" others live and encouraged to appreciate their own advantages, but those advantages are very rarely curtailed.

Instead of limiting material entitlements, these parents are giving their children a "sense of their place."[26] In showing their children what is "'normal'" for others, these parents implicitly delineate another kind of normal for themselves. And, as they help their kids locate themselves in the world, these practices and discourses cultivate their children to be capable of inhabiting that space appropriately, in a behavioral and emotional sense. Having a good work ethic, being a nice person, and knowing how to navigate difference are useful skills, so fostering these traits is a form of giving children the tools to survive in an uncertain world. But, I have argued, this cultivation also produces a particular set of dispositions, a *habitus* that helps them occupy their social advantages with moderation, appreciation, effort, and reciprocity. As Donovan said, about his children's education around money, "I do think that I've done the most important things. Which is modeling behavior for them, again about appropriateness, about being grateful for what you have, about recognizing that it can in fact disappear fairly easily if it's not handled prudently." Affluent parents want their kids to see that they have more than others but not to feel that they are better than others. They try to pass down the sense of obligation they feel to make themselves worthy of their privilege. And, as they produce good people, parents also become good people.

CONCLUSION

In November 2016, James B. Stewart wrote a *New York Times* column in which he tried to pin down the net worth of British writer J. K. Rowling, author of the fantastically successful Harry Potter series.[1] In the piece he attributes his interest in her assets to the fact that she is "that all-too-rare commodity in the ranks of the ultrawealthy—a role model." He continues, "Not only has she made her fortune largely through her own wits and imagination, but she also pays taxes and gives generously to charity. At a time of bitter disputes over rising income inequality, no one seems to resent Ms. Rowling's runaway success." What struck me about this piece, first, is that Stewart invokes two of the characteristics of the good wealthy person that I have described: Rowling is hard-working, as indicated by her upward mobility, and she gives back liberally.[2] He doesn't mention her lifestyle, but a 2006 *Daily Mail* article describes her relatively moderate consumption as "a valuable and uplifting counterpoint to the circus of pointless and continuous spending" of other celebrities, and it seems unlikely that Stewart would think she was such a role model if she were perceived as an ostentatious consumer.[3]

Even more notable is Stewart's claim that "no one seems to resent" Rowling's success, despite widespread critiques of extreme economic inequality, because she acquired her fortune meritoriously and uses it to help others. The implication is that if she had inherited her money or otherwise obtained it without working, and if she were not generous with it, she would be resented—perhaps rightly so. Instead, because she is deserving, she is not part of the problem of increasing inequality. It is precisely this connection, between how affluent people inhabit their wealth and how they are seen and see themselves as legitimately entitled to it, that I have explored in this book.

My conversations with affluent New York parents reveal the challenges of managing privilege in a society that prides itself on egalitarianism and meritocracy at a historical moment of extreme and increasingly visible inequality. Some people, especially those who were downward-oriented, spoke more openly with me than others about feeling uncomfortable with their privilege and perhaps felt it more intensely. But all the people I talked with signaled discomfort. They struggle, with others and with themselves, to define their own entitlements and obligations and those of their partners and children. These struggles engage a broad range of objects and experiences, from sofas to schools, handbags to houses, vacuum cleaners to vacations.

I have argued that as they grapple with these questions, these New Yorkers are trying to see themselves as "good people" by cultivating particular practices and affects. Good people work hard. They live prudently, within their means. Their lifestyles are focused on their families and on meeting needs they construe as basic and reasonable. Self-indulgent purchases are exceptional "treats" that they could live without. They "give back" through work, philanthropy, volunteering, and everyday practices of generosity to others. They don't brag or show off, and they treat other people respectfully regardless of social differences, but they maintain an internal awareness of and appreciation for their advantages. And they raise children who will not feel or act "entitled." Whether or not my interviewees actually adhere consistently to the imperatives of good personhood they describe (an issue I discuss in the appendix), the fact that they work so hard to *interpret* themselves as doing so is key to understanding how inequality is legitimated.

CULTURAL LEGITIMATION
AND INDIVIDUAL JUDGMENT

My findings illuminate a real cultural ambivalence about privilege in the United States. Confusing representations of wealthy people proliferate, invoking both aspiration to and judgment of high-end consumption. These images sit uncomfortably next to social norms of not talking generally about social class and specifically about one's own advantages over others. Despite the ideological prominence of the American Dream and the assumption that *pursuing* wealth is unequivocally desirable, *having* wealth is not simple and straightforward.

The accounts of my respondents clearly show that there are right and wrong ways to inhabit wealth, what I call a *cultural logic of legitimate entitlement*. This logic is not limited to the people I spoke with. It resonates precisely because it constitutes common sense more broadly. It means, first, working hard, consuming prudently, and giving back; second, being both aware of and modest about privilege; and third, not feeling as if one deserves more than others. This logic draws fundamentally on the symbolism of the morally worthy middle class. The most visible elite lifestyles—those of "real" housewives or wolves of Wall Street—are widely seen as over the top, unnecessary and thus worthy of critique. In contrast, in their appeals to ordinariness, my respondents move to occupy the cultural legitimacy of the middle class. They want to be in the middle, not in a *distributional* sense but rather in the *affective* sense of having the habits and desires of the middle class. As long as the wealthy can distance themselves from images of "bad" rich people, their entitlement is acceptable. In fact, it is almost as if they are *not rich*.

It is especially striking that the middle is symbolically available to everyone, even if they have $50 million and are thus actually at the tippy-top of the income distribution, as long as they can claim a particular kind of disposition and lifestyle. This availability matters because it forms part of the *normalization of affluence*, the larger cultural process by which the top comes to seem like the middle. If people at the top are those who buy $20 million houses in the Hamptons, those in the middle can be the people who earn $2 million per year and have $5 million in assets. This normalization of affluence is also visible in U.S. popular culture, in which lifestyles that would actually be quite expensive (including spacious homes, domestic employees, family vacations, and fashionable clothing) appear in ostensibly "middle-class" settings on television and in the movies.[4] Certain kinds of consumption thus come to seem "normal" in general, as they do to my respondents. The wealth that supports these "reasonable" lifestyles is made harder to see and thus to critique. At the same time, the actual middle class and the poor disappear from public view.

As I have argued, legitimate entitlement is based on individual moral worth, established through particular modes of sentiment, disposition, and behavior. It's about what people do and how they feel, not what they have. It is therefore located in moral judgments of the behavior and affect of individuals rather than of distributions of resources. As we judge rich people for consuming well or badly, working hard or being lazy, giving money away or keeping it, we create distinctions that legitimate the system. Even negative judgments of individual behavior reproduce the logic of legitimate entitlement, because to say someone is inhabiting privilege incorrectly is also to say that it is *possible* to inhabit it correctly. This focus on distinctions among individuals draws attention away from institutions and social processes such as the systematic unequal distribution of resources.

Yet social structures and institutions do shape the possibilities of wealthy people—as they do those of all people—in crucial ways. On the one hand, economic privilege is itself anchored in labor markets that offer extremely high rewards for particular forms of labor and low rewards for others, and also in labor law that disadvantages workers relative to employers. Elites accrue cultural capital and networks, which are useful in entering those same high-paying labor markets, in particular social and educational environments. Economic advantage further rests on tax policies that favor holders of economic capital and higher earners relative to lower ones, as well as those who want to bequeath wealth to their children. White wealthy people, the vast majority of the privileged, also benefit from individual and institutional racism and white privilege.

On the other hand, the sense of risk that many of the people I talked with feel is also a product of particular institutional arrangements. High earners often face unstable employment conditions and fluctuating incomes. The lack of significant state support for education, housing, heath care, and retirement makes individuals responsible for their own security.[5] Crucially, such conditions both drive the fears of the wealthy and result from their actions. Those who work in finance and related industries contribute to the same volatile markets that make them nervous about their own economic situations. Wealthy people often advocate policies, such as lower taxation, that weaken the state and hence increase individuals' responsibility for their own welfare. Although in the short term such measures seem rational, as they allow rich people to keep more of their money, in the long term they create a system that spawns anxieties among the wealthy themselves.

Scholars and activists have long pointed out that people often interpret structural problems—in this case, a radically unequal distribution of resources—as individual ones.[6] It is common, for example, to blame poor people for their own poverty, suggesting that they do not work hard enough or are otherwise morally deficient when in fact they face structural disadvantages in educational and legal institutions as well as in labor markets. People who struggle economically are also apt to blame themselves rather than the system for their failure to advance.[7] The wealthy people I talked with vary in how much they *explain* their social position solely with reference to hard work and other individual attributes. But they *manage their discomfort with privilege* by turning inward, toward managing affect and behavior, rather than outward, toward social structure and distribution. Of course, trying to be worthy of privilege at the top of the income distribution is not the same as blaming oneself or being blamed for economic struggle at the bottom. But the failure to connect what C. Wright Mills called "personal troubles of milieu," by which he meant problems of individuals in their immediate social environments, to "public issues of social structure" is the same.[8] To put it more succinctly: the personal is political.

WHAT IS TO BE DONE?

Despite their discomfort with their wealth, the people I interviewed never ratchet *down* their spending or change their lifestyles significantly. In fact, the opposite is true. As they get older, they spend more and more on dresses, sofas, or homes, in the process Beatrice described as "luxury creep." They gain practice carrying out large consumption projects such as renovations and become comfortable spending the amounts of money required for these. They continue or begin to employ housekeepers, nannies, designers, architects, personal shoppers, personal assistants, personal trainers, tutors, and therapists, among others. As their children get older, parents turn away from the possibility of giving them sustained exposure to difference or paid work in order to give them other kinds of opportunities. Even those who have been most uncomfortable with affluent lifestyles grow accustomed to their advantages. Their social networks often become more homogenous as they come to consist largely of other private-school parents or their affluent neighbors. Yet, at the same time, these affluent New Yorkers consolidate their deserving identities. They see themselves as retaining the "mindset" and affect of hard workers and reasonable consumers, even though they may not work for pay, and even as their consumption spirals upward. Those who have had deep misgivings about their privilege come to frame such qualms as "unproductive" and allow them to fade into the background.

But what else could they do? Would it matter if they consumed less? If they "gave back" more? Or if they "gave up" something of more substance? A few of my interviewees thought so, as we saw in chapter 4. But many did not see taking meaningful action as possible. Even those who worried about inequality were not willing to sacrifice individual advantage for a slim shot at improving the collective good, for example by putting their children in public school. Yet maybe if there were clearer ways to attach some of this ambivalence to alternative political ideas or practices, these people would support them. Of course, as we have seen, most weren't interested in changing the system, despite the conflicts they felt.

However, I think the larger political task highlighted by these findings has less to do with prescribing how wealthy people should act and more to do with deconstructing this logic of legitimate privilege, which focuses on individual actions and measures behavior and feeling, not distribution, with a moral yardstick. What would happen if we stopped distinguishing between individual good and bad rich people and engaged questions about a more egalitarian distribution of material and experiential resources? What would it mean, for example, to say that we should be critical of the fact that J. K. Rowling is a billionaire—regardless of how she came by her fortune, how she spends it, or whether she gives it away—just on the basis of the idea that such wealth is inseparable from extreme inequality, which is both pernicious to society and itself immoral?

To some extent recent public discourses critical of inequality emerging from the Occupy movement, the Fight for Fifteen struggle for a $15 minimum wage, and the Bernie Sanders presidential campaign have raised exactly these questions. As we have seen, the people I talked with sometimes responded quite negatively to these critiques, interpreting them as personal judgments, as when high earners reacted defensively after President Obama advocated repealing high-wage tax cuts. But this tendency to feel *personally* affronted by public criticism of inequality also has to do with exactly the same process of attaching entitlement to individual merit. That is to say, to believe that J. K. Rowling should not have a billion dollars when other people have nothing is not to suggest she is a bad person for having the billion dollars. The distribution of the assets is the problem, not the individual behavior, disposition, or feelings—or any other characteristic—of the person holding the assets. If it were possible to separate critiques of inequality from those of individual behavior, wealthy people might not take such critiques so personally.

To divorce questions of distribution from those of individual merit does not mean separating them from moral criteria, of course. A more egalitarian distribution of resources across communities (national or otherwise) can be defended as a morally better form of social organization because it benefits more people and, ultimately, society as a whole. But advancing such a perspective is still no easy task. Wealthy people tend to resist giving up their short-term advantages, and their outsize political and media power means that they disproportionately control both the terms and the outcomes of the debates on these issues. Perhaps more important, the idea that people deserve resources based on individual moral affect and action is broadly taken for granted in the United States across the gamut of political opinion or economic position. Nonetheless, to raise issues of distributional justice means to challenge the legitimacy of distinctions among individuals based on moral worth, as much at the top of the income scale as at the bottom.

MONEY TALKS

This book is the result of the most difficult research project I have ever worked on. To take just the most extreme example: I found interviewing and writing about affluent people, most of whom live within ten miles of my home, more challenging than interviewing and writing about Chilean fishing industry workers who lived in remote areas, with unpredictable schedules, in Spanish, when I was 22 years old and working almost entirely on my own. This project was not only logistically complicated and time-consuming but also emotionally draining and anxiety-producing, as I have struggled with questions of research design, access, analysis, and ethics.

There are undoubtedly many reasons that I found this research so challenging. But a central one is that many of the taken-for-granted ideas and discourses about wealth and wealthy people that I have tried to deconstruct in this book also affected my capacity to collect and analyze evidence. First, I was myself subject to many of those ideas (recall the old saw about fish not being able to see the water they swim in). For example, I, like many others, intuitively imagined "real" rich people as only the super-rich. Also like many others, I was inclined to think of professionals earning $500,000 as "upper-middle-class." I now see this as a function of some of the cultural tendencies I have identified here, such as the attachment of "middle-ness" to certain kinds of lifestyles, especially in contexts like New York, where life is expensive and the super-wealthy abound. I have also felt constrained by the same logics of moral judgment that I have tried to illuminate. It has been challenging to interpret what my interviewees were saying while retaining some kind of consciousness of my own affective and normative responses to them.

Second, the delicacy and privacy of the subject matter also affected my methodological practice. Social silences about money and class made it hard to find people to talk with as well as to bring up these sensitive issues in these conversations. It was difficult to know how participants might read my class position and how those readings might influence how they talked with me. In the writing, I have struggled with how to most effectively maintain confidentiality, which I also feel more concerned about breaching than I have in previous projects, given the intimate nature of these questions of money and privilege.

In this appendix I offer a fairly standard account of the methodological choices I made, including more detail on the people I talked with, how I recruited them, and the mechanics of the interviews and analysis. But I also reflect on how the issues I have analyzed in the body of the book came into play.

RESEARCH DESIGN

I came to this project through both previous research and personal experience. In a previous study I had interviewed people who often stayed in luxury hotels, which had revealed ambivalent feelings about their entitlement to consume luxury service and in some cases about class entitlement more generally.[1] Both the interviews and my ethnographic work in hotels had also illuminated a strong norm of reciprocity among guests, who felt that they had a moral responsibility to treat workers well. Although I did not see it in these terms at the time, I would say now that these consumers wanted to be worthy of their entitlement to luxury service. I was also raised with class privilege, so I was familiar with these feelings both because I shared them and because I had seen them among family members and friends, especially those with liberal politics. So I was interested in investigating these affects and practices in more depth. Research I had conducted on the personal concierge and lifestyle management industry also raised questions about how people with the disposable income to hire this type of service provider understood the value of aesthetic and reproductive labor.[2] Therefore, exploring consumption of goods and services seemed like one avenue into understanding these experiences of privilege.

In-depth interviewing is the best method for investigating, in the words of Lamont and Swidler, "where people live imaginatively—morally but also in terms of their sense of identity—what allows them to experience themselves as good, valuable, worthwhile people."[3] As Allison Pugh points out, in-depth interviews also illuminate emotions, including anxieties, in particular cultural and social contexts.[4] In-depth interviews were therefore the logical method to use to explore how respondents made lifestyle choices and how these choices were shaped by and connected to their feelings about privilege and entitlement. (Later I discuss some of the trade-offs of this approach.)

As noted in the introduction, I wanted to speak with privileged parents of relatively young children, expecting that they would be making important lifestyle decisions, possibly for the first time, particularly regarding where and how to live and how to care for and educate their children. I imagined that younger people would be thinking less about long-term questions of lifestyle; they were also likely to have less money and hence fewer options. Older people seemed more likely to have made these decisions long before and not to be considering them so explicitly now. (This frame, of course, excludes people making alternative choices, who might not rely as heavily on "family" rhetorics of legitimation as these subjects ultimately did.)

One critical question, as I have noted, was how to define privileged people, given that privilege is relative. Because I thought it would be difficult to get people to talk with me and it would be impossible to sample on the basis of precise income or asset numbers, I wanted to be flexible. And I wanted to cast a somewhat broader net than is commonly used. The public focus on the top 1 percent had not emerged when I began this study in 2009, and in any case, as I explained in the introduction, I think this definition of privilege is too restrictive. I find it odd to suggest that anyone between the bottom 20 percent or so and the top 1 percent is somehow in the same group.[5]

I decided to begin by looking for people with household incomes of $250,000, which was in the top 5 percent in 2010.[6] I also chose this income criterion because it was the level over which the Obama administration was proposing to eliminate the Bush tax cuts. As such, it had acquired both symbolic and material significance. People often remark to me that "$250,000 is middle-class in New York." This is empirically false, at least if we take the median as the middle, because the median income in New York City is about $52,000.[7] Furthermore, the idea that $250,000 is middle-class *assumes* a level of legitimate need rather than investigating it. For example, a 2009 *New York Times* headline trumpeted, "You Try to Live on 500K in This Town."[8] The corresponding article took for granted that the hypothetical earner's family's "needs" included a Manhattan apartment, a summer home, two vacations a year, a nanny, a personal trainer, and private school. Designing research on needs on the basis of assumptions about needs seemed unwise to me. Additionally, as we have seen, wealthy people often assert that they are not "really" rich, pointing to even wealthier people. I did not want to build this justification into my sample. I also sought respondents with assets (not including home value) of over $1 million, which was an arbitrary decision. Ultimately, most of the people I talked with had income and wealth well above this level.

I believed that occupation, class background, political beliefs, gender, race, and sexual orientation were important potential sources of variation in how respondents would feel and talk about consumption and privilege. But adjudicating among the effects of these covarying characteristics would not be possible in a sample of this size. Ultimately I decided to make a virtue out of this messiness, sample for range, and look broadly at themes and variations that emerged in interviews. I focused primarily on obtaining variation in whether wealth was inherited or earned.

FINDING RESPONDENTS

It is notoriously difficult to gain access to elites for research purposes.[9] Many qualitative studies of wealthy people identify subjects according to their affiliation with organizations such as schools, exclusive clubs, or charitable groups.[10] Such studies take this affiliation as a proxy for wealth or affluence and seek subjects through this filter, which was not logical in my case. A few studies use random sampling within a previously defined population.[11] Such sampling was not appropriate for a study as exploratory as mine, especially given the covariation of possible factors described above combined with my desire for in-depth conversation, and poses significant challenges in any case.[12] I thus decided to use snowball sampling.[13] This choice sacrifices generalizability and representativity in favor of depth. However, my goal was not to make generalizable claims about all people in a certain income or wealth bracket but rather to explore the ways they talked about their lifestyle decisions and social positions, as explained in the introduction. Indeed, I was and remain more interested in mapping differences comparatively than in making broad claims about this very diverse population.

With the previously stated parameters in mind, I sought people to interview primarily through friends and colleagues who had attended elite colleges or lived in affluent neighborhoods, asking them to give me the names of their friends or acquaintances. I initially said that I was looking to interview people who were making or had recently made major lifestyle decisions, including buying homes or choosing children's schools. Because I imagined that potential participants might not want to identify themselves as wealthy (a supposition ultimately borne out by the responses to the word "affluent," as I discussed in chapter 1), I did not use this criterion explicitly with potential respondents, instead saying I sought "professional" families. The vagueness of what I was looking for, I think, made it hard for me to identify people to talk with, though I did conduct about twelve of the total fifty interviews in this phase.

I eventually realized that several of these people had carried out home renovations. I knew that home renovation was very common in New York and that it was a topic people are often eager to discuss. And from what I had already heard, I believed that this topic would raise the financial, aesthetic, and lifestyle issues I was interested in. Doing a major renovation also indicated that these people owned their homes and had significant disposable income.

I therefore shifted my focus to people doing renovations. Like any sampling frame, this approach excluded some possible respondents, notably renters and owners who had not renovated. On the positive side, using this frame allowed me to include people farther removed from my own network in the sample and possibly less similar to each other. That is, people I knew or had interviewed recommended others they did not necessarily know very well, particularly their neighbors, which meant I was not only tapping into their close networks.

As noted in the introduction, I also met a few people (ultimately seven in the core sample of fifty and all five of the noncore sample of unmarried people without children) via organizations that represent progressive wealthy people. (Such organizations include Patriotic Millionaires, Resource Generation, Responsible Wealth, and Wealth for the Common Good, as well as foundations such as Astrea Lesbian Foundation for Justice, Bread & Roses Community Fund, Haymarket People's Fund, and the North Star Fund.) I contacted staff of these organizations, who contacted possible respondents on my behalf. In one case, at the beginning of the project, the staff member chose particular people to approach and then gave me their names once they had agreed. In the other organization—which I contacted further into the project—the staff member sent an email I had composed to about forty-five members. (I asked him if I should use specific numbers for assets and income, and he responded, "I think numbers are good . . . otherwise people think 'I'm not wealthy' or 'I'm not upper income.' I see it all the time." Later I realized that this response anticipated my claim that many affluent people do not want to characterize themselves as such.) Only five people contacted me expressing interest, of whom I ultimately interviewed four.

In general, even after changing the topical focus of the interviews to renovation, I had trouble finding people willing to talk with me, despite the promised confidentiality of their responses. Some friends, colleagues, and acquaintances asked others who refused. One or two who were in these categories told me that they themselves wouldn't want to do it if I had asked them. Some people who had said they would participate did not respond to repeated emails.

One woman who had initially agreed to participate told me she was "swamped" with her kids and therefore too busy, when it turned out that the kids were at summer camp. A few people I contacted through the progressive groups eventually stopped responding to my emails, even though they had agreed to be interviewed. Even more notable was the lack of snowballing after interviews. People I had interviewed who said they would find friends for me to talk with either failed to respond to my follow-up emails or told me the people they'd asked didn't want to do it. A few women said their husbands would be happy to talk with me, but when I followed up they told me their husbands had refused.

These overt and implicit refusals seemed at least partly related to the fact that affluence and money were topics of the interview. I suspect that the interviewees realized that recruiting other participants would mean that they would have to talk to their peers or friends about money themselves and admit that they had talked about it with me. Occasionally this suspicion was confirmed explicitly. For example, a colleague offered to connect me to a family member who worked in finance but later rescinded the offer, saying that she felt "protective" of him, given the subject matter. Two potential interview subjects, both women, said they didn't want to talk with me because the money issues in their lives were too "private" for their husbands (echoing what female respondents I did talk with said about their own husbands).

INCOME AND ASSETS

I have described the sample in the introduction, including both the "core" sample of fifty and the "noncore" sample of five people without children, who were also either younger or older than the core respondents. Here I offer more of a breakdown of their financial situations. I have estimated their total assets given what they told me about their income, savings and investments, spending, and debt, including mortgages—and, in a few cases, based on likely earnings in their occupations. I used public records on housing prices to confirm what respondents told me about their housing costs. I did not use a consistent instrument for asking about financial information, although I should have (another way in which I allowed discomfort with talking about money to affect my practice). In the best cases I was able to ask specific questions about income, assets, debt, and monthly spending, as well as about home values, and I believed that the respondents knew the answers to those questions. In those cases, I am relatively confident that I have a good sense of these people's finances. But in other cases I do not have comprehensive information. This might be because I did not ask, they would not tell me, or—most often—they said they did not know. Many of my respondents were able to tell me their earned income but not their assets. People from families with wealth have often not inherited the assets they will receive upon the deaths of their parents or other family members. Calculating income for earners with significant assets invested in their businesses is difficult. For example, one respondent's husband had foregone his salary in changing his private equity business, but he had also recently received a windfall payment of over $5 million. As I have noted, respondents seemed very likely to underreport their assets, and I have also been more comfortable estimating them conservatively. So I believe I have probably underestimated these numbers.

In order to avoid reporting data I am not sure about, I have classified respondents by the primary types of assets they talked about living on—earned income or accumulated assets, usually inherited. Three respondents in the sample claimed that their households had over $5 million in earned income annually; three earned over $3 million; six had over $2 million; and three more earned over $1 million. These are minimum numbers, as in several cases I am sure my respondents were underestimating their incomes and/or not including capital gains income. These fifteen households also had net assets of at least $1 million, although I suspect the number was much higher for most (certainly it rose to $50 million in several cases). In most of these families the wives did not work for pay; in all cases except one, the only or primary income came from finance, corporate, real estate, or consulting work. Seven additional house-holds had incomes of over $500,000 annually. Of these twenty-two total families, I believe at least five had inherited or would inherit wealth in the millions of dollars. Five of the remaining families in the sample earned $250,000–$400,000; two of these had some inher-ited wealth, but in both cases the respondents told me they had spent most of it. Most of these families still obtained their income through finance, law, and business, but a few had earners working in creative occupations such as advertising, architecture, and nonprofits.

Of the families who lived primarily on income from their assets, eight had assets, mostly inherited, of over $8 million (significantly over in several cases). Two additional families had assets of over $5 million, and four more had assets of over $3 million. Of these four-teen families, ten had inherited the bulk of these assets. A few of these families also earned or had earned incomes of over $500,000. The last inheritor household had an inheritance I estimate at over $1 million. Most people in these households currently worked in the arts, nonprofits, or academia, although a few (those with accumu-lated rather than inherited assets) either had worked or currently worked in finance, technology, or related occupations.

EXPERT SERVICE PROVIDERS

In the book I also draw on interviews with thirty providers of life-style services to elites in a range of fields. These service providers (what Goffman called "curator groups" and Bourdieu called "cul-tural intermediaries"[14]) have intimate knowledge of their clients' decisions and thought processes around lifestyle and play an active role in their choices about spending, accumulating, and giving away money. Many service providers talked at length about their clients, which broadened my data on consumers, and for the most part what they described echoes what I heard.

I had conducted a project on the personal concierge and lifestyle management industry before beginning this research.[15] Therefore, interviews with personal concierges as well as ethnography among them preceded those with wealthy consumers and indeed shaped some of my interests in this project. I do not draw on all of those interviews here; I include only those with the twelve concierges who owned or worked in relatively successful businesses and thus had extensive experience with clients. Two of these had also worked as personal assistants.[16] Concomitant with the wealthy-consumer interviews, I pursued interviews with eighteen expert service providers in financial and philanthropic advising, interior design, art advising, tutoring, real estate, architecture, personal cooking, wedding photography, and therapy. These interviews were generated by snowball sampling, and these respondents were much easier to find than the wealthy ones. The interviews lasted, on average, 90 minutes and were recorded, transcribed, and coded.

THE INTERVIEW PROCESS

As noted, I come from a privileged background myself, which includes being educated in elite institutions. So I was in some ways quite similar to my interviewees, especially those in more creative-class jobs with progressive politics. Because they were closer to my own social networks and to progressive organizations, I connected with these respondents first. Although I was nervous about talking about money with these people, I did not worry too much about sharing a common language or style. Many of my interviewees lived in Brooklyn, as I do (though none of them lived in my neighborhood), so we shared a local context. When meeting them, I wore standard academic-professional clothing, which is relatively casual; they tended to be informally dressed.

When it came to interviewing people in single-earner wealthy families, however, I was more intimidated, as this was not a world I knew. The first time I planned to drive out to the suburbs to conduct an interview, I felt anxious about my 1994 Honda Civic. It had giant white patches on the roof and hood, products of years of East Coast winter street parking, which stood out against the dark blue of the rest of the car. I was afraid the state of the car might make my interviewees see me as impoverished and thus not talk openly with me. I felt so self-conscious about this that I took the car to two different body shops to find out how much it would cost to have it repainted. The lower quote was $800, which seemed like a lot to spend on an ancient car I rarely drove simply to assuage my status anxiety for a few hours. In the end, I'm not sure anyone I interviewed even noticed the car, which I used to get to only a few of the interviews.

I also felt the need to upgrade my wardrobe for these encounters. I went to the Eileen Fisher outlet store in Secaucus, New Jersey, to buy (on sale!) the kind of expensive yet relaxed clothes that I thought would be appropriate for summertime interviewing of elite people, mostly women. I thought I should seem a little dressy without appearing formal, and ultimately I believe this was the right approach. However, most of the women I interviewed, especially the stay-at-home mothers, dressed quite informally for our meetings. Several met with me in exercise clothes because they had just come from working out—something the upper-class women Susan Ostrander interviewed would never have done. In the end, I felt more comfortable talking with these participants than I had expected to.

Our conversations flowed partly because I possessed the same cultural capital as my interviewees in many areas. I understood their references to elements of their backgrounds and lifestyles, such as boarding schools and colleges, local restaurants and leisure pursuits, and the basics of investments. Having lived in New York for years, I knew the differences among neighborhoods in Manhattan and Brooklyn and something about jobs in finance (and much more, of course, about those in academia and nonprofits). Surely there were more issues that I might have tripped over if I had not been from the same background, but these were invisible to me. Some of this implicit knowledge became explicit when my research assistant was unfamiliar with certain luxury goods and services, such as NetJets, the private airplane rental service. Transcribers likewise lacked certain referents of elite consumption and education, such as—to take four examples that came up in a single interview—Chippendale furniture, RISD (the Rhode Island School of Design), Hermès, and Groton (an elite boarding school).

I did try to signal my own cultural capital in these areas, to avoid the possibility that interviewees would construct me as too far outside their worlds. But when it came to furniture, clothing, and accessories, my ignorance became manifest. Although I had heard of mainstream brands and designers, I often did not understand the finer distinctions among them. For the most part I did not reveal my lack of knowledge to respondents, but sometimes my naïveté was helpful in getting them to explain, for example, the characteristics of the suburb they lived in or the stores where they shopped.

The interviews were essentially conversations, focused primarily on consumption practices and definitions of needs, though also covering personal histories and characteristics. These practices included the purchase, design, and renovation of homes; child care and schooling; leisure expenditures; daily consumption of goods and services such as food, clothing, and personal care; and personal services. This approach encouraged respondents to talk about how they think about spending money, where they feel uncomfortable about these decisions, and how lifestyle choices are implicated in family and social relationships. My focus on home and family also presumably led respondents to talk about their concerns about their children and all the issues related to family that I have described. It is possible that if I had been more focused on talking about their choices of goods such as cars or clothing, the conversation would have been different.

In terms of the rhythm and mechanics of the interviews, I had a list of interview questions, but I used it to guide the interviews only in a very general way. Near the end of an interview I would check the guide to make sure I had covered all the central themes. I do have more data on some topics than on others in certain cases, especially when the interviews were time-limited by the respondents. Once I shifted focus in the interviews to look at moral conflicts more specifically, I would ask about entitlement and feelings of deservingness at the end of an interview if the respondent had not brought these issues up already. I also asked about income and assets at the end if these topics had not arisen.

As noted, I usually sensed some kind of discomfort with talking about money, though less so with the people I had found through the progressive organizations and others who were downward-oriented. With practice, I improved at asking people about money, especially about specific income and asset numbers. But in two cases, both with inheritor women married to earners, I felt a kind of interactive barrier, like an invisible wall, preventing me from inquiring about numbers (especially total assets), and thus I did not ask.[17] Two or three people refused to share income and/or asset numbers with me even when I did ask. Some of them talked about money euphemistically, referring to "saving our acorns" or "a little boodle of money." Willa told me the amount of her renovation ($1.5 million) but referred to it as "a lot of beans." These are formulations with a kind of homey, down-to-earth connotation—the opposite of expressions of excess. Service providers I talked with told me their clients often had trouble talking about money. As I described previously, however, some people expressed relief at being able to discuss these issues.

The interviews ranged from one to four hours in length; the vast majority lasted about two hours. All but one were conducted in person,[18] most commonly in the respondent's home (thirty-three of fifty), in a café or restaurant, or in an office (mine or the respondent's). All were digitally recorded. With two exceptions, the interviews were professionally transcribed, and they were all coded using Dedoose, by me or by a research assistant.[19] I analyzed the information by reading and rereading both complete interviews and groups of coded excerpts.

One often hears the advice to continue interviewing until one reaches "saturation."[20] I did indeed begin to hear the same kinds of narratives and concerns over and over again, especially among two populations: stay-at-home mothers married to earners and liberal inheritors of wealth working in creative-class occupations. I also got to a point at which respondents' networks began to overlap, especially as I interviewed parents with children at the same school who had been introduced to me through different channels. I feel relatively confident that if I continued interviewing people in these populations I would not hear anything significantly different from what I have already heard. However, I would have liked to be able to interview more earners, male and female. Because high earners typically work so many hours, they are a very hard population to reach. I would also have liked to talk with more spouses of inheritors. And I could have continued pursuing access to the old-money New York families who are better known for their philanthropy. This lack of comprehensiveness is another price I pay for not having limited the categories to begin with, but it leaves plenty of room for others to pursue more precisely delineated research with particular populations.

POSSIBLE CRITIQUES

Scholars of interviewing methods might offer a number of critiques of this research.[21] First, they could say that my respondents' talk might not match their behavior.[22] We already know that they consume at a level that is unattainable for the vast majority of people in New York and elsewhere. Maybe they also lie around "eating bon-bons all day," in Stephanie's words, instead of working hard. And perhaps they violate the behavioral norms they claim to adhere to, treating other people rudely or constantly bragging about money. But their actions are not my central interest. Perhaps these people do not live up to the values they express; but the fact that they do espouse these values of hard work, reasonable consumption, and giving back is key to understanding cultural legitimations of inequality. I read their discourses not as shallow justifications but as portraits of the worthy people they want to be and descriptions of what this worth consists of. Whether their behaviors matched their accounts is less important for my purposes. Furthermore, as I have said, I think trying to adjudicate whether wealthy people are "really" good people not only is impossible but also reproduces individual-level judgments that ultimately legitimate inequality.

Second, one might argue that my respondents' accounts, even at the level of discourse, do not represent the truth of their experience. These responses could simply be strategic justifications of privilege. Or they might have been elicited by the artificial interview situation and therefore not be rooted in "real" feelings. Perhaps the interviewees assumed that I was less advantaged than they and therefore shaped their responses to minimize their status-competitiveness or conspicuousness and emphasize their being "down to earth." It is impossible to know exactly what was going on in the minds of interview participants or to know how my presence affected these conversations, so some of this might be going on. And people do take different stances in different contexts and with different interlocutors, although this possibility does not make what they say untrue.

However, even to the extent that respondents were telling me what they imagined I wanted to hear, *what they imagined I wanted to hear* is precisely the object of interest—what they think constitutes worthy personhood. These accounts of good personhood were consistent and often emerged without my asking about them. As Sherry Ortner has noted, through interviews one can see "cultural patterns across texts" that "amount to a cultural discourse."[23]

More important, my respondents gave many kinds of examples, though not always intentionally, to support my sense that they felt conflicted. They also communicated indecision and struggle through various elements of their speech, particularly hesitation, vehemence, and word choice, which I have noted in various places throughout the book.[24] Their explicit expressions of relief to be talking about these issues and their tendency to look to me for validation also suggest that the worries they talked about were truly felt. More concretely, as noted, I verified assets (especially housing prices) wherever possible and never came across an instance of people having exaggerated their worth, though some had *underestimated* their home value, supporting my claim that they tend to minimize their affluence. And, as I have shown, the service providers I interviewed independently recounted seeing their clients struggle with these tensions around money and privilege.

A third critique might be that even if one accepts my claims about these respondents, they were probably unusual relative to other privileged people. As I have suggested, most media representations of wealthy and affluent people do not describe the conflicted, morally striving wealthy parents I have written about in this book. They resemble instead the stereotypical "entitled" wealthy. Furthermore, my interviewees constantly invoked such "bad" rich people, in their social networks or their families, as foils for themselves. So perhaps the liberal New Yorkers I have studied are exceptions, and most wealthy people do not share these fears about being illegitimately entitled or care about being morally worthy.

However, such a possibility seems counterintuitive to me. It stands to reason that most privileged people (like people in other social classes[25]) want to feel morally worthy. In the United States, as noted, such people are responding to a long tradition of egalitarianism, as well as to a more recent shift to meritocratic criteria for moral worth. And these shifts are occurring in the midst of rising, and increasingly publicly discussed, inequality. It would be hard not to have to deal with moral challenges to entitlement in this context in some way, even if these challenges are not apparent to others. Again, wanting to interpret oneself as morally worthy can coexist with other kinds of beliefs and behaviors.

Nonetheless, a range of characteristics probably shapes how people both feel and talk about privilege and their ideas about deserving it. My interviewees are not only politically liberal but also largely secular, highly educated, and professional, and their discourses may differ from those of people who vary on these dimensions. Even within the group of people I interviewed, discourses and practices differ based on some combination of political views, source of wealth, class background, and social networks. Furthermore, being at a life stage of family formation has influenced their thinking on these issues relative to that at earlier moments in their lives, as we have seen.[26]

Further research could, and should, explore differences in orientations among wealthy people more systematically on the basis of these characteristics and at different life stages, as well as on the basis of gender and race/ethnicity. Microcultures of wealth are likely to differ in different locales, even within the United States. National contexts probably also influence the discourses and actions of elites around their privilege because cultural repertoires of merit and entitlement vary and are, in fact, reflected in and reproduce systems of economic distribution.[27] Finally, it would be useful to investigate change over time in elites' self-conceptions, although such an approach would face a challenging dearth of evidence. These ideas may respond both to long-term changes in cultural notions of meritocracy and to shorter-term economic and political cycles that influence the prevalence and salience of inequality.

CONFIDENTIALITY

I have been extremely concerned about preserving anonymity in writing about these respondents, given the intimacy and privacy of some of what they told me. My central concern has not been that they would be identifiable to the general reader, which I believe is essentially impossible, but rather that people who knew I had interviewed their friends or neighbors would be able to identify them. Thus I have been less concerned about the people who came to the study in such a way that they are unlikely to be identifiable—that is, no one knows they spoke with me—and more concerned about those who entered through their own close friends, who may recognize them in these pages.

I refer to the participants with pseudonyms, and I have modified some of their characteristics. I do not describe people physically or link them to identifiable features of their homes, a necessity that unfortunately precludes including richer ethnographic detail. I do not include a table of all of the participants and their characteristics because it could be used to identify respondents through the process of elimination. And I do not always identify which respondents were married to each other. As readers will have noticed, I sometimes refer to individuals without pseudonyms in order to avoid creating characters who can be identifiable across the text. (That is, if a certain characteristic is likely to identify a respondent to someone who knows she spoke with me, I usually do not attach a name to the characteristic.) In order to avoid identifying respondents who had built new homes, I refer to their projects as renovations. In masking certain characteristics, I have been attentive to the possible consequences of my decisions and have avoided making changes that are likely to affect the reader's capacity to evaluate my argument (such as major changes to demographic or biographical characteristics of my informants).[28]

The most complicated and perhaps controversial decision in this regard is not to identify named respondents by race. This choice leads to the risk that racial differences will not be acknowledged and that the reader will assume that all speakers are white. It also removes the reader's ability to imagine that certain characteristics may have to do with race. But because I interviewed several clusters of people of color who knew each other, I felt that the risk of mutual identification was high enough that I was obliged ethically to mask them this way. (Indeed, several people of color worried that they would be identifiable to the larger world if I used their real characteristics; for example, one woman asked me not to identify her Manhattan neighborhood because so few affluent people of color live there that she thought she would be identifiable if I did.) As I have said, the small number of people of color in the sample and their variation in terms of other characteristics meant that I found few systematic differences related to race. Where I have found such differences or possible patterns, I have described them without identifying particular respondents by race or by using pseudonyms assigned just for that section of text.

JUDGMENT

As I have suggested, popular representations of wealth, wealthy people, and especially wealthy consumption are often voyeuristic. Such representations also mobilize images of rich people as—at least potentially—morally unworthy. Indeed, it is precisely these kinds of representations that my respondents are struggling against. I have struggled with them, too. Ultimately, of course, my point has been to illuminate the normative issues surrounding these discussions, but to work in the midst of them was hard. It has felt almost impossible to write and talk about these consumers without participating in exoticizing, sensationalistic curiosity about wealth and/or making, or seeming to make, moral evaluations. Just describing some of their consumption practices can feel prurient, and simply stating how much money they have or describing their homes can feel judgmental. It is hard to write that certain people nearly always travel first class or spent a million dollars on a home renovation without participating in preexisting cultural ideas about legitimate needs. I have tried to find a tone that avoids judgment entirely, though I have doubtless not always succeeded. Sometimes I have struggled even to choose particular words. For example, when describing my respondents' lifestyles, I have been tempted to use the word *cushy*, but it seems slightly negative. I have usually chosen *comfortable*, which sounds to me less negative but more euphemistic.

I have also wondered whether the empathy I feel for the people I talked with is blinding me to the contradictions in their accounts or, conversely, if my own critical politics are standing in the way of my comprehension of them. I have tried to be attentive to both these tendencies as well as to follow standard procedures for coding, returning to interview text repeatedly, and sharing my work with others.

I have experienced a wide variety of responses to this work from readers and audiences. Many readers have acknowledged that they felt judgmental of respondents while reading this work, and some have encouraged me to try to forestall potential judgments by highlighting this tendency up front, as I did in the introduction. Some friends and colleagues, usually those from less privileged backgrounds, have thought I was being too generous to respondents because they judged them harshly ("What assholes!"). Other friends, especially those who have more class privilege, were more sympathetic to these interviewees. One friend said it was "like reading about myself." I have also sometimes felt that I have struck a nerve among academic readers who may be using some of the same interpretative moves I describe here to avoid feeling privileged themselves.

I still feel anxious that my respondents will feel their trust has been violated, even if they are not identifiable, because they may feel that they are being judged or that their private emotions and struggles have been brought to light here in a way they did not expect. My anxiety about this is another indicator of the strength of the prohibition on talking publicly about money and privilege. However, I hope that these people will not think I have written about them sensationalistically or gratuitously. And I believe that it is culturally, politically, and sociologically important to try to foster conversations about money, morality, and selfhood in the context of the vast class inequalities that mark the contemporary United States.

NOTES

INTRODUCTION

1. John, a young progressive person with wealth, told me a similar story, of a friend who was buying a penthouse apartment but insisted as a condition of the sale that the *PH* be removed from the elevator and replaced by the floor number.
2. Fussell 1983, chapter 1.
3. Keller 2005, ix; see also Ortner 2003.
4. Of course this equality has always been, and remains, imaginary, given the long and multifaceted history of the marginalization and oppression of Native Americans, people of color, women, immigrants, and workers of all kinds. See, e.g., Nakano Glenn 2002; Zinn 1980.
5. On the American Dream, see Cullen 2004; Hochschild 1995; McCall 2013.
6. Nakano Glenn 2002.
7. DeMott 1990. See also Kendall 2005 on "consensus framing."
8. See, e.g., Bartels 2008; Cooper 2014; David and Kim 2015; Hacker 2006; Hacker and Pierson 2011; Heiman 2015; Katz 2012; Lane 2011; Pugh 2015; Schor 2016; Sennett 2007; Standing 2011.
9. E.g., Krugman 2002.
10. "In 2010, the top one percent owned more than 34% of net worth, and the next 9% owned an additional 40%, leaving just over 25% of net worth for the remaining households" (Keister 2014, 353). See also Hacker and Pierson 2011; Keister 2005; Keister and Moller 2000; Piketty 2014; Saez 2015.
11. Chetty et al. 2015; Norton and Ariely 2011.
12. Frank 2007; Kenworthy 2015; Wilkinson and Pickett 2009.
13. Pew Research Center 2016. They define "middle-income" people as those adults with annual adjusted household incomes of between two-thirds of the national median and double the median.
14. Dwyer and Wright 2012; Wright and Dwyer 2003.
15. There was always some tension between the type of work seen as middle class (nonmanual work usually) and these lifestyle possibilities, which, when unions were stronger, were more often available even to manual workers considered "working class" (see Halle 1984). For a recent discussion of the concept of the middle class, see Heiman et al. 2012.
16. Anat Shenker-Osorio (2013) argues that "middle class" is "a frozen phrase, no longer rooted in the meaning of component parts that ought to designate

economic status between two others. Instead, it has become a status, a brand—a label you opt to adopt."

17. Max Weber (2003 [1958]) famously argued that American Puritans, influenced by Calvinist theology, worked hard to show that they had been "chosen" by God to be among the "elect." Closely coupled with disciplined hard work was disciplined consumption. Weber drew on the wisdom of Benjamin Franklin's Poor Richard, whose *Almanac* brimmed with aphorisms promoting industry and economy and eschewing excessive consumption. Franklin's maxims included, "Early to bed, early to rise, makes a man healthy, wealthy, and wise," "Beware of little expenses; a small leak will sink a great ship," and "Many a man thinks he is buying pleasure when he is really selling himself a slave to it." Hard work and prudent consumption led, in Weber's view, to the accumulation of capital that was the foundation of capitalism in the United States.

18. See, e.g., Gilens 1999; Katz 2013.

19. Veblen 1994 [1899]. In Veblen's model, even leisure became conspicuous. Women and servants, for example, wore impractical clothes, such as corsets and uniforms, to show that they didn't need to work, which reflected positively on the husband/master.

20. Fan 2016; Levin 2016. Perhaps ironically, both articles refer to, and were likely inspired by, a reality TV show, *Ultra Rich Asian Girls of Vancouver*. For a comprehensive analysis of the portrayal of wealthy people in the media, including a discussion of this type of "price-tag framing," see Kendall 2005. For scholarly research on the new rich in China and their moral quandaries, see Osburg 2013.

21. Piff 2014; Piff et al. 2010; Piff et al. 2012; Vohs et al. 2006. See Korndörfer et al. 2015 for a review of this literature and a contradictory set of findings. See Lamont 2000 on working-class men's views of "people above" as, among other things, snobbish, competitive, and uncaring.

22. See Khan 2011, whose definition matches that of my interviewees. Annette Lareau (2011) uses the term in a different way: to describe a sense of belonging in particular environments and the feeling that one has the right to ask questions and receive attention from others. See Sherman 2017.

23. Frank 2008; Freeland 2012.

24. Sengupta 2012.

25. This term is typically defined as describing someone with investable assets of $1 million or more (see Hay 2013, 3).

26. See McCall 2013 for a nuanced discussion of media coverage of income inequality since 1980.

27. McCall 2016. Her data show that the level of concern with inequality was also high in the mid-1990s.

28. Bourdieu 1984; Daloz 2012; Khan 2012; Mears 2014; Schor 1998, 2007; Veblen 1994 [1899]. On the super-rich, see, e.g., Beaverstock and Hay 2016. Given the difficulty of accessing elites, scholars tend to look at what is visible (e.g., Mears 2014; Spence 2016). Some recent research looks at men's "consumption" of women's sexual and embodied capital in their pursuit not only of distinction but also of economic and social capital (e.g., Hoang 2015; Mears 2015b).

29. See Khan 2012; Ostrander 1984; Ostrower 1995. Research on membership in social clubs, for example, tends to highlight the exclusionary aspects of these organizations and spaces (Chin 2011; Holden Sherwood 2013; Kendall 2002). Recent research on French social clubs has examined these spaces of elite positioning comparatively, noting a corresponding variation in (and struggle over) forms of sociability and social capital accumulation and deployment, but this work retains a concern with distinction and exclusion (Cousin and Chauvin 2014). Research on schooling primarily focuses on how parents seek a leg up for their children in educational institutions (Johnson 2006; Lareau and Weininger 2008; in the UK context, see, e.g., Devine 2004; Reay 1998, 2005a; Vincent and Ball 2007).

Furthermore, researchers have shown that even as social institutions become more outwardly meritocratic and diverse in terms of race/ethnicity and gender, they still function as sites of exclusion in less obvious ways. Lauren Rivera (2015), for example, shows that even as more people of color graduate from college, and even as elite firms pay lip service to hiring them, privileged white interviewers often, though not consciously, exclude these newcomers in favor of candidates more similar to themselves culturally. Shamus Khan (2011) has argued that despite the increasingly diverse population of students in elite schools such as St. Paul's and the use of "hard work" (rather than entitlement through birth) as a justification for privilege, those who show themselves to have a sense of "ease" are more likely to be seen as truly belonging to the elite. Thus the exclusion once based on obvious mechanisms such as explicitly restricted admission to country clubs or elite colleges, or on the refusal to hire certain kinds of people for certain jobs, has become more embedded in less visible cultural processes.

30. Khan 2011; Khan and Jerolmack 2013.

31. Lamont 1992. See also Sayer 2005; Sherman n.d.

32. Reay 2005b. On working-class people's lived experience, see, e.g., Bettie 2003; Hochschild 2016; Jensen 2004; Kefalas 2003; Lewis 1993; MacLeod 1995; Rubin 1992 [1976]; Sennett and Cobb 1993 [1973]; Silva 2013; Skeggs 1997; Willis 1979. For work on poverty, see Desmond 2016; Edin and Kefalas 2005; Edin and Lein 1997; Edin and Shaefer 2015; Goffman 2014; Hays 2003; Newman and Massengill 2006; J. Sherman 2009; Young 2004. On the middle

class in the United States, see Ehrenreich 1989; Heiman 2015; Newman 1999. On race and the middle class, see Jackson 2001; Lacy 2007; Pattillo 2007, 2013.

33. Many studies compare "middle-class" people to those who are "working class"; in such studies the middle-class person is usually defined as having a college education and/or a professional or managerial job. Because the comparison of interest is to those below, these studies usually do not differentiate between middle class and upper middle or upper class (e.g., Cucchiara 2013; Lareau 2011; Streib 2015). Studies explicitly focused on the "professional middle" may use education as the differentiating factor (Nelson 2010), which makes it difficult to see how to define an "upper class" (because there are limits to how much education a person can have); others focus on the "upper middle class" without clearly defining it (Johnson 2006). Defining class according to education, without reference to income, actually makes an "upper-class" categorization impossible (see Sherman 2017). On parenting and/or education, see also Ball et al. 2004; Devine 2004; Irwin and Elley 2011; Johnson 2006; Pugh 2009.

34. Founded in the late nineteenth century, the *Social Register* was a directory of the names, addresses, and other information pertaining to the elite; inclusion defined membership in the establishment in much of the twentieth century.

35. Ostrander 1984. See also Kaplan Daniels 1988 for a study of women in a similar class position, focusing on their work as volunteers.

36. Baltzell 1964, 1991.

37. For a discussion of this transition, see Khan 2011, chapter 1. See also Ostrower 1995; Savage and Williams 2008.

38. See Karabel 2005; Lemann 1999.

39. Hay 2013; Reay et al. 2007; Rothkopf 2009; Sklair 2001.

40. Brooks 2000; Khan 2011. For recent synopses of the literature on cultural omnivorousness, see Karademir Hazir and Warde 2016 and Warde 2015.

41. Sassen 1988, 1990.

42. Fiscal Policy Institute 2010; McGeehan 2012; Roberts 2014.

43. Gregory 2014.

44. Roberts 2014. Roberts also shows that in 2013 the citywide poverty rate was 21 percent, meaning that 1.7 million people were living below the poverty line. In 2015 a *New York Times* poll found that 51 percent of New Yorkers felt they were "not getting by" (Burns and Russonello 2015).

45. Fry and Taylor 2012. The level of residential racial segregation, though high, is actually decreasing somewhat. See Alba and Romalewski 2017.

46. Martin 2015.

47. The city has particular cultural characteristics, and its residents are likely to differ from their counterparts elsewhere. But this is true in any location, and I thought it made sense to keep a cultural context constant rather than aim for

representativity across a broad population (impossible in a sample of this size, in any case, and especially hard to obtain when looking at elites) (Page et al. 2013; Small 2009). See appendix.

48. On "elites," conceptualized as those with social, economic, cultural, and political power, see Khan 2012. Social class is a complicated concept to define and to measure. It can be defined in terms of one's location in a distribution of income and wealth; in terms of various features related to occupation; in terms of ownership of various forms of capital; or (especially when it comes to the middle class) in terms of particular kinds of consumption. For discussions of these possibilities, see Halle 1984; Lacy 2007; Lareau and Conley 2008; Wright 2005. Typically, empirical researchers using the concept of class deploy some combination of income, education, and occupation (which usually cluster together, though see Halle 1984) to indicate class position. The "upper class" in the United States has traditionally been defined not by income (though high income, wealth, and control of capital were presumed) but by belonging to particular elite institutions (Domhoff 1971; Ostrander 1984). As those institutions have waned in importance and elites have become more diverse, the "top 1 percent" has become a more common category of analysis (e.g., Page et al. 2013). Such a focus on distribution, like my focus here, fails to theorize the differences among class *locations* of people whose wealth is earned versus inherited, who have different relationships to capital or different levels of autonomy and authority, or who possess different ratios of economic to cultural capital (Bourdieu 1984). It would be useful to revisit this question. There are meaningful theoretical as well as empirical differences in my sample—for example, between families that control large amounts of global capital and those who are salaried and could be thought of as "upper middle class" or "professional-managerial class" (Ehrenreich and Ehrenreich 1979). However, I believe the distributional definition is appropriate for my primary purpose here of looking at lived experience.

49. See, e.g., Khimm 2011. Defining elites as the top 1 percent or the top .1 percent may make sense for studies of political influence. But those in the top 5 percent or even 10 percent, despite garnering lower returns in recent years than the top .1 percent, remain extremely privileged relative to the rest of the population. To imply that there is no meaningful difference in lived experience between the top 5 or 10 percent and the median, for example, is problematic.

50. Rivera 2014.

51. Estimates of the top percentages vary significantly depending on how and when they are calculated (see Bricker et al. 2016). Lisa Keister uses data from the 2010 Survey of Consumer Finances (SCF) to place the cutoff for the top 5 percent of income nationally at $205,335 in 2010 (personal communication).

Emmanuel Saez (2015) claims that in 2012 an income of $394,000 was the bottom of the top 1 percent nationally; $161,000 was the bottom of the top 5 percent. According to *Business Insider*, in 2015, to be in the top 1 percent in New York City required an income of $608,584, whereas being in the top 5 percent required $246,596 (Elkins 2015). Liu (2012) uses data on New York City tax filers (not the same as households) to suggest that the cutoff for the top 1 percent in 2008 was $595,029, whereas in 2009 it had dropped to $492,422.

The top strata of wealth are also hard to define; Keister (2014) draws on SCF data to set the top 1 percent at $6.8 million in 2010, in which year she also calculates that the threshold for the top 5 percent was $1,863,800 (personal communication). Bricker et al. (2016) show estimates of the threshold for the top 1 percent in net worth as varying from almost $4 million to almost $8 million in 2012. Reports of the average incomes or assets of the top 1 percent are skewed because of the extremely high values at the very top, which is why I use thresholds. And medians are a better indicator of the middle of the category. On the question of whether $250,000 is "really" privileged in New York City, see the appendix.

52. The sampling process and all my methodological decisions are described in detail in the appendix.

53. I also interviewed five wealthy people who were unmarried and childless, either younger or older than the rest of the sample. I refer to people in this "noncore" sample occasionally throughout the book, and their discourses are broadly similar to those of the others.

54. U.S. Census Bureau 2016. See also Roberts 2014.

55. Keister 2014. I have estimated net worth based on what respondents told me about their incomes, assets, monthly spending, and debt and on public records of property values. See appendix.

56. Khan 2011.

57. Several interviewees who did not have advanced degrees were married to spouses who did.

58. Two of these women worked very occasionally for pay.

59. Page et al. 2013.

60. Those who did not own homes had owned homes previously and were between places or were seriously considering buying expensive homes.

61. For example, Margaret worked in a nonprofit; her husband worked in the entertainment industry. Her household income at the time I interviewed her was almost exactly $250,000; they had assets of $80,000, a few thousand dollars in debt, and no family money. She and her husband owned their home (though they paid about $4,000 to the bank every month for the mortgage), but it

was in a less affluent Brooklyn neighborhood. Their children were in public school, and Margaret expected them to remain there. They rarely traveled and were the only people in my sample who did not have a housecleaner. A couple of additional respondents had been wealthy but had encountered financial problems; for example, Rebecca's renovation and unexpected medical bills had nearly bankrupted her when she and her husband both lost their lucrative jobs in the 2008 recession, although she had some inherited wealth to fall back on.

62. On "consumption work," see Weinbaum and Bridges 1976.

63. Bourdieu 1984.

64. For more detail on these interviews, see the appendix. On the relations between expert service workers and their clients, see Sherman 2014. On personal concierges specifically, see Sherman 2010 and 2011.

65. See, e.g., Domhoff 2010; Johnson 2006, 123–124; Ortner 2003, 10.

66. In some cases this refusal was quite productive because it allowed me to ask *why* they didn't want to talk about it.

67. See Chin 2011 for a similar finding.

68. Ostrander 1984, 35, 26.

69. Ibid., 101.

70. Service providers I interviewed tried to refrain from being judgmental of how their clients spent money, often saying, "Well, I don't want to be judgmental, but . . ." Both the idea that it is inappropriate to judge others and the desire to avoid exposure because it can lead to judgment produce silences around money, entitlement, and inequality. See Strieb (2015, 35) on avoiding class judgment in a different context.

71. Streib 2015, 36; see also Bonilla-Silva 2006.

72. Kluegel and Smith 1986; Lamont 1992, 2000; McCall 2013; McNamee and Miller 2004; Schulz 2012.

73. See McNamee and Miller 2004. Note that it is often referred to as the "Protestant work ethic," which minimizes the consumption dimension.

74. In the sense in which Khan (2011) uses the term. On money and morality, see Carruthers and Espeland 1998; Kornhauser 1994; Lamont 1992, 2000; Zelizer 1994.

75. Hochschild 1989b.

76. This concept comes from Gramsci (1971). For an ethnography of classed "common sense" in the United States, see Heiman 2015.

77. This focus on selfhood mirrors, in a sense, a similar phenomenon among working-class young people in the "mood economy," who blame themselves for failing to achieve the trappings of adulthood, such as a home, steady job, and family (Silva 2013; see also Lewis 1993).

78. See Small 2009.

79. Graham 1999; Lacy forthcoming. Annette Lareau has begun a qualitative interview study comparing white and African American high-net-worth families, but it is too early to have results (personal communication).

CHAPTER ONE: ORIENTATIONS TO OTHERS

1. I did not ask my respondents explicitly about what social class they thought they were in. The concept of social class is complicated, and it is hard to know how people understand it. Furthermore, we know that Americans tend to identify as middle class and to think that their income is average. Instead, I attended carefully to how they talked about their class location and about their sense of themselves as privileged or not. I paid special attention to what other people they tended to talk about and in what ways, and I occasionally asked who they compared themselves to. Sometimes toward the end of interviews I asked direct questions about their feelings about people with less or more than they had if they had not mentioned this theme.

2. See Leach et al. 2002 for a social-psychological typology of characteristics they argue predict different forms of recognition or denial of advantage.

3. Leach et al. 2002; Pratto and Stewart 2012. On whiteness, see also Frankenberg 1993; Lipsitz 1998; McIntosh 1988.

4. See Harth et al. 2008.

5. For a review, see Smith and Pettigrew 2014. See also Frank 2007.

6. "The maternalistic dynamic is based on the assumption of a superordinate-subordinate relationship" (Rollins 1985, 186). Maternalism is a "unilateral positioning of the employer as a benefactor who receives personal thanks, recognition, and validation of self from the domestic worker" (Hondagneu-Sotelo 2001, 172).

7. Rivera (2014) also makes this point.

8. See Cooper 2014; Pugh 2015.

9. In this discussion I have assigned different pseudonyms to these women than those they are given elsewhere in the book to avoid making them identifiable. See appendix.

10. I think of *affluent* as meaning less wealthy than *wealthy*, and also as a euphemism for *wealthy*. Friends and colleagues I have asked about this, however, often disagree, believing that the two words are essentially equivalent, which is what Pam and Beverly seemed to believe as well.

11. See, e.g., Jackson 2001; Lacy 2007; Pattillo 2013.

12. One woman's father had married into extreme wealth when she was in middle school, creating in her what she called a "dual consciousness" as both a wealthy

and a not-wealthy person. Another respondent had lived in a more lower-middle-class style for several years after his wealthy grandfather got angry at his parents and cut them off.

13. It is impossible to say with this kind of evidence which comes first—one's orientation to privilege or the diversity of one's relationships (or politics or job). As the quotations I have shared show, once people enter certain kinds of environments, such as jobs or schools, those environments will provide reference points in the form of people with more or fewer resources. But of course one has made the choice between public or private school, or between working in one sector or the other, in the first place—choices that presumably have come from some preexisting orientation.

14. Leach et al. (2002, 156) refer to "strategic modesty" about privilege as one way people deal with guilt over their advantages.

CHAPTER TWO: WORKING HARD OR HARDLY WORKING?

1. Unless these issues came up on their own—which they often did—I usually saved this question for the end of the interview. I thought it might provoke negative responses, because it so directly alluded to the interviewees' privilege and could imply that I thought they did not deserve what they had.

2. See McCall 2013.

3. Gaztambide-Fernández 2009; Ho 2009; Khan 2011; Khan and Jerolmack 2013; Lacy 2007; McNamee and Miller 2004. For similar discourses in France and England, see Power et al. 2016. McCall (2016) finds that the top 1 percent are especially likely, relative to other income groups and other possible factors, to agree that hard work is important for getting ahead. Khan 2011 shows how young people at an elite boarding school learn to deploy this discourse.

4. Folbre 1991; Kaplan Daniels 1987; Sherman 2010.

5. Kaplan Daniels 1987, 1988.

6. As we will see in chapter 5, her husband was careful to recognize her labor as contributing, which helped her frame herself this way.

7. Lareau 2011; Rivera 2015.

8. Power et al. 2016, 311.

9. Brown et al. 2016, 200.

10. Heather Beth Johnson (2006) has also shown that affluent people simultaneously recognize and deny their advantages. Her interviewees agreed that having educational advantages provided a leg up but also asserted a strong belief in

the American Dream and equality of opportunity, even when confronted very explicitly with this contradiction.

11. I do not include Vera in the core sample of fifty because she is not a parent. See appendix.

12. On media framing of structural issues as individual ones, see Kendall 2005.

13. Respondents with inherited wealth who also earned significant amounts of money were typically less conflicted about it than those who lived primarily on their inherited wealth. These respondents were able to rely on the "earner" discourse of moral worth while also avoiding the anxiety felt by earners who lacked a safety net.

14. Odendahl 1990; Ostrander 1995a.

15. Ostrower (1995, 108) also makes this point.

16. Thaler 1999. See also Zelizer 1994 on "special monies" and Zelizer 2012 on "relational accounting." On the changing of the meaning of money according to the source, see Carruthers and Espeland 1998; Kornhauser 1994.

17. Ostrander 1984; see also Kaplan Daniels 1988.

18. Two of these women had some paid part-time work, but very few hours, and they spent most of their time on unpaid household and family work. They would not have defined themselves as "stay-at-home mothers," partly for the reasons I describe in this section.

19. Stone 2007. See also Blair-Loy 2003.

20. Weinbaum and Bridges (1976) coined this term, although they are not referring to the lifestyle work of wealthy women but rather to everyday consumption tasks such as grocery shopping.

21. Folbre 1991; Sherman 2010.

22. Folbre and Nelson 2000; Strasser 1982; Weinbaum and Bridges 1976.

23. Kaplan Daniels 1988.

24. African American women have worked for pay since the end of slavery in much greater numbers than white women and have been morally judged on the basis of not doing so, which has implications for their decisions about leaving paid work (Barnes 2015).

25. She had chosen this amount not because it reflected the market value of her work, which she thought would in fact be higher, but because it was the amount of dividend income she could generate from her assets while also paying taxes and her children's private school tuition. Hence, to call it a "salary" was purely symbolic.

26. Macdonald 2011.

27. See Silva 2013 for a related argument about working-class youth: that the "mood economy" leads them to explain their economic position in terms of individual affect, thus assigning responsibility only to themselves.

CHAPTER THREE: "A VERY EXPENSIVE ORDINARY LIFE"

1. On "ordinariness," see Savage et al. 2001; Sayer 2005.
2. The same is true of judgments we might make of their lifestyle choices.
3. Zelizer 1994, 2012.
4. Bourdieu 1984.
5. Ellen was one of the expert service providers I interviewed, not part of the sample of fifty wealthy parents, because she lives in another city, but I did talk with her about her experience of privilege as well as about her work.
6. On managing feeling, see Hochschild 1989a.
7. See Frank 2007.
8. See Pugh 2009 on children's consumption as a mechanism of belonging.
9. Because he had no children, I include Nathan in the noncore sample. See appendix.
10. Sherman 2011.
11. Many of these experts work on commission or otherwise receive a percentage of what the client spends, so in that sense they have a monetary incentive to encourage higher levels of spending. However, those I interviewed described themselves as more concerned with making clients happy than with persuading them to buy the more expensive items. On how luxury hotel workers similarly cultivate entitlement among hotel guests, see Sherman 2007.
12. The majority estimated that they spent $240,000–$360,000 ($20,000–$30,000 per month). These estimates were imprecise, often simply referring to the monthly total on the credit card statement, not always including kids' school tuition, which was sometimes paid for by grandparents or other family members, or mortgages.

CHAPTER FOUR: "GIVING BACK," AWARENESS, AND IDENTITY

1. Other researchers have also identified this cultural imperative. See, e.g., Ostrander 1984, p. 36 and chapter 6; Power et al. 2016; Whillans et al. 2016.
2. See Sayer 2005, chapter 7, on egalitarianism and interpersonal relations across class.
3. Scholars such as Diana Kendall (2002), for example, have pointed out the tension between the attempts of the upper-class women she studied to help others and the exclusive organizations they construct through which to do this. Furthermore, as some of these researchers have noted, most of these women's charitable giving benefits their own communities. On these issues

see also Chin 2011; Odendahl 1990; Ostrander 1984, 1995a; Ostrower 1995; Silver 2007.

4. Note that the "hair shirt" is a religious image of extreme self-sacrifice and discomfort, not unlike Ellen's reference to a "vow of poverty" in the previous chapter.

5. Nicole similarly suggested that "nice" people should not be judged. As I noted in chapter 3, she was upset that her husband's family members judged her for consuming in a way they found excessive but she thought was reasonable in New York. She said, "I think the reason why I feel like, really annoyed at being judged, is because it feels really unfair. I tried very hard to not, like—I can't afford to be that kind of person. And I'm not that kind of person. And if you want to meet that kind of person, I'll introduce you to them. And guess what? They're really nice, and you shouldn't give them grief either, you know?" Nicole suggested that being "that kind of person"—illegitimately entitled and thus worthy of critique—is based not only on how much one has but also on how "nice" one is.

6. I found this symbolic requirement in my study of luxury hotels (Sherman 2007); workers understood reciprocity and niceness as the basis for entitlement to highly personalized luxury service. Reciprocity from guests to workers was one of the key means by which the obvious inequality between them came to seem normal. When guests treated workers with friendliness and gratitude, the class difference between them faded into the background. See also Sayer 2005, chapter 7.

7. This is according to my very rough calculations, which were especially difficult to make in the case of inheritors. Many interviewees could not estimate with confidence how much they gave away. See appendix.

8. Although I tried to ask all interviewees about their charitable habits, I did not address the topic in as much detail as I did some of the other issues. Thus I cannot make precise claims about recipient organizations or amounts.

9. For example, one African American man worked to "bring fitness to communities of color." Creating this access is one way he could "give back and make a difference," which mattered to him partly because of health problems in his family.

10. Ostrander 1984; see also Kaplan Daniels 1988; Odendahl 1990.

11. Chin 2011; Domhoff 1971; Kaplan Daniels 1988; Odendahl 1990; Ostrower 1995. See Silver 2007 for a review.

12. See Kaplan Daniels 1988 for an in-depth study of the "invisible careers" of wealthy women volunteers.

13. One suburban woman explained to me about the Junior League: "I moved here, and I was like, 'What am I going to do,' right? And I don't know anyone.

So what the Junior League really does—it's a bunch of women that just want to volunteer. And a way to do it. They need a forum, to [do it]—so, it's all about giving back. But you need a forum to do it. So they already have set up things that you can do."

14. Many New York elites are, of course, deeply invested in being patrons of the arts and other social and educational institutions. These are likely to be the old-money and super-rich elites I did not interview (see, e.g., Ostrower 1995).

15. There were a couple of notable exceptions. Wendy, for example, felt that giving to her alma mater was unnecessary. She said, "I've been given all the opportunity in the world, and I'm going to give my money to people who haven't been, not to me twenty years ago."

16. A donor-advised fund is a charitable fund usually administered by a public organization such as a nonprofit in which the giving is directed by the donor over time.

17. Resource Generation exists, like some other similar organizations, partly in order to create spaces where people can not only talk about these issues but also come up with giving priorities and plans (Wernick 2009).

18. Donovan also explicitly connected the moral dimension of the question of how much to give to his own spending rather than his assets. He said, "I mean, what's the right metric? Should you be focusing on giving away a percentage of your assets? What's ethically interesting to me is not what percentage of your wealth you're giving away but what's the connection between what you're spending on yourself and what you're giving away. Again, I don't spend a lot as a percentage of my wealth, [and] I don't give a lot as a percentage of my wealth. But I give a lot as a percentage of what I spend on myself."

19. See Whillans et al. 2016 on the idea of "giving back" as linked to taxes.

20. It is interesting that Nadine chooses the language of "death tax" over "estate tax," because "death tax" is more often used by opponents of the tax.

21. As Ira Silver (2007) has argued, the organizations of the type supported by the most progressive in my sample do tend to challenge inequalities of various kinds rather than only reproduce privilege. Yet he shows that the structures of these organizations (in his case, progressive groups that make grants to smaller organizations), despite the best efforts of staff, donors, and activists, often still reproduce class divisions between funders and activists and/or reproduce donors' claims to have particular kinds of identities validated. See also Ostrander 1995a; Roelofs 2003; Wernick 2009. For a philosophical discussion of this dilemma, see Cohen 2000.

22. This link between individual entitlement or advancement and awareness of systematic inequality has also been noted, in a different context, by Heather Beth Johnson (2006).

23. See Mogil and Slepian with Woodrow 1991.
24. As noted in the introduction, these respondents are not included in the core sample of fifty parents.

CHAPTER FIVE: LABOR, SPENDING, AND ENTITLEMENT IN COUPLES

1. See Acker 1988 on the ways interpersonal relations in the family deflect attention from the gendered distribution of resources.
2. See, e.g., Blumberg 1988; Blumberg and Coleman 1989; Blumstein and Schwartz 1991; Burgoyne 1990; Chang 2010; Dema-Moreno 2009. Additional literature looks at how couples manage money, especially whether they share it or separate it; whether pooling systems lead to equal access to and control over money; and how members of couples spend similarly or differently (Kenney 2006; Klawitter 2008; Ludwig-Mayerhofer et al., 2011; Pahl 1983, 1990; Treas 1993; Vogler 2005; Vogler and Pahl 1993, 1994; Vogler et al. 2008; Yodanis and Lauer 2007). Though pooling seems more egalitarian, it actually can mean less independence for women; because both partners feel that earning confers greater control, male earners spend more and women nonearners less (but when women earn more, men still spend it) (Schwartz et al. 2012, 259–60). See also Chang (2010) on the barriers to wealth accumulation for women.
3. For an overview, see Shockley and Shen 2016 and Zelizer 2005, 244. For a recent discussion of gender identity specifically, see Schneider 2012.
4. This is in a sense an economy of *recognition* of each person's contribution, similar to Hochschild's (1989a) concept of the "economy of gratitude."
5. See, e.g., Acker 1988; Coulson et al. 1975; DeVault 1991; Folbre 1991; Fraser 2014; Laslett and Brenner 1989; Molyneux 1979; Nakano Glenn 1992; Schwartz Cowan 1984; Secombe 1974; Weinbaum and Bridges 1976; Zelizer 2005. See also Raxlen and Sherman 2016.
6. I have more data on relations in these households because I have seventeen such households in the sample; the dual-earner, dual-contributor, and inherited-wealth categories all include fewer households, which vary more in terms of the gender of the person bringing the wealth. I thus go into more depth on the single-earner households here. I have masked some identifying characteristics in this chapter because many interviewees said that these issues were the most private.
7. By this I mean the few women who worked very part-time, usually freelance. These women would not characterize themselves as stay-at-home mothers

(avoiding the stigma of that label) but spent the vast majority of their time on family rather than paid labor.

8. Nearly all had joint bank accounts, at least for daily living, and pooled savings in retirement and college accounts. But many also maintained their own individual accounts (occasionally in secret, as we'll see). Practices of daily money management varied. In some cases, one person of the couple paid all the bills; in others, each partner was responsible for different expenses.

9. Although in a few cases this claim rang untrue—I suspected that they were saying it in order to avoid disclosing numbers—many seemed genuinely not to know. Julia, for example, underestimated the cost of her $600,000 renovation by $200,000, and her husband corrected her. When men worked in some finance or legal jobs or owned their own businesses, this lack of clarity was compounded by the fact that bonuses or unpredictable windfalls constituted a large share of their income and/or that their assets were invested in their companies. Thus they either did not receive a conventional salary or it was only a small part of their total compensation.

10. In a few of these families, the man had participated more actively in the decision making. But in only one case did the husband take the lead role across the board (partly because his wife was pregnant).

11. In some cases this was another facet of concern regarding the prudent use of money. For example, one woman said her husband had insisted on high-end kitchen appliances because he cared about resale value, although they were planning to live in their renovated house long-term.

12. I suspect that my interviewees in general were likely to underestimate or keep silent about the amount of conflict they had with their partners over spending. Those who did talk about it usually emphasized that it was deeply private.

13. On "consumption work," see Weinbaum and Bridges 1976.

14. The wealthy women volunteers Kaplan Daniels (1988, 33) studied similarly had to prioritize their husbands' needs over their volunteer work.

15. It seems that Alice was going to say she "proved" she could work. This is the same kind of interpretive move I described in chapter 2, in which because Alice "did that" she can *feel like* a worker, or have a worker's "mindset," even without currently working for money.

16. With limited variation in the gender of inheritors, it is difficult to draw comparative conclusions. I also interviewed more inheritors than spouses of inheritors, so it is hard to make claims about spouses' views.

17. She told me, "Thank God my kids learned to write in cursive. 'Cause you know they don't teach that in public schools anymore. Because they will need to sign their names a lot."

18. Ehrenreich 2002; Hochschild 1989b; Rollins 1985.
19. DeVault 1991, 1999; Streib 2015.
20. A few women in inheritor households also worked full-time, but they typically had more flexible jobs.
21. See Tichenor 2005.
22. Tichenor 2005.
23. On the family myth, see Hochschild 1989b.
24. Zelizer 2005, 243; see also Zelizer 2012.
25. See, e.g., Bittman et al. 2003; Brines 1994; Evertsson and Nermo 2004; Hochschild 1989b; Schneider 2012; Tichenor 2005.
26. Yodanis and Lauer 2007.
27. See Chang 2010.
28. See Zelizer 2005 on the relationship of legal categories and processes to family relations around money.
29. Acker 1988, 487.

CHAPTER SIX: PARENTING PRIVILEGE

A modified version of this chapter has been published as Sherman 2017.

1. See Khan 2011; Lareau (2011) uses this word to mean a more positive sense of empowerment. See the introduction and Sherman 2017 on this point.
2. See, e.g., Cooper 2014; Katz 2008, 2012; Nelson 2010.
3. See Cucchiara and Horvat 2014 for a discussion of school choice as identity construction for parents.
4. Nelson 2010, 6. See also Katz 2001, 2008, 2012; Lareau 2002, 2011; Streib 2013. On the pursuit of educational advantages specifically, see Calarco 2011; Johnson 2006; Lareau and Weininger 2008. For the UK context, see, e.g., Devine 2004; Reay 1998, 2005a; Vincent and Ball 2007; Weis et al. 2014. For more detailed engagement with this literature, see Sherman 2017. For popular literature on questions of entitlement, see Carlyle 2012; D'Amico 2010; Gallo and Gallo 2001; Hausner 1990; Lieber 2015.
5. As I discuss later in the chapter, they also taught children to observe the behavioral prohibition on talking about money.
6. As others have pointed out, being a good parent means being a good consumer in the sense of both consuming for children and guiding their consumption (see Cucchiara 2013; Pugh 2009; Schor 2003).
7. See also Pugh 2009.
8. Kolbert 2012.
9. This scheme cultivates not only the child's willingness to work for what he wants but an ethic of self-improvement: he chooses both the type of

self-improvement he engages in to *obtain* the points (participating in school) *and* the type of self-improvement for which he *redeems* them (the art class).

10. Pugh 2009.

11. Allison Pugh (2009) has described similar practices and feelings of ambivalence among the upper-income parents she studied, who used "symbolic deprivation" and "rules and allowances" to manage their children's consumption and their own anxieties about that consumption. Those parents also expressed concerns, linked to their own histories, about how restricting consumption affected their children's dignity. Pugh (2009, 119) theorizes the tension between indulging children's desires and constraining them primarily as having to do with parents' fear of raising kids without self-control and anxiety about materialism as morally unworthy. My complementary interpretation extends this view into the realm of managing affluence more generally by avoiding "entitlement."

12. It is possible that the family travels with a domestic worker accompanying the children in coach class, as I have been told some families do. Unfortunately this possibility did not occur to me during the interview, so I did not ask Allison about it.

13. Gaztambide-Fernández and Howard 2013, 3.

14. Reay et al. 2007 call this "an act of appropriation"; see also Pugh 2009.

15. See Jackson 2001; Pattillo 2013.

16. Pugh 2009; Lacy forthcoming. As Karyn Lacy (2007, 152) has noted in writing about black middle-class parents, "In addition to teaching their children to negotiate the black-white boundary, these parents must also prepare their children to manage class-based boundaries between different groups of blacks." Pugh (2009) also finds that affluent African American parents intentionally place their children in diverse environments, creating what she calls "exposed childhoods."

17. Writing about white middle-class parents who send their children to urban comprehensive schools (which in the United States are known as public schools), they argue, "The white middle-class interest in difference and otherness can thus also be understood as describing a project of cultural capital through which these white middle-class families seek to display their liberal credentials and secure their class position. The ability to move in and out of spaces marked as 'other' becomes part of the process through which this particular fraction of the white middle classes come to know themselves as both privileged and dominant" (Reay et al. 2007, 1047).

18. Reay et al. 2007. See also Gillies 2005; Khan 2011.

19. Some of the less affluent parents also worried that their kids would feel bad about *themselves* if they thought they were the "only ones without a country house," in Linda's words.

20. See also Cucchiara 2013; Cucchiara and Horvat 2014; Johnson 2006.
21. Pugh 2009, 194.
22. One such parent told me the boarding schools were actually more diverse than the public school in her elite, nearly all-white suburb.
23. This is the sense in which Lareau (2011) uses the word. See Sherman 2017.
24. Pugh 2009.
25. Coined by Allison Pugh (2009, 178), the term "pathway consumption" means "spending on the opportunities that shape children's trajectories," especially including school and activities such as summer camp.
26. Bourdieu 1990.

CONCLUSION

1. Stewart 2016.
2. Indeed, much of the press coverage of Rowling has highlighted her status as a struggling single mother on the dole when she wrote the first Harry Potter book.
3. Boshoff 2006.
4. See Schor 1998.
5. See Cooper 2014; Pugh 2015.
6. See, e.g., Lewis 1993.
7. For a recent example, see Silva 2013.
8. Mills 2000 [1959], 8.

METHODOLOGICAL APPENDIX

1. Sherman 2007.
2. Sherman 2010, 2011.
3. Lamont and Swidler 2014, 159.
4. Pugh 2013.
5. Rivera (2014) challenges the idea that the top 1 percent is the "elite"; she uses the top 20 percent because of their greater access to education. Pew Research Center (2016) defines "upper-income" as earning double the national median.
6. Elkins 2015.
7. See Roberts 2014.
8. Salkin 2009.
9. Page et al. 2013. On interviewing elites in general, see Harvey 2011; Mikecz 2012; Ortner 2003; Ostrander 1995b.
10. On schools, see, e.g., Cookson and Persell 1985; Gaztambide-Fernández 2009; Gaztambide-Fernández and Howard 2013; Howard 2010; Khan 2011. On clubs,

see Chin 2011; Cousin and Chauvin 2014; Holden Sherwood 2013; Kendall 2002. On charitable organizations and foundations, see Ostrander 1995a; Ostrower 1995; Silver 2007.

11. Lamont 1992; Ostrower 1995; Page et al. 2013.

12. These multiple factors could be analyzed and perhaps disaggregated in a large-N study, which would not only require more resources than I had and pose sampling challenges, but would also require a survey-style format that would reduce complexity. See Page et al. 2013; Small 2009.

13. Snowball sampling is a sampling method whereby future study subjects are recruited by existing subjects from among people they know.

14. Bourdieu 1984; Goffman 1951.

15. This project included twenty-three interviews with personal concierges and 180 hours of participant observation in the lifestyle management industry, primarily spent working in a high-end Manhattan company offering personal assistant and concierge services (see Sherman 2010, 2011).

16. Many people (nearly always women) who start concierge businesses are quite unsuccessful, as my research has shown (Sherman 2010).

17. See Ostrander 1995b on interactions with elites in interviews.

18. I conducted one interview with a male respondent over the phone because he did not have time to meet with me in person.

19. The exceptions were two people whose interviews had included a lot of extraneous material, so I listened to the interviews and transcribed relevant sections myself. Only one research assistant coded service-provider interviews, and only one coded wealthy-consumer interviews. Both of them did coding alone only after becoming deeply familiar with my coding process, partly by reviewing my codes on many interviews before coding independently.

20. E.g., Small 2009.

21. For recent discussions of these issues, see Jerolmack and Khan 2014; Khan and Jerolmack 2013; Lamont and Swidler 2014; Pugh 2013; Vaisey 2009, 2014.

22. Jerolmack and Khan 2014; Khan and Jerolmack 2013.

23. Ortner 2003, 6.

24. Pugh 2013; also see DeVault 1990; Scott and Lyman 1968.

25. See, e.g., Kefalas 2003; Lamont 1992, 2000; Sayer 2005; Sherman 2009; Silva 2013.

26. This finding is consistent with research on younger affluent people. My respondents differ from the young, wealthy men in the international "VIP party scene" studied by Ashley Mears (2014, 2015a). Mears suggests that participants in this global jet set are highly invested in the public display of wealth (although even they do not talk about particular amounts of money). But as they get

older they may become more similar to my respondents. On the other hand, given that most of them are not from the United States, they may develop other repertoires of merit.

27. Lamont 1992, 2000.

28. See Murphy and Jerolmack 2016.

REFERENCES

Acker, Joan. 1988. "Class, Gender, and the Relations of Distribution." *Signs* 13 (3): 473–497.

Alba, Richard, and Steven Romalewski. 2017. "The End of Segregation? Hardly." New York: Center for Urban Research, Graduate Center, City University of New York. https://www.gc.cuny.edu/Page-Elements/Academics-Research -Centers-Initiatives/Centers-and-Institutes/Center-for-Urban-Research/CUR -research-initiatives/The-End-of-Segregation-Hardly. Accessed February 28, 2017.

Ball, Stephen J., Carol Vincent, Sophie Kemp, and Soile Pietikainen. 2004. "Middle Class Fractions, Childcare and the 'Relational' and 'Normative' Aspects of Class Practices." *Sociological Review* 52 (4): 478–502.

Baltzell, E. Digby. 1964. *The Protestant Establishment: Aristocracy & Caste in America*. New York: Random House.

———. 1991. *The Protestant Establishment Revisited*. New Brunswick, NJ: Transaction.

Barnes, Riché. 2015. *Raising the Race: Black Career Women Redefine Marriage, Motherhood, and Community*. New Brunswick, NJ: Rutgers University Press.

Bartels, Larry. 2008. *Unequal Democracy: The Political Economy of the New Gilded Age*. New York: Russell Sage.

Beaverstock, Jonathan V. and Iain Hay (eds). 2016. *Handbook on Wealth and the Super-Rich*. Cheltenham, UK: Edward Elgar.

Bettie, Julie. 2003. *Women without Class: Girls, Race, and Identity*. Berkeley: University of California Press.

Bittman, Michael, Paula England, Nancy Folbre, Liana Sayer, and George Matheson. 2003. "When Does Gender Trump Money? Bargaining and Time in Household Work." *American Journal of Sociology* 109: 186–214.

Blair-Loy, Mary. 2003. *Competing Devotions: Career and Family among Women Executives*. Cambridge, MA: Harvard University Press.

Blumberg, Rae Lesser. 1988. "Income under Female versus Male Control: Hypotheses from a Theory of Gender Stratification and Data from the Third World." *Journal of Family Issues* 9 (1): 51–84.

Blumberg, Rae Lesser, and Marion Tolbert Coleman. 1989. "A Theoretical Look at the Gender Balance of Power in the American Couple." *Journal of Family Issues* 10 (2): 225–250.

Blumstein, Philip, and Pepper Schwartz. 1991. "Money and Ideology: Their Impact on Power and the Division of Household Labor." Pp. 261–288 in *Gender, Family and Economy: The Triple Overlap*, edited by Rae Lesser Blumberg. Newbury Park, CA: Sage.

Bonilla-Silva, Eduardo. 2006. *Racism without Racists: Color-Blind Racism and the Persistence of Racial Inequality in the United States*. Lanham, MD: Rowman and Littlefield.

Boshoff, Alison. 2006. "What Does JK Rowling Do with Her Money?" *Daily Mail*, August 24. Available at http://www.dailymail.co.uk/femail/article-402027/What-does-JK-Rowling-money.html.

Bourdieu, Pierre. 1984. *Distinction*. Cambridge, MA: Harvard University Press.

———. 1990. *The Logic of Practice*. Cambridge, UK: Polity Press.

Bricker, Jesse, Alice Henriques, Jacob Krimmel, and John Sabelhaus. 2016. "Measuring Income and Wealth at the Top Using Administrative and Survey Data." *Brookings Papers on Economics Activity* (Spring): 261–312. Available at https://www.jstor.org/stable/43869025?seq=1#page_scan_tab_contents.

Brines, Julie. 1994. "Economic Dependency, Gender, and the Division of Labor at Home." *American Journal of Sociology* 100: 652–688.

Brooks, David. 2000. *Bobos in Paradise: The New Upper Class and How They Got There*. New York: Simon & Schuster.

Brown, Phillip, Sally Power, Gerbrand Tholen, and Annabelle Allouch. 2016. "Credentials, Talent and Cultural Capital: A Comparative Study of Educational Elites in England and France." *British Journal of Sociology of Education* 37 (2): 191–211.

Burgoyne, Carol. 1990. "Money in Marriage: How Patterns of Allocation both Reflect and Conceal Power." *Sociological Review* 38: 634–665.

Burns, Alexander, and Giovanni Russonello. 2015. "Half of New Yorkers Say They Are Barely or Not Getting By, Poll Shows." *New York Times*, November 18. Available at http://www.nytimes.com/2015/11/19/nyregion/half-of-new-yorkers-say-they-are-barely-or-not-getting-by-poll-shows.html.

Calarco, Jessica McCrory. 2011. "'I Need Help!' Social Class and Children's Help-Seeking in Elementary School." *American Sociological Review* 76 (6): 862–882.

Carlyle, Erin. 2012. "Father's Day Advice from Billionaires: How to Not Raise Spoiled Kids." *Forbes*, June 15. Available at http://www.forbes.com/sites/erincarlyle/2012/06/15/billionaire-advice-how-to-not-raise-spoiled-kids/.

Carruthers, Bruce, and Wendy Espeland. 1998. "Money, Meaning, and Morality." *American Behavioral Scientist* 41 (10): 1384–1408.

Chang, Mariko Lin. 2010. *Shortchanged: Why Women Have Less Wealth and What Can Be Done about It*. Oxford, UK: Oxford University Press.

Chetty, Raj, Nathaniel Hendren, Patrick Kline, and Emmanuel Saez. 2015. "Economic Mobility." *Pathways Magazine*, Stanford Center for the Study of Poverty and Inequality, Winter: 55–60. Available at http://inequality.stanford.edu/sotu/SOTU_2015_economic-mobility.pdf.

Chin, Fiona. 2011. "Inequality among the Affluent." Paper presented at Eastern Sociological Society Annual Meeting, Philadelphia, February.

Cohen, G. A. 2000. "If You're an Egalitarian, How Come You're So Rich?" *Journal of Ethics* 4 (1–2): 1–26.

Cookson, Peter, and Caroline Hodges Persell. 1985. *Preparing for Power: America's Elite Boarding Schools.* New York: Basic Books.

Cooper, Marianne. 2014. *Cut Adrift: Families in Insecure Times.* Berkeley: University of California Press.

Coulson, Margaret, Branka Magas, and Hilary Wainwright. 1975. "The Housewife and Her Labour under Capitalism: A Critique." *New Left Review* 89: 59–71.

Cousin, Bruno, and Sébastien Chauvin. 2014. "Globalizing Forms of Elite Sociability: Varieties of Cosmopolitanism in Paris Social Clubs." *Ethnic and Racial Studies* 37 (12): 2209–2225.

Cucchiara, Maia. 2013. "'Are We Doing Damage?' Choosing an Urban Public School in an Era of Parental Anxiety." *Anthropology and Education Quarterly* 44 (1): 75–93.

Cucchiara, Maia, and Erin Horvat. 2014. "Choosing Selves: The Salience of Parental Identity in the School Choice Process." *Journal of Education Policy* 29 (4): 486–509.

Cullen, Jim. 2004. *The American Dream: A Short History of an Idea That Shaped a Nation.* New York: Oxford University Press.

Daloz, Jean-Pascal. 2012. *The Sociology of Elite Distinction.* New York: Palgrave Macmillan.

D'Amico, James V. 2010. *Affluenza Antidote: How Wealthy Families Can Raise Grounded Children in an Age of Apathy and Entitlement.* CreateSpace Independent Publishing Platform.

David, Gerald F., and Suntae Kim. 2015. "Financialization of the Economy." *Annual Review of Sociology* 41: 203–221.

Dema-Moreno, Sandra. 2009. "Behind the Negotiations: Financial Decision-Making Processes in Spanish Dual-Income Couples." *Feminist Economics* 15 (1): 27–56.

DeMott, Benjamin. 1990. *The Imperial Middle.* New York: William Morrow.

Desmond, Matthew. 2016. *Evicted: Poverty and Profit in the American City.* New York: Crown.

DeVault, Marjorie. 1990. "Talking and Listening from Women's Standpoint: Feminist Strategies for Interviewing and Analysis." *Social Problems* 37 (1): 96–116.

———. 1991. *Feeding the Family: The Social Organization of Caring as Gendered Work.* Chicago: University of Chicago Press.

———. 1999. "Comfort and Struggle: Emotion Work in Family Life." *Annals of the American Academy for Political and Social Sciences* 561: 52–63.

Devine, Fiona. 2004. *Class Practices: How Parents Help Their Children Get Good Jobs*. Cambridge, UK: Cambridge University Press.

Domhoff, William. 1971. *The Higher Circles: The Governing Class in America*. New York: Vintage Books.

———. 2010. *Who Rules America: Challenges to Corporate and Class Dominance* (Sixth Edition). New York: McGraw-Hill.

Dwyer, Rachel E., and Erik Olin Wright. 2012. "Job Growth and Job Polarization in the United States and Europe, 1995–2007." Pp. 52–74 in *Transformation of the Employment Structure in the EU and USA, 1995–2007*, edited by Enrique Fernández-Macías, John Hurley, and Donald Storrie. Hampshire, UK: Palgrave Macmillan.

Edin, Kathryn, and Maria Kefalas. 2005. *Promises I Can Keep: Why Poor Women Put Motherhood before Marriage*. Berkeley: University of California Press.

Edin, Kathryn, and Laura Lein. 1997. *Making Ends Meet: How Single Mothers Survive Welfare and Low-Wage Work*. New York: Russell Sage.

Edin, Kathryn J., and H. Luke Shaefer. 2015. *$2.00 A Day: Living on Almost Nothing in America*. Boston: Houghton Mifflin Harcourt.

Ehrenreich, Barbara. 1989. *Fear of Falling: The Inner Life of the Middle Class*. New York: Harper Perennial.

———. 2002. "Maid to Order." Pp. 85–103 in *Global Woman: Nannies, Maids, and Sex Workers in the New Economy*, edited by Barbara Ehrenreich and Arlie R. Hochschild. New York: Henry Holt.

Ehrenreich, John, and Barbara Ehrenreich. 1979. "The Professional-Managerial Class." In *Between Labor and Capital*, edited by Pat Walker. Boston: South End Press.

Elkins, Kathleen. 2015. "Here's What You Need to Earn to Be in the Top 1% in 13 Major US Cities." *Business Insider*, August. Available at http://www.businessinsider.com/income-top-one-percent-us-cities-2015-8.

Evertsson, Marie, and Magnus Nermo. 2004. "Dependence within Families and the Division of Labor: Comparing Sweden and the United States." *Journal of Marriage and Family* 66: 1272–1286.

Fan, Jiayang. 2016. "The Golden Generation." *New Yorker*, February 22. Available at http://www.newyorker.com/magazine/2016/02/22/chinas-rich-kids-head-west.

Fiscal Policy Institute. 2010. "Grow Together or Pull Farther Apart? Income Concentration Trends in New York." Available at http://fiscalpolicy.org/wp-content/uploads/2010/12/FPI_GrowTogetherOrPullFurtherApart_20101213.pdf. Accessed November 16, 2016.

Folbre, Nancy. 1991. "The Unproductive Housewife: Her Evolution in Nineteenth-Century Economic Thought." *Signs* 16 (3): 463–484.

Folbre, Nancy, and Julie Nelson. 2000. "For Love or Money—Or Both?" *Journal of Economic Perspectives* 14 (4): 123–140.

Frank, Robert H. 2007. *Falling Behind: How Rising Inequality Harms the Middle Class*. Berkeley: University of California Press.

Frank, Robert. 2008. *Richistan: A Journey through the American Wealth Boom and the Lives of the New Rich*. Three Rivers, CA: Penguin Random House.

Frankenberg, Ruth. 1993. *White Women, Race Matters: The Social Construction of Whiteness*. Minneapolis: University of Minnesota Press.

Fraser, Nancy. 2014. "Behind Marx's Hidden Abode: For an Expanded Conception of Capitalism." *New Left Review* 86: 1–17.

Freeland, Chrystia. 2012. *Plutocrats: The Rise of the New Global Super-Rich and the Fall of Everyone Else*. New York: Penguin.

Fry, Richard, and Paul Taylor. 2012. "The Rise of Residential Segregation by Income." Pew Research Center report, August 1. Available at http://www.pewsocialtrends.org/2012/08/01/the-rise-of-residential-segregation-by-income/.

Fussell, Paul. 1983. *Class: A Guide through the American Status System*. New York: Simon & Schuster.

Gallo, Ellen, and Jon Gallo. 2001. *Silver Spoon Kids: How Successful Parents Raise Responsible Children*. New York: McGraw-Hill.

Gaztambide-Fernández, Rubén. 2009. *The Best of the Best: Becoming Elite at an American Boarding School*. Cambridge, MA: Harvard University Press.

Gaztambide-Fernández, Rubén, and Adam Howard. 2013. "Social Justice, Deferred Complicity, and the Moral Plight of the Wealthy." *Democracy & Education* 21 (1): Article 7.

Gilens, Martin. 1999. *Why Americans Hate Welfare: Race, Media and the Politics of Antipoverty Policy*. Chicago: University of Chicago Press.

Gillies, Val. 2005. "Raising the 'Meritocracy': Parenting and the Individualization of Social Class." *Sociology* 39 (5): 835–853.

Goffman, Alice. 2014. *On The Run: Fugitive Life in an American City*. Chicago: University of Chicago Press.

Goffman, Erving. 1951. "Symbols of Class Status." *British Journal of Sociology* 2: 294–304.

Graham, Lawrence Otis. 1999. *Our Kind of People: Inside America's Black Upper Class*. New York: Harper.

Gramsci, Antonio. 1971. *Selections from the Prison Notebooks*. New York: International Publishers.

Gregory, Kia. 2014. "Citing 'Inequality Crisis,' Mayor Names Top Legal Adviser and Fills 2 Other Jobs." *New York Times*, February 18. Available at http://www.nytimes.com/2014/02/19/nyregion/citing-inequality-crisis-mayor-names-top-legal-adviser-and-fills-2-other-jobs.html.

Hacker, Jacob. 2006. *The Great Risk Shift: The New Economic Insecurity and the Decline of the American Dream*. New York: Oxford University Press.

Hacker, Jacob, and Paul Pierson. 2011. *Winner-Take-All Politics*. New York: Simon & Schuster.

Halle, David. 1984. *America's Working Man: Work, Home, and Politics among Blue Collar Property Owners*. Chicago: University of Chicago Press.

Harth, Nicole Syringa, Thomas Kessler, and Colin Wayne Leach. 2008. "Advantaged Groups' Emotional Reactions to Intergroup Inequality: The Dynamics of Pride, Guilt, and Sympathy." *Personality and Social Psychology Bulletin* 34: 115–128.

Harvey, William S. 2011. "Strategies for Conducting Elite Interviews." *Qualitative Research* 11: 431–441.

Hausner, Lee. 1990. *Children of Paradise: Successful Parenting for Prosperous Families*. New York: St. Martin's Press.

Hay, Iain (ed.). 2013. *Geographies of the Super-Rich*. Cheltenham UK: Edward Elgar.

Hays, Sharon. 2003. *Flat Broke with Children: Women in the Age of Welfare Reform*. New York: Oxford University Press.

Heiman, Rachel. 2015. *Driving after Class: Anxious Times in an American Suburb*. Berkeley: University of California Press.

Heiman, Rachel, Carla Freeman, and Mark Liechty. 2012. "Introduction: Charting an Anthropology of the Middle Classes." Pp. 3–29 in *The Global Middle Classes: Theorizing Through Ethnography*, edited by Rachel Heiman, Carla Freeman, and Mark Liechty. Santa Fe: SAR Press.

Ho, Karen. 2009. *Liquidated: An Ethnography of Wall Street*. Durham, NC: Duke University Press.

Hoang, Kimberly Kay. 2015. *Dealing in Desire: Asian Ascendancy, Western Decline, and the Hidden Currencies of Global Sex Work*. Berkeley: University of California Press.

Hochschild, Arlie R. 1989a. "The Economy of Gratitude." Pp. 95–113 in *The Sociology of Emotions: Original Essays and Research Papers*, edited by David D. Franks and E. Doyle McCarthy. Greenwich, CT: JAI Press.

———. 1989b. *The Second Shift: Working Parents and the Revolution at Home*. New York: Viking Penguin.

———. 2016. *Strangers in Their Own Land*. New York: New Press.

Hochschild, Jennifer. 1995. *Facing Up to the American Dream: Class, Race, and the Soul of the Nation*. Princeton, NJ: Princeton University Press.

Holden Sherwood, Jessica. 2013. *Wealth, Whiteness, and the Matrix of Privilege: The View from the Country Club*. Lanham, MD: Lexington.

Hondagneu-Sotelo, Pierrette. 2001. *Doméstica: Immigrant Workers Cleaning and Caring in the Shadows of Affluence*. Berkeley: University of California Press.

Howard, Adam. 2010. *Learning Privilege: Lessons of Power and Identity in Affluent Schooling*. New York: Routledge.

Irwin, Sarah, and Sharon Elley. 2011. "Concerted Cultivation? Parenting Values, Education and Class Diversity." *Sociology* 45 (3): 480–495.

Jackson, John. 2001. *Harlemworld*. Chicago: University of Chicago Press.

Jensen, Barbara. 2004. "Across the Great Divide: Crossing Classes, Clashing Cultures." Pp. 168–184 in *What's Class Got to Do with It?*, edited by Michael Zweig. Ithaca, NY: Cornell University Press.

Jerolmack, Colin, and Shamus Khan. 2014. "'Talk Is Cheap': Ethnography and the Attitudinal Fallacy." *Sociological Methods & Research* 43: 178–209.

Johnson, Heather Beth. 2006. *The American Dream and the Power of Wealth*. New York: Routledge.

Kaplan Daniels, Arlene. 1987. "Invisible Work." *Social Problems* 34 (5): 403–415.

———. 1988. *Invisible Careers: Women Civic Leaders from the Volunteer World*. Chicago: University of Chicago Press.

Karabel, Jerome. 2005. *The Chosen: The Hidden History of Admission and Exclusion at Harvard, Yale, and Princeton*. New York: Houghton Mifflin.

Karademir Hazir, Irmak, and Alan Warde. 2016. "The Cultural Omnivore Thesis: Methodological Aspects of the Debate." Pp. 77–89 in *The Routledge Handbook of the Sociology of Arts and Culture*, edited by Laurie Hanquinet and Mike Savage. New York: Routledge.

Katz, Cindi. 2001. "The State Comes Home: Local Hyper-Vigilance of Children and the Global Retreat from Social Reproduction." *Social Justice* 28 (3): 47–55.

———. 2008. "Childhood as Spectacle: Relays of Anxiety and the Reconfiguration of the Child." *Cultural Geographies* 15: 5–17.

———. 2012. "Just Managing: American Middle-Class Parenthood in Insecure Times." Pp. 169–188 in *The Global Middle Classes*, edited by Rachel Heiman, Carla Freeman, and Mark Liechty. Santa Fe, NM: SAR.

Katz, Michael. 2013. *The Undeserving Poor: America's Enduring Confrontation with Poverty; Fully Updated and Revised*. New York: Oxford.

Kefalas, Maria. 2003. *Working-Class Heroes*. Berkeley: University of California Press.

Keister, Lisa. 2005. *Getting Rich: America's New Rich and How They Got That Way*. Cambridge, UK: Cambridge University Press.

———. 2014. "The One Percent." *Annual Review of Sociology* 40: 347–367.

Keister, Lisa, and Stephanie Moller. 2000. "Wealth Inequality in the United States." *Annual Review of Sociology* 26: 63–81.

Keller, Bill. 2005. "Introduction." Pp. ix–xviii in *Class Matters*, edited by correspondents of the *New York Times*. New York: Times Books.

Kendall, Diana. 2002. *The Power of Good Deeds: Privileged Women and the Social Reproduction of the Upper Class*. Lanham, MD: Rowman and Littlefield.

―――. 2005. *Framing Class: Media Representations of Wealth and Poverty in America*. Lanham, MD: Rowman & Littlefield.

Kenney, Catherine. 2006. "The Power of the Purse: Allocative Systems and Inequality in Couple Households." *Gender and Society* 20 (3): 354–381.

Kenworthy, Lane. 2015. "Is Income Inequality Harmful?" In *The Good Society*. https://lanekenworthy.net/is-income-inequality-harmful/. Last accessed January 2017.

Khan, Shamus. 2011. *Privilege*. Princeton, NJ: Princeton University Press.

―――. 2012. "The Sociology of Elites." *Annual Review of Sociology* 38 (1): 361–377.

Khan, Shamus, and Colin Jerolmack. 2013. "Saying Meritocracy, Doing Privilege." *Sociological Quarterly* 54: 9–19.

Khimm, Suzy. 2011. "Who Are the 1 Percent?" *Washington Post*, October 6. Available at https://www.washingtonpost.com/blogs/ezra-klein/post/who-are-the-1-percenters/2011/10/06/gIQAn4JDQL_blog.html.

Klawitter, Marieka. 2008. "The Effects of Sexual Orientation and Marital Status on How Couples Hold Their Money." *Review of Economics of the Household* 6 (4): 423–446.

Kluegel, James R., and Eliot R. Smith. 1986. *Beliefs about Inequality: Americans' Views of What Is and What Ought to Be*. New Brunswick, NJ: Transaction.

Kolbert, Elizabeth. 2012. "Spoiled Rotten: Why Do Kids Rule the Roost?" *New Yorker*, July 2. Available at http://www.newyorker.com/magazine/2012/07/02/spoiled-rotten.

Korndörfer, Martin, Boris Egloff, and Stefan C. Schmukle. 2015. "A Large Scale Test of the Effect of Social Class on Prosocial Behavior." *PLoS ONE* 10 (7): e0133193. doi:10.1371/journal.pone.0133193.

Kornhauser, Marjorie E. 1994. "The Morality of Money: American Attitudes Toward Wealth and the Income Tax." *Indiana Law Journal* 70 (1): Article 5.

Krugman, Paul. 2002. "For Richer." *New York Times Magazine*, October 20. Available at http://www.nytimes.com/2002/10/20/magazine/for-richer.html

Lacy, Karyn. 2007. *Blue-Chip Black: Race, Class, and Status in the New Black Middle Class*. Berkeley: University of California Press.

―――. Forthcoming. *Black Like Us*. New York: Russell Sage.

Lamont, Michèle. 1992. *Money, Morals and Manners*. Chicago: University of Chicago Press.

―――. 2000. *The Dignity of Working Men*. Cambridge, MA: Harvard University Press.

Lamont, Michèle, and Virág Molnár. 2002. "The Study of Boundaries in the Social Sciences." *Annual Review of Sociology* 28: 167–195.

Lamont, Michèle, and Ann Swidler. 2014. "Methodological Pluralism and the Possibilities and Limits of Interviewing." *Qualitative Sociology* 37: 153–171.

Lane, Carrie. 2011. *A Company of One*. Ithaca, NY: Cornell University Press.

Lareau, Annette. 2002. "Invisible Inequality: Social Class and Child Rearing in Black and White Families." *American Sociological Review* 67: 747–776.

———. 2011. *Unequal Childhoods* (Second Edition). Berkeley: University of California Press.

Lareau, Annette, and Dalton Conley (eds.). 2008. *Social Class: How Does It Work?* New York: Russell Sage.

Lareau, Annette, and Elliot B. Weininger. 2008. "Time, Work, and Family Life: Reconceptualizing Gendered Time Patterns through the Case of Children's Organized Activities." *Sociological Forum* 23 (3): 419–454.

Laslett, Barbara, and Johanna Brenner. 1989. "Gender and Social Reproduction: Historical Perspectives." *Annual Review of Sociology* 15: 381–404.

Leach, Colin, Nastia Snider, and Aarti Iyer. 2002. "Poisoning the Consciences of the Fortunate: The Experience of Relative Advantage and Support for Social Equality." Pp. 136–163 in *Relative Deprivation: Specification, Development, and Integration*, edited by Iain Walker and Heather J. Smith. New York: Cambridge University Press.

Lemann, Nicholas. 1999. *The Big Test: The Secret History of the American Meritocracy*. New York: Farrar, Straus & Giroux.

Levin, Dan. 2016. "Chinese Scions' Song: My Daddy's Rich and My Lamborghini's Good-Looking." *New York Times*, April 12. Available at http://www.nytimes.com/2016/04/13/world/americas/canada-vancouver-chinese-immigrant-wealth.html.

Lewis, Michael. 1993. *The Culture of Inequality* (Second Edition). Amherst, MA: University of Massachusetts Press.

Lieber, Ron. 2015. *The Opposite of Spoiled*. New York: HarperCollins.

Lipsitz, George. 1998. *The Possessive Investment in Whiteness*. Philadelphia: Temple University Press.

Liu, John C. 2012. "Income Inequality in New York City." New York City Comptroller's Office. http://comptroller.nyc.gov/wp-content/uploads/documents/NYC_IncomeInequality_v17.pdf. Last accessed January 2017.

Ludwig-Mayerhofer, Wolfgang, Jutta Allmendinger, Andreas Hirseland, and Werner Schneider. 2011. "The Power of Money in Dual-Earner Couples: A Comparative Study." *Acta Sociologica* 54 (4): 367–383.

Macdonald, Cameron Lynne. 2011. *Shadow Mothers: Nannies, Au Pairs, and the Micropolitics of Mothering*. Berkeley: University of California Press.

MacLeod, Jay. 1995. *Ain't No Makin' It: Aspirations and Attainment in a Low-Income Neighborhood*. Boulder, CO: Westview.

Martin, Wednesday. 2015. *Primates of Park Avenue: A Memoir*. New York: Simon & Schuster.

McCall, Leslie. 2013. *The Undeserving Rich: American Beliefs about Inequality, Opportunity, and Redistribution*. Cambridge, UK: Cambridge University Press.

———. 2016. "Political and Policy Responses to Problems of Inequality and Opportunity: Past, Present, and Future." Pp. 415–442 in *The Dynamics of Opportunity in America: Evidence and Perspectives*, edited by Irwin Kirsch and Henry Braun. Springer Open Access.

McGeehan, Patrick. 2012. "More Earners at Extremes in New York than in U.S." *New York Times*, May 20. Available at http://www.nytimes.com/2012/05/21/nyregion/middle-class-smaller-in-new-york-city-than-nationally-study-finds.html.

McIntosh, Peggy. 1988. "White Privilege: Unpacking the Invisible Knapsack." *Race, Class, and Gender in the United States: An Integrated Study* 4: 165–169.

McNamee, Stephan J., and Robert K. Miller. 2004. *The Meritocracy Myth*. Lanham, MD: Rowman & Littlefield.

Mears, Ashley. 2014. "The Collective Accomplishment of Conspicuous Consumption: Doing Display among the New Global Elite." Paper presented at the Council of European Studies, Washington, DC, March.

———. 2015a. "Girls as Elite Distinction: The Appropriation of Bodily Capital." *Poetics* 53: 22–37.

———. 2015b. "Working for Free in the VIP: Relational Work and the Production of Consent." *American Sociological Review* 80 (6): 1099–1122.

Mikecz, Robert. 2012. "Interviewing Elites: Addressing Methodological Issues." *Qualitative Inquiry* 18 (6): 482–493.

Mills, C. Wright. 2000 [1959]. *The Sociological Imagination*. New York: Oxford University Press.

Mogil, Christopher, and Anne Slepian with Peter Woodrow. 1991. *We Gave Away a Fortune: Stories of People Who Have Devoted Themselves and Their Wealth to Peace, Justice, and the Environment*. Philadelphia: New Society.

Molyneux, Maxine. 1979. "Beyond the Domestic Labor Debate." *New Left Review* 116: 3–27.

Murphy, Alexandra, and Colin Jerolmack. 2016. "Ethnographic Masking in an Era of Data Transparency." *Contexts* 15 (2): 14–17.

Nakano Glenn, Evelyn. 1992. "From Servitude to Service Work: Historical Continuities in the Racial Division of Paid Reproductive Labor." *Signs* 18 (1): 1–43.

———. 2002. *Unequal Freedom: How Race and Gender Shaped American Citizenship and Labor*. Cambridge, MA: Harvard University Press.

Nelson, Margaret. 2010. *Parenting Out of Control: Anxious Parents in Uncertain Times*. New York: New York University Press.

Newman, Katherine. 1999. *Falling from Grace: Downward Mobility in the Age of Affluence*. Berkeley: University of California Press.

Newman, Katherine S., and Rebekah Peeples Massengill. 2006. "The Texture of Hardship: Qualitative Sociology of Poverty, 1995–2005." *Annual Review of Sociology* 32: 423–446.

Norton, Michael, and Dan Ariely. 2011. "Building a Better America—One Wealth Quintile at a Time." *Perspectives on Psychological Science* 6 (1): 9–12.

Odendahl, Teresa. 1990. *Charity Begins at Home: Generosity and Self Interest among the Philanthropic Elite*. New York: Basic Books.

Ortner, Sherry. 2003. *New Jersey Dreaming: Capital, Culture, and the Class of '58*. Durham, NC: Duke University Press.

Osburg, John. 2013. *Anxious Wealth: Money and Morality among China's New Rich*. Stanford, CA: Stanford University Press.

Ostrander, Susan. 1984. *Women of the Upper Class*. Philadelphia: Temple University Press.

———. 1995a. *Money for Change: Social Movement Philanthropy at Haymarket People's Fund*. Philadelphia: Temple University Press.

———. 1995b. "'Surely You're Not in This Just to Be Helpful': Access, Rapport, and Interviews in Three Studies of Elites." Pp. 133–150 in *Studying Elites Using Qualitative Methods*, edited by R. Hertz and J. B. Imber. Thousand Oaks, CA: Sage.

Ostrower, Francie. 1995. *Why the Wealthy Give*. Princeton, NJ: Princeton University Press.

Page, Benjamin, Larry Bartels, and Jason Seawright. 2013. "Democracy and the Policy Preferences of Wealthy Americans." *Perspectives on Politics* 11 (1): 51–73.

Pahl, Jan. 1983. "The Allocation of Money and the Structuring of Inequality within Marriage." *Sociological Review* 31 (2): 237–262.

———. 1990. "Household Spending, Personal Spending and the Control of Money in Marriage." *Sociology* 24 (1): 119–138.

Pattillo, Mary. 2007. *Black on the Block*. Chicago: University of Chicago Press.

———. 2013. *Black Picket Fences* (Second Edition). Chicago: University of Chicago Press.

Pew Research Center. 2016. "America's Shrinking Middle Class: A Close Look at Changes within Metropolitan Areas." http://www.pewsocialtrends.org/2016/05/11/americas-shrinking-middle-class-a-close-look-at-changes-within-metropolitan-areas/. Accessed November 5, 2016.

Piff, Paul K. 2014. "Wealth and the Inflated Self: Class, Entitlement and Narcissism." *Personality and Social Psychology Bulletin* 40 (1): 34–43.

Piff, Paul K., Michael W. Krauss, Stéphane Côté, Bonnie Hayden Cheng, and Dacher Keltner. 2010. "Having Less, Giving More: The Influence of Social Class on Prosocial Behavior." *Journal of Personality and Social Psychology* 99 (5): 771–784.

Piff, Paul K., Daniel M. Stancato, Stéphane Côté, Rodolfo Mendoza-Denton, and Dacher Keltner. 2012. "Higher Social Class Predicts Increased Unethical

Behavior." *Proceedings of the National Academy of Sciences of the United States of America* 109 (11): 4086–4091.

Piketty, Thomas. 2014. *Capital in the Twenty-First Century*. Cambridge, MA: Harvard University Press.

Power, Sally, Annabelle Allouch, Phillip Brown, and Gerbrand Tholen. 2016. "Giving Something Back? Sentiments of Privilege and Social Responsibility among Elite Graduates from Britain and France." *International Sociology* 31 (3): 305–323.

Pratto, Felicia, and Andrew L. Stewart. 2012. "Group Dominance and the Half-Blindness of Privilege." *Journal of Social Issues* 68 (1): 28–45.

Pugh, Allison. 2009. *Longing and Belonging: Parents, Children, and Consumer Culture*. Berkeley: University of California Press.

———. 2013. "What Good Are Interviews for Thinking about Culture? Demystifying Interpretive Analysis." *American Journal of Cultural Sociology* 1: 42–68.

———. 2015. *The Tumbleweed Society*. New York: Oxford University Press.

Raxlen, Jussara, and Rachel Sherman. 2016. "Working Hard or Hardly Working? Elite Stay-at-Home-Moms and the Labor of Lifestyle." Paper presented at the American Sociological Association annual meetings, Seattle, August.

Reay, Diane. 1998. *Class Work: Mothers' Involvement in Their Children's Primary Schooling*. London: UCL.

———. 2005a. "Doing the Dirty Work of Social Class? Mothers' Work in Support of Their Children's Schooling." Pp. 104–116 in *A New Sociology of Work?*, edited by Lynne Pettinger, Jane Perry, Rebecca Taylor, and Miriam Glucksmann. Oxford, UK: Blackwell.

———. 2005b. "Beyond Consciousness? The Psychic Landscape of Social Class." *Sociology* 39 (5): 911–928.

Reay, Diane, Sumi Hollingworth, Katya Williams, Gill Crozier, Fiona Jamieson, David James, and Phoebe Beedell. 2007. "A Darker Shade of Pale? Whiteness, the Middle Classes and Multi-Ethnic Schooling." *Sociology* 41 (6): 1041–1059.

Rivera, Lauren. 2014. "The Have-Nots versus the Have-a-Lots: Who Is Economically Elite in America?" Paper presented at the American Sociological Association meetings, August, San Francisco.

———. 2015. *Pedigree: How Elite Students Get Elite Jobs*. Princeton, NJ: Princeton University Press.

Roberts, Sam. 2014. "Gap between Manhattan's Rich and Poor Is Greatest in U.S., Census Finds." *New York Times*, September 17. Available at http://www.nytimes.com/2014/09/18/nyregion/gap-between-manhattans-rich-and-poor-is-greatest-in-us-census-finds.html

Roelofs, Joan. 2003. *Foundations and Public Policy: The Mask of Pluralism*. Albany, NY: State University of New York Press.

Rollins, Judith. 1985. *Between Women: Domestics and Their Employers*. Philadelphia: Temple University Press.

Rothkopf, David. 2009. *Superclass: The Global Power Elite and the World They Are Making*. New York: Farrar, Straus & Giroux.

Rubin, Lillian. 1992 [1976]. *Worlds of Pain: Life in the Working-Class Family*. New York: Basic Books.

Saez, Emmanuel. 2015. "Striking It Richer: The Evolution of Top Incomes in the United States. (Updated with 2013 preliminary estimates)." https://eml.berkeley.edu/~saez/saez-UStopincomes-2013.pdf. Last accessed January 2017.

Salkin, Allen. 2009. "You Try to Live on 500K in This Town." *New York Times*, February 8. Available at http://www.nytimes.com/2009/02/08/fashion/08halfmill.html?_r=0. Accessed July 6, 2016.

Sassen, Saskia. 1988. *The Mobility of Labor and Capital: A Study in International Investment and Labor Flow*. Cambridge, UK: Cambridge University Press.

———. 1990. *The Global City: New York, London, Tokyo*. Princeton, NJ: Princeton University Press.

Savage, Mike, and Karel Williams (eds.). 2008. *Remembering Elites*. Oxford, UK: Blackwell.

Savage, Mike, Gaynor Bagnall, and Brian Longhurst. 2001. "Ordinary, Ambivalent and Defensive: Class Identities in the Northwest of England." *Sociology* 35 (4): 875–892.

Sayer, Andrew. 2005. *The Moral Significance of Class*. Cambridge, UK: Cambridge University Press.

Schneider, Daniel. 2012. "Gender Deviance and Household Work: The Role of Occupation." *American Journal of Sociology* 117 (4): 1029–1072.

Schor, Juliet. 1998. *The Overspent American: Upscaling, Downshifting and the New Consumer*. New York: Basic Books.

———. 2003. *Born to Buy*. New York: Scribner.

———. 2007. "In Defense of Consumer Critique: Revisiting the Consumption Debates of the Twentieth Century." *Annals of the American Academy of Political and Social Science* 611 (1): 16–30.

———. 2016. "Debating the Sharing Economy." *Journal of Self-Governance and Management Economics* 4 (3): 7–22.

Schulz, Jeremy. 2012. "Talk of Work: Transatlantic Divergences in Justifications for Hard Work among French, Norwegian, and American Professionals." *Theory & Society* 41 (6): 603–634.

Schwartz, Pepper, Davis Patterson, and Sara Steen. 2012. "The Dynamics of Power: Money and Sex in Intimate Relationships." Pp. 253–275 in *Gender, Power and Communication in Human Relationships*, edited by Pamela J. Kalbfleisch and Michael J. Cody. New York: Routledge.

Schwartz Cowan, Ruth. 1984. *More Work for Mother: The Ironies of Household Technology from the Open Hearth to the Microwave*. New York: Basic Books.

Scott, Marvin B., and Stanford M. Lyman. 1968. "Accounts." *American Sociological Review* 33 (1): 46–62.

Secombe, Wally. 1974. "The Housewife and Her Labor under Capitalism." *New Left Review* 83: 3–24.

Sengupta, Somini. 2012. "Preferred Style: Don't Flaunt It in Silicon Valley." *New York Times*, May 17, A1. Available at http://www.nytimes.com/2012/05/18/technology/a-start-up-is-gold-for-facebooks-new-millionaires.html. Accessed November 21, 2016.

Sennett, Richard. 2007. *The Culture of New Capitalism*. New Haven, CT: Yale University Press.

Sennett, Richard, and Jonathan Cobb. 1993 [1973]. *The Hidden Injuries of Class*. New York: W. W. Norton.

Shenker-Osorio, Anat. 2013. "Why Americans All Believe They Are 'Middle Class.'" *Atlantic*, August 1. Available at http://www.theatlantic.com/politics/archive/2013/08/why-americans-all-believe-they-are-middle-class/278240/. Accessed July 2, 2016.

Sherman, Jennifer. 2009. *Those Who Work, Those Who Don't*. Minneapolis: University of Minnesota Press.

Sherman, Rachel. 2007. *Class Acts: Service and Inequality in Luxury Hotels*. Berkeley: University of California Press.

———. 2010. "'Time Is Our Commodity': Gender and the Struggle for Occupational Legitimacy among Personal Concierges." *Work and Occupations* 37 (1): 81–114.

———. 2011. "The Production of Distinctions: Class, Gender, and Taste Work in the Lifestyle Management Industry." *Qualitative Sociology* 34 (1): 201–219.

———. 2014. "Caring or Catering? Emotions, Autonomy and Subordination in Lifestyle Work." In *Caring on the Clock: The Complexities and Contradictions of Paid Care Work*, edited by Mignon Duffy, Amy Armenia, and Clare Stacey. New Brunswick, NJ: Rutgers University Press.

———. 2017. "Conflicted Cultivation: Parenting, Privilege, and Moral Worth in Wealthy New York Families." *American Journal of Cultural Sociology* 5 (1): 1–33.

———. n.d. "A Very Expensive Ordinary Life: Symbolic Boundaries and Aspiration to the Middle among New York Elites." Unpublished paper.

Shockley, Kristen, and Winny Shen. 2016. "Couple Dynamics: Division of Labor." Pp. 125–139 in *The Oxford Handbook of Work and Family*, edited by Tammy D. Allen and Lillian T. Eby. Oxford, UK: Oxford University Press.

Silva, Jennifer. 2013. *Coming Up Short*. New York: Oxford University Press.

Silver, Ira. 2007. "Disentangling Class from Philanthropy: The Double-Edged Sword of Alternative Giving." *Critical Sociology* 33: 537–549.

Skeggs, Beverly. 1997. *Formations of Class & Gender: Becoming Respectable.* London: Sage.

Sklair, Leslie. 2001. *The Transnational Capitalist Class.* Oxford: Blackwell.

Small, Mario. 2009. "How Many Cases Do I Need?" *Ethnography* 10 (1): 5–38.

Smith, Heather J., and Thomas F. Pettigrew. 2014. "The Subjective Interpretation of Inequality: A Model of the Relative Deprivation Experience." *Social and Personality Psychology Compass* 8 (12): 755–765.

Spence, Emma. 2016. "Performing Wealth and Status: Observing Super-Yachts and the Super-Rich in Monaco." Pp. 287–301 in *Handbook on Wealth and the Super-Rich,* edited by Jonathan V. Beaverstock and Iain Hay. Cheltenham, UK: Edward Elgar.

Standing, Guy. 2011. *The Precariat: The New Dangerous Class.* London: Bloomsbury.

Stewart, James B. 2016. "In the Chamber of Secrets: J. K. Rowling's Net Worth." *New York Times,* November 25, A1. Available at http://www.nytimes.com/2016/11/24/business/in-the-chamber-of-secrets-jk-rowlings-net-worth.html. Accessed November 26, 2016.

Stone, Pamela. 2007. *Opting Out? Why Women Really Quit Careers and Head Home.* Berkeley: University of California Press.

Strasser, Susan. 1982. *Never Done: A History of American Housework.* New York: Pantheon Books.

Streib, Jessi. 2013. "Class Origin and College Graduates' Parenting Beliefs." *Sociological Quarterly* 54: 670–693.

———. 2015. *The Power of the Past: Understanding Cross-Class Marriages.* New York: Oxford University Press.

Thaler, Richard H. 1999. "Mental Accounting Matters." *Journal of Behavioral Decision Making* 12: 183–206.

Tichenor, Veronica. 2005. *Earning More and Getting Less: Why Successful Wives Can't Buy Equality.* New Brunswick, NJ: Rutgers University Press.

Treas, Judith. 1993. "Money in the Bank: Transaction Costs and the Economic Organization of Marriage." *American Sociological Review* 58 (5): 723–734.

U.S. Census Bureau. 2016. "QuickFacts, New York City, New York." https://www.census.gov/quickfacts/table/PST045215/3651000. Last accessed January 2017.

Vaisey, Steven. 2009. "Motivation and Justification: A Dual-Process Model of Culture in Action." *American Journal of Sociology* 114 (6): 1675–1715.

———. 2014. "Is Interviewing Compatible with the Dual-Process Model of Culture?" *American Journal of Cultural Sociology* 2: 150–158.

Veblen, Thorstein. 1994 [1899]. *The Theory of the Leisure Class.* New York: Penguin.

Vincent, Carol, and Stephen J. Ball. 2007. "'Making Up' the Middle-Class Child: Families, Activities and Class Dispositions." *Sociology* 41 (6): 1061–1077.

Vogler, Carolyn. 2005. "Cohabiting Couples: Rethinking Money in the Household at the Beginning of the Twenty-first Century." *Sociological Review* 53 (1): 1–29.

Vogler, Carolyn, and Jan Pahl. 1993. "Social and Economic Change and the Organization of Money within Marriage." *Work, Employment & Society* 7 (1): 71–95.

———. 1994. "Money, Power and Inequality within Marriage." *Sociological Review* 42 (2): 263–288.

Vogler, Carolyn, Clare Lyonette, and Richard D. Wiggins. 2008. "Money, Power and Spending Decisions in Intimate Relationships." *Sociological Review* 56 (1): 117–143.

Vohs, Kathleen D., Nicole L. Mead, and Miranda R. Goode. 2006. "The Psychological Consequences of Money." *Science* 314 (5802): 1154–1156.

Warde, Alan. 2015. "The Sociology of Consumption: Its Recent Development." *Annual Review of Sociology* 41: 117–134.

Weber, Max. 2003 [1958]. *The Protestant Ethic and the Spirit of Capitalism.* New York: Dover.

Weinbaum, Batya, and Amy Bridges. 1976. "The Other Side of the Paycheck: Monopoly Capital and the Structure of Consumption." *Monthly Review* 28 (3): 88–103.

Weis, Lois, Kristin Cipollone, and Heather Jenkins. 2014. *Class Warfare: Class, Race, and College Admissions in Top-Tier Secondary Schools.* Chicago: University of Chicago Press.

Wernick, Laura. 2009. "How Young Progressives with Wealth Are Leveraging Their Power and Privilege to Support Social Justice: A Case Study of Social Justice Philanthropy and Young Donor Organizing." Ph.D. diss., University of Michigan, Ann Arbor.

Whillans, Ashley V., Nathan J. Wispinski, and Elizabeth W. Dunn. 2016. "Seeing Wealth as a Responsibility Improves Attitudes towards Taxation." *Journal of Economic Behavior & Organization* 127: 146–154.

Wilkinson, Richard, and Kate Pickett. 2009. *The Spirit Level: Why Greater Equality Makes Societies Stronger.* Bloomsbury Press.

Willis, Paul. 1979. *Learning to Labor: How Working Class Kids Get Working Class Jobs.* New York: Columbia University Press.

Wright, Erik Olin (ed.). 2005. *Approaches to Class Analysis.* Cambridge, UK: Cambridge University Press.

Wright, Erik Olin, and Rachel E. Dwyer. 2003. "The Patterns of Job Expansions in the USA: A Comparison of the 1960s and 1990s." *Socio-Economic Review* 1 (3): 289–325.

Yodanis, Carrie, and Sean Lauer. 2007. "Managing Money in Marriage: Multilevel and Cross-National Effects of the Breadwinner Role." *Journal of Marriage and Family* 69 (5): 1307–1325.

Young, Alford A. 2004. *The Minds of Marginalized Black Men: Making Sense of Mobility, Opportunity, and Future Life Chances*. Princeton, NJ: Princeton University Press.

Zelizer, Viviana. 1994. *The Social Meaning of Money*. New York: Basic Books.

———. 2005. *The Purchase of Intimacy*. Princeton, NJ: Princeton University Press.

———. 2012. "How I Became a Relational Economic Sociologist and What Does That Mean?" *Politics & Society* 40 (2): 145–174.

Zinn, Howard. 1980. *A People's History of the United States*. New York: Harper & Row.

INDEX

Acker, Joan, 195

activism, political, 62, 134, 142–43, 152, 153, 234

affluence, 232–33; anxiety linked to, 20–25, 50; and freedom from economic anxiety, 37–38, 159; normalization of (*see* normalization of affluence); as subject of research, 11–18, 245; as term, 41, 42, 266n10

African Americans, 15, 39–42, 55–56, 67, 132, 136, 219; and exposure to diversity, 215, 221–22, 275n16; giving back and, 219, 270n9; and work as value, 268n24. *See also* race and ethnicity

American Dream, 5–10, 12, 22, 59–61, 70–71, 232, 267n10

anxiety: affluence linked to, 20–25, 50; downward or upward social orientation and, 30, 38–39; earners and, 22, 26, 38–39, 67–70, 90, 179, 233–34, 268n13; economic climate and, 6, 37–38, 90, 151–52, 233–34; and financial insecurity or risk, 39, 67–70, 73, 151–52; freedom from economic, 37–38, 46; inheritors and, 26, 152, 179, 268n13; interview process and exploration of, 233–34; job insecurity and, 6, 22, 38, 179, 194–95; and marital disagreements over money, 110, 156, 158–59, 177; parenting and, 22, 198, 226–27, 275n11; privilege deflected by, 69, 227; provider role and, 67–68

appreciation: and appropriate inhabiting of wealth, 228–29; awareness of privilege and, 47–48, 126–30, 199, 207–9, 212, 231; and giving back, 212; gratitude, 76, 113, 127, 231; and legitimate entitlement, 23–24, 76, 113, 126–27, 131, 228; of luxuries, 127, 205

Baltzell, E. Digby, 12

body labor, 99, 168

boundaries, symbolic, 60–61, 74, 81, 83, 94, 103, 104

Bourdieu, Pierre, 121, 199, 247

budgets, 69, 98, 120, 122, 161–63, 173, 176–78, 183, 224

charity. *See* giving back

children: awareness and appreciation of privilege as parental goal, 207–10, 212, 216, 228–29; care of (*see* nannies; stay-at-home parents); college expenses, responsibility for, 29, 66, 68, 167, 223–24; constraint as parental strategy, 198, 203–7, 223–24, 227–28, 275n11; and consumption, 99–101, 118–19; as contribution to society, 123; enrichment for (expansion), 199, 204, 224, 228–29, 235; entitlement as parental concern, 24, 198–202, 227–29, 275n11; and exposure as parental strategy, 102–3, 211–14, 217–22; financial provisions for, 107, 151, 186, 197; and legitimate

ostentation, 3, 150; consumption choices and, 50–51, 87, 105–6, 110 (*see also* luxuries); and domestic employees, 48, 105–6, 116–17; and downward social orientation, 30, 105; inequality and, 10–11, 149, 230–31; inheritors and, 26, 60, 71–73, 71–78, 122–23, 151–52; and middle class/working background, 26, 50–51; as motivation for work, 73–74; "new money" and, 120; normalization of affluence and, 3, 117, 142; philanthropic "giving back" and, 141–42, 149–54; and privilege, 20–21, 39, 41, 60, 234; reciprocity and, 132–33; and social isolation, 56, 105; stay-at-home parents and, 60–61, 82, 84–85, 173–74; talk of money as uncomfortable, 5–6, 18–22, 40–41, 50–51, 54–55, 72, 87, 130–31, 215, 240, 251, 258, 265; as unproductive, 122; and upward mobility, 26; and upward social orientation, 30. *See also* anxiety; symbolic boundaries

display of wealth. *See* ostentation

distinction, as motive for consumption. *See* status competition

distributional justice, 233–37

diversity: downward or upward orientation and, 29–32, 48–50; "economic diversity" as value, 102–3; and exposure as parental strategy, 102–3, 222; of interviewees, 26; as value of the "new elite," 14–15, 20

domestic employees, 35; discomfort with, 48, 54–55, 105–6, 116–17; maternalism, 35, 266n6; reciprocity and relationship with, 270n6;

and self-reliance, 86; as social interlocutors, 105–6; stay-at-home parents and, 85–86, 179, 266n6; structural inequality in relationships with, 35, 48, 266n6; wages and value of, 35, 134–35. *See also* nannies

downward orientation, 21, 23, 44–52, 56–57, 62; attitudes toward taxes, 147–48; and awareness of privilege, 29–32; consumption choices and, 92–93; and discomfort with wealth, 105; and diversity of social networks, 32, 48–50; philanthropy and, 125, 139–40

earmarking, 101. *See also* treats (self-indulgent consumption)

earned wealth: and anxiety, 22, 26, 38–39, 67–70, 90, 179, 233–34, 268n13; and entitlement, 58–59, 61–62, 71–72, 157, 159; gender and provider role, 160–61; and merit, 64, 230; and moral worth, 32, 268n13; and prudence, 69–70; self-sufficiency and, 62–63; work and legitimacy of, 9–10, 58–63, 70–71, 74–76, 81, 83, 90, 122–23, 127, 146, 157, 159, 196, 223–24, 234, 267n3

economic crisis of 2008, 67–69

education: as class identifier, 262n33; and economic inequality, 7, 12, 25, 65; elites and access to, 12, 20, 62–63, 208, 219, 233; giving back and educational institutions, 135–36, 138, 140–41, 142, 150, 152, 271n15; of interviewees, 15; school choice (public *vs.* private), 5, 20, 102–3, 208, 214, 217–22, 221, 261n29; as value, 208, 225

DISCUSSION QUESTIONS

As the distance between rich and poor widens, *Uneasy Street* not only explores the real lives of those at the top but also sheds light on how extreme inequality comes to seem ordinary and acceptable to the rest of us. The questions below are intended to enhance group discussion about this remarkable book.

1. Sherman discusses the challenges of defining "the elite," and she describes the set of criteria for choosing her participants. Who do you count as "elite"? Is that status based on income, wealth, education, or job? In what ways do public figures such as politicians and celebrities seem "elite" or not?

2. Sherman notes that there is an American cultural taboo against discussing money and class. Some of her respondents even suggested that they would not tell their partners that they had shared details with her. How do you feel about discussing your own financial situation? With whom are you comfortable discussing it? Are there other topics that are similarly "off limits"?

3. Sherman conducted her interviews in New York City, one of the most unequal cities in the United States, at a time when economic disparities were especially prominent. How might the story have changed if she had interviewed people in a different city?

4. Sherman identifies "upward-oriented" and "downward-oriented" people in her sample. Do you tend to compare yourself to people who have as much or more than you, or to those who have less? Do you think of yourself as privileged? Why or why not?

5. Do the criteria Sherman identifies for being a morally worthy wealthy person—working hard, consuming prudently, giving

back, and in general trying to be "normal"—resonate with you? Do you make these distinctions or see them in the culture at large?

6. In explaining their success, Sherman's respondents often referred to how hard they have worked. They often emphasized the role of luck, too. Sherman suggests that this obscures other advantages, such as elite educations, lack of debt, financial support from their parents, et cetera. Do you agree? What is the difference between "hard work" and "luck" as explanations for having wealth?

7. When asked what "giving back" means, Sherman's interviewees talked about charitable giving, volunteering, and having awareness of privilege. How do you define giving back? What do you think the purpose of "giving back" is?

8. Sherman's respondents had mixed feelings about the value of teenagers working for pay in high school and college. Some felt it was a necessary experience. Others felt that a job would take away from other activities, including schoolwork. Do you think it is important for teenagers to hold paying jobs? Why or why not?

9. In the appendix, Sherman notes that she comes from a privileged background, which was useful in connecting with some of her interviewees. How might her interviewees have responded differently if she had a different background?

10. Have your perceptions of wealthy Americans changed after reading *Uneasy Street*? In what ways?